Understanding Bhagat Singh

Some of the Books by Chaman Lal

1. Bhagat Singh Aur Unke Sathiyon Ke Dastavej (Co-edited) (Hindi) 1986
2. Bhagat Singh Ke Sampooran Dastavej (Edited) (Hindi) 2004
3. Bhagat Singh ke Rajnitik Dastavez (Edited), NBT, New Delhi (Hindi) 2007
4. Shaheed Bhagat Singh: Dastavezon ke Aiane Mein (Edited) (Hindi) 2007
5. Jail Note book and Other Writings: Bhagat Singh (Compiled and Introduction) 2007
6. Bhagat Singh: Vicharvan Inqlabi, (Punjabi), Navyug Press, New Delhi, 2009
7. Bhagat Singh, Medha publications Delhi, 2009
8. Bhagat Singh:Sampuran Vangmay (Edited) (Marathi) 2007
9. Ghadar Party Nayak-Kartar Singh Sarabha (Hindi) 2007
10. Ghadar party Naik Kartar Singh Sarabha (Punjabi), NBT, New Delhi, 2008
11. Ghadar Party Hero: Kartar Singh Sarabha (English), NBT, New Delhi, 2011
12. Inqlabi Itihas De Sunehari Panne (History) (Punjabi) 2005
13. Krantiveer Bhagat Singh, 'Abhyuday aur Bhavishya' 2012
14. Jail Note Book Ani Anya Lekhan: Bhagat Singh (Edited) (Bengali) 2012
15. The Punjabi and Dalit Images in Indian literature (Criticism) 1998
16. Gurmukhi Manuscripts in Patiala. 1990
17. Storms Never Know Defeat-Paash(Edited) 1989
18. Dalit and Woman in Indian Literature (edited-bilingual) 2001

Understanding Bhagat Singh

Chaman Lal

UNDERSTANDING BHAGAT SINGH
Chaman Lal

First Published, 2013

ISBN 978-93-5002-222-1 (Hb)

Published by
AAKAR BOOKS
28 E Pocket IV, Mayur Vihar Phase I, Delhi 110 091
Phone : 011 2279 5505 Telefax : 011 2279 5641
info@aakarbooks.com; www.aakarbooks.com

Printed at
Mudrak, 30 A, Patparganj, Delhi 110 091

Contents

PART I – ARTICLES

PART II – ANNEXURES

Acknowledgements

The first draft of *Understanding Bhagat Singh* was ready in 2008. I was planning to give it to some other publisher, when Prof. Abhai Maurya became founder Vice-Chancellor of the newly established/ upgraded University—English and Foreign Languages University (EFLU), Hyderabad and he expressed the desire to publish the book from EFLU. The manuscript was sent to EFLU and Prof. Maurya got it vetted by EFLU Prof. L. Balagopal, who gave many valuable suggestions as well. The press copy of the earlier manuscript was prepared by Prof. Balagopal, when Prof. Maurya's term as VC came to an end. After he left, EFLU delayed the publication of the book, when I requested them to return the manuscript, which was duly sent back to me. In the meantime, I had many new writings on Bhagat Singh and the manuscript grew in size as well. Later Shri K.K. Saxena of Aakar Books expressed his desire to publish the book, which I happily accepted.

I acknowledge Prof. Abhai Maurya and Prof. L. Balagopal's role in initiating the process of publication of the book and Shri K.K. Saxena of Aakar Books for actually bringing it out for the benefit of readers.

Chaman Lal

Preface

Understanding Bhagat Singh is a collection of my articles on Bhagat Singh written during the last many years, but more in the last 6-7 years, when I launched a campaign for celebrating Bhagat Singh's 75th martyrdom year and birth centenary a year later. A few of these articles were published in papers/journals like *Analytical Monthly Review*, *Economic and Political Review* (EPW), *Mainstream*, *Frontier*, *The Hindu*, *The Tribune*, etc., while a few were presented at some national and international academic conferences, some are like personal musings or memoirs, published or unpublished! I have been working on Bhagat Singh's documents since 1984 and by now I have brought out many collections in Hindi, Punjabi and English, some of which are already translated in Marathi, Bengali and Urdu as well. In the process, I have gone through lots of material—published and unpublished, on revolutionary movements in general, and Bhagat Singh in particular. Being in Jawaharlal Nehru University (JNU), New Delhi since 2005 helped me to consult Nehru Memorial Museum and Library and National Archives, both rich storehouses of material and documents on the national freedom struggle. I collected for my own use, several books and documents about Bhagat Singh. It was a pleasant surprise to know that a number of publications about Bhagat Singh in many Indian languages is so high, which you can see in the reading list provided at the end of this book. Till now I have been able to collect references or actual publications of more than 400 books, out of which half are in Hindi alone. The range of languages is spread not only throughout India; it has crossed national boundaries as well, there are publications in Pakistan and one book reference I could get even from Germany in the German language. Apart from Hindi, Punjabi and English, which have many books on Bhagat Singh, he is a no less popular figure for writings in other Indian languages as well—Urdu, Tamil, Marathi, Bengali, Sindhi, Kannada, Telugu, Malayalam, Gujarati, Manipuri, etc., all have books on Bhagat Singh. The largest numbers of books on Bhagat Singh were proscribed by British colonial rulers, some of which now find place in the British Library London! I found in this process that Bhagat Singh is a more misunderstood and less understood political personality of India. Yet Bhagat Singh is hugely popular in India and he is remembered fondly in Pakistan as well. Many people are anguished that 'a mere young boy is being blown up to the skies'. They would have been contented to keep Bhagat Singh's image alive as 'a brave patriot'. Anything more than that hurts them. But Bhagat Singh's writings and actions speak otherwise. These writings and actions project Bhagat Singh as one of the most mature and developing thinkers and activists with a tremendous quality of leadership. Those who want to belittle Bhagat Singh's maturity owing to his relative youth, conveniently forget that Dobrolubov like young philosophers in pre-revolutionary Russia contributed so much to the growth of materialist philosophy in Russia, though he died at the age of only 24. Victims of inferiority complex in India, think Russia or Europe can produce Dobrolubov, but not India, a thinker in that age.

I have tried to present Bhagat Singh's actions and writings in an objective manner through these articles. I have also included some other personalities' views on Bhagat Singh, such as Periyar (E.V. Ramaswamy Naicker), whose views on Bhagat Singh have remained largely unknown till now. Bhagat Singh's own thoughts have also been presented here just symbolically, in order to know his quality of thinking. My focus is more on documentation to clear the air about many myths or half-truths. Thus the very first publication of his seminal essay—'Why I Am an Atheist' is produced here in scanned form, as some right wingers and religious fundamentalists have tried to spread that this essay was not written by Bhagat Singh, it is 'interpolation' later by 'leftists' as per their interpretation! However I could locate its original first publication in *The People* issue of September 27, 1931, which incidentally marked Bhagat Singh's first birth anniversary as well, after his martyrdom! Bhagat Singh had handed over a bag full of his papers to Kumari Lajjawati(Secretary, Bhagat Singh Defence Committee at that time and in close touch with Jawaharlal Nehru, later Principal of a Jalandhar College) from Lahore jail, before his impending execution, to be handed over to his comrade and friend Bejoy Kumar Sinha, who was imprisoned in the Lahore Conspiracy case at that time, after his release from prison. However, Kumari Lajjawati had shown these papers to Feroze Chand, who was a Socialist and editor of *The People* founded by Lala Lajpat Rai in English, along with *Bande Matram* in Urdu from Lahore. Feroze Chand, also biographer of Lala Lajpat Rai, later published many of Bhagat Singh's writings from this bagful of papers, as is clear from the small editorial note given at the beginning of 'Why I Am an Atheist', ascribing the copyrights to his father S. Kishan Singh. The family, though largely did not become atheist like Bhagat Singh, except for a few, yet never questioned Bhagat Singh's views and upheld these, as were expressed by the martyr. Bhagat Singh wrote this essay in response to the Ghadrite revolutionary Bhai Randhir Singh, who was deeply religious and was undergoing imprisonment in the same jail in Lahore, where Bhagat Singh and his comrades were kept. Unfortunately, Bhai Randhir Singh twisted this meeting to say that at his persuasion, Bhagat Singh reaffirmed his faith in Sikhism and grew a beard in jail and had a 2-3 inch beard at the time of his execution. Bhagat Singh was so conscious of his own views/ideas not being distorted/misinterpreted after his death, that he put such sensitive and ideology-related matters not only on record, he even ensured that these writings reached the concerned people and were published well in time, so that they could not be subjectively distorted! His other important document 'Letter to Young Political Workers', dated February 2, 1931, where he gives a clear socialist revolutionary programme based on Marxist ideology, was also published by *The People* and many Hindi papers like *Bhavishya*, almost immediately after his martyrdom. The success of his political adversaries lies that these documentary evidences of his ideological orientation, his intellectual competence, his leadership qualities, which made him immensely popular among the Indian masses, were soon clouded by the imposed image of 'A Brave Patriot with selfless sacrifice for the Nation', showing him in distorted paintings, with a bomb-pistol holding image, thus completely over shadowing his real personality. In one of the recent books, though with a more 'sympathetic' attitude, acknowledging some of his qualities, questioned his competence in 'English', as he was not even a 'graduate' formally, the doubt expressed by trial British judge as well in the Delhi Bomb case! While 'Why I Am an Atheist' is produced here in scanned form from *The People*, the letters written by Bhagat Singh to British executive and judicial officers, including the High Court, are also produced here in his own handwriting in scanned form. These letters were first brought into focus in the Supreme Court exhibition—'The Trial of Bhagat Singh' in 2008, the digital copy of which was kindly provided by Supreme Court Museum officials with the permission to use it with acknowledgement, and were published for the first time in *The Hindu* of August 15, 2011 very prominently, with my introduction to the letters with due courtesy to the Honourable Supreme Court. My introduction here is reproduced along with letters in original scanned form, while *The Hindu* at that time has published all the letters in print form, with one specimen letter in original scan. In my view the authentic documents are the best source to study and understand history and historical processes/ personalities. So with support from original documents, I hope to understand Bhagat Singh properly, this book will be of some use.

I am happy that Aakar, which has a reputation for bringing out world and Indian classics of historical movements/ideas, particularly of left orientation, is bringing out the book in the shortest time.

February 27, 2013
Chandershekhar Azad
Martyrdom Day

Chaman Lal
Prof.chaman@gmail.com
blog-bhagatsinghstudy.blogspot.com

PART I
ARTICLES

1

Revolutionary Legacy of Bhagat Singh*

The threat of neo-imperialism of America is looming large not only over India, but on the whole world, particularly on Asia, Africa, the Arab countries, and Latin America. At some places like in Iraq, Lebanon and Palestine, this threat has taken the form of direct military intervention. USA, Israel, Iran and North Korea like countries face all sorts of bullying, whereas Cuba and Venezuela have to fight conspiracies all the time, India and some other countries are faced with the pressures on their economic and political policies, threatening their independence in conducting relations with foreign countries as well as framing their own domestic economics and political policies according to the needs of their own people. And the thought just goes to Bhagat Singh along with Che Guevara, at such difficult times, both of whom fought an uncompromising war against all forms of imperialism and colonialism, and both of whom were absolutely fearless and sincerely dedicated to the cause, more dear to them than their own life, and both of them set a shining example in laying down their life in such brave manner that it inspires the youth everywhere. While the glorious story of Che Guevara is known the world over, the story of Bhagat Singh's fight against British imperialism has not yet reached the struggling people the world over. It needs to be told, as it inspires not only Indian youth, it has the potential of inspiring struggling people everywhere, as much as the Che Guevara saga inspires.

---

* Earlier published in *Economic and Political Weekly.*

It was on April 8, 1929 when Bhagat Singh and B.K. Dutt, threw harmless bombs with a view 'to make the deaf hear' in the Central Assembly called Parliament of today. It was on that occasion, two slogans caught the imagination of the Indian people–*Inqlab Zindabad* and 'Down with Imperialism'.

In fact these two slogans arose out of a qualitative change in the perception of the Indian revolutionary movement at that point of time. These two slogans replaced the earlier popular slogan of revolutionaries – 'Bande Matram'. It was not just a change of slogan at the linguistic level, from Sanskrit language slogan to Hindustani and English mixed slogans, it was a sign of growth of consciousness at a higher level in the revolutionaries and revolutionary movement of the country. And the catalyst of this change was none else than Bhagat Singh, who, by now through his experience of revolutionary movement and from the systematic study of the revolutionary movement the world over, particularly from the study of Soviet revolutionary experience, had reached this conclusion that it is not just enough to 'free the mother India from the chains of foreign slavery'. It was much more important to know the whole system of enslaving and exploiting other nations, that is system of imperialism and then to understand the mechanism of making revolution against imperialism. It is quite interesting to know that Bhagat Singh had started making this study from as early an age as 14 or 15. At no other point in the life of India since 1947, has the reference to these two slogans of Bhagat Singh been more important than today in the wake of the old UK imperialism being replaced by the more vicious and dangerous neo-imperialism of USA.

Born on September 28, 1907 at Chak No. 105 of Lyallpur Banga, now in Pakistan, Bhagat Singh was nurtured and brought up not only on the milk of his mother, he drank deeply the milk of patriotism from almost the day of his birth. In his home the day of his birth brought the good news of release of his father Kishan Singh and two uncles, the revolutionary Ajit Singh and young Swaran Singh from British prisons. Swaran Singh who caught tuberculosis in jail, died shortly after his release, at the young age of about 24. And his revolutionary uncle Ajit Singh, the founder of Bharat Mata Society, along with Lala Lajpat Rai and a peasant organizer, was forced to leave the country in 1909, when Bhagat Singh was just two years old, to return only after 38 years at the verge of independence day and die on the very day of independence, that is August 15, 1947 at Dalhousie. Ajit Singh spent his exiled life mostly in Latin America in revolutionary activities for the freedom of the country. In fact, he tried to get Bhagat Singh out of the country as he knew about his revolutionary activities in India. According to late Baba Bhagat Singh Bilga, the veteran Ghadarite revolutionary Living in Argentina in the 1930s, where Ajit Singh also stayed with them many times, told this writer that Ajit Singh had three letters of Bhagat Singh with him, which were given to someone for safe custody and which were lost as some documents sent from jail by Bhagat Singh, before his execution, were lost.

At the age of four, Bhagat Singh as an innocent child talking to Mehta Anand Kishore, a well known freedom fighter and friend of his father in the Congress Party S. Kishan Singh, that he 'would sow rifles in fields in order to reap a fruit of fulsome crop to drive the British out of the country'. At the age of 12, he had visited Jallianwala Bagh in Amritsar in April 1919, after the massacre of people and brought 'blood soaked sand'. At the age of 14, while studying in school in Lahore, he informed his grandfather about the preparations being made by railwaymen to go on strike in 1921. Bhagat Singh had joined National College, Lahore at the age of 15 in the F.A. class, after passing the ninth class. Prior to that he had welcomed the protesting Akali workers in his village, as on February 20, 1921 more than 140 devout Sikhs were killed by Mahant Narain Dass in collaboration with the British authorities at Gurdwara Nankana Sahib. And it was the time that Bhagat Singh learnt the Gurmukhi script and Punjabi language. Since his grandfather Sardar Arjan Singh was a staunch Arya Samajist, despite being a Sikh, his emphasis was on learning the Sanskrit language, which Bhagat Singh did learn in school along with Urdu, Hindi and English.

Worried at the revolutionary traits of Bhagat Singh's growing personality, the family particularly his father, thought of 'controlling him through marriage'. There were already two young women in the house, widow of Bhagat Singh's younger uncle Swaran Singh and Bibi Harnam Kaur, wife of his exiled revolutionary uncle Ajit Singh. If marriage could not control Ajit Singh, who, had no child himself, how could it control Bhagat Singh? And Bhagat Singh was too sensitive to the sufferings of both his aunts. He was particularly attached to his aunt Harnam Kaur, wife of Ajit Singh. According to the account of one of his close schoolmate friends Jaidev Gupta, available in the Nehru Memorial Museum and Library (NMML), Bhagat Singh was given to Harnam Kaur as her 'son' on account of being childless, while her husband Ajit Singh lived in exile for an uncertain period. Bhagat Singh in any case was like the mental son of Ajit Singh, with whom, he was much attached without living with him. At the level of ideas, Ajit Singh was much advanced than Congress perception of freedom of India and he was much more revolutionary in thought than Congress as he wanted to awaken and organize the peasantry on the basis of their economic exploitation at the hands of big feudal lords and the colonial system. Bhagat Singh took further steps on this advanced thinking of his uncle and reached the logical end of adopting the Marxist ideology of liberation.

At the age of 15, Bhagat Singh questioned his father about the withdrawal of the non-cooperation movement by Mahatma Gandhi on the pretext of the 'Chauri Chaura' incident. In fact withdrawal of the non-cooperation movement after 'Chauri Chaura' in 1922 had disillusioned the youth and revolutionaries all over India. Chandershekhar Azad, who had got the punishment of flogging by shouting 'Mahatma Gandhi Ki Jai' was one among those youths, who were very bitter at this development and later during their revolutionary activities could never trust Gandhi. More of them had relations with leaders such as C.R. Das, Jawaharlal Nehru, Subhas Chandra Bose, Lala Lajpat Rai, Madan Mohan Malviya and many others, but no revolutionary had claimed closeness to Gandhi, though correspondence had some time taken place and the reply to Sukhdev's letter to Gandhi, before execution was given by Gandhi only through *Young India*, after his execution. To be fair, Gandhi received the letter, though written earlier, only after his execution along with Bhagat Singh and Rajguru.

In a way, the withdrawal of the non-cooperation movement in 1922, gave an impetus to the revolutionary movement throughout the country, the pockets of which already existed in Bengal in the form of Anushilan and Yugantar, HRA, in UP, et cetera. Bhagat Singh reached Kanpur in 1923, after informing his father through a letter that his life was dedicated to the nation, so he could not think of marrying. His teacher in National College, Jai Chander Vidyalankar had given an introductory letter for Ganesh Shankar Vidyarthi, editor of *Pratap*, Kanpur and Congress leader of UP. Bhagat Singh not only joined *Pratap* a Hindi paper, he also joined the underground revolutionary organization Hindustan Republican Association, organized by Sachinder Nath Sanyal, the author of *Bandi Jivan* who, had already gone through one round of transportation to the Andamans. Bhagat Singh had met him at Lahore. It was at Kanpur that Bhagat Singh met Bejoy Kumar Sinha, Shiv Verma, Jaidev Kapoor, B.K. Dutt and Ajoy Ghosh, the revolutionary comrades of HRA. Sukhdev and Bhagwati Charan Vohra were his comrades in Lahore. After spending about six months, writing under the pen name of Balwant in *Pratap*, working sometime for flood relief and also performing the duties of headmaster in a national school around Aligarh, Bhagat Singh returned to Lahore on hearing the news of his grandmother's illness and getting the assurance that no one in the house would talk about his marriage any more. By the age of 17, Bhagat Singh had matured so much that he wrote an essay in Hindi on the language issue of Punjab in competition writing and won a prize. In 1924 and 1925, he wrote *Vishv Prem*—love with the world and *Yuvak*, which were published in Matwala, both under the assumed name of Balwant Singh. And then on the execution of six Babbar Akali revolutionaries, in 1926 his article, the Blood Drops on Holi Day (*Holi ke Din Rakt ke Chhinte*) was published in the name of 'One Punjabi Youth'. And in *Why I Am an Atheist*, written in 1930, Bhagat Singh had referred to the development of ideas in his personality by saying that he had become an atheist by the end of 1926 itself, when he was yet to be 19 years old. These development in his personality had taken place in the backdrop of considerable Marxist literature reaching Dwarka Dass Library, Lahore, where Bhagat Singh had become a voracious reader from 1924 or so and he did not stop at just being an atheist.

Bhagat Singh was searching for the ultimate ideology of human liberation from all kinds of yokes and he had become almost a committed Marxist, through his contacts with the Kirti group of Ghadrite revolutionaries of Punjab.

He had contributed articles regularly to *Kirti* (Punjabi) on various issues like 'Communalism and its Solution', 'Problem of Untouchability', 'Religion and Our Freedom Struggle', et cetera. If he had any differences with them, these were only about the programme of the revolutionary party and Bhagat Singh and his comrades were convinced that to awaken the country from slumber, the youth needed to perform some daring revolutionary nationalist actions and make sacrifices to advance the movement.

By 1928 not only Bhagat Singh, even Sukhdev and Bhagwati Charan Vohra in Punjab, Bejoy Kumar Sinha, Shiv Verma and Jaidev Kapoor in UP were getting more and more convinced about the need of the socialist agenda of their revolutionary party and they gave a practical shape to it by calling an urgent meeting of the central committee of HRA on September 8 and 9, 1928 at Ferozeshah Kotla ground in Delhi, where after long deliberations and at the suggestion of Bhagat Singh, supported by Sukhdev, Bejoy Kumar Sinha, Shiv Verma and Jaidev Kapoor, HRA was rechristened as HSRA. The addition of the word socialist was not just ornamental as was done by Indira Gandhi during the emergency adding socialist to the preamble of Indian Constitution. It was a well thought out qualitative change of perception about the goal of the Indian revolution which had the sanction of Chandershekhar Azad as well, who was not that well read but who trusted Bhagat Singh absolutely.

Before the formation of HSRA, Bhagat Singh trained himself in mass organizational work. Naujawan Bharat Sabha, on the pattern of youth organization in Italy inspired by Mazzini and Garibaldi was formed in 1926. Bhagat Singh was its general secretary and Bhagwati Charan Vohra was propaganda secretary. NBS worked to organize lantern shows of patriots' pictures. They were particularly inspired by the sacrifice of Kartar Singh Sarabha, as he was executed at the young age of 19, in 1915 at Lahore and whose photograph Bhagat Singh always kept in his pocket. In all their public meetings they used to garland Sarabha's picture, put on the dais. During this period, Ghadrite revolutionaries returned from Moscow, trained in Communist theory in the Eastern university, had formed the Kirti group and Santokh

Singh had started *Kirti*, a journal in Punjabi with which Bhagat Singh was associated as writer. After Sohan Singh Josh, became its editor at the untimely death of Santokh Singh in relative youth, Bhagat Singh even formally worked on the *Kirti* staff for a while, as he was in touch with Sohan Singh Josh, in connection with Naujawan Bharat Sabha activities. Even before forming NBS in Lahore, Bhagat Singh was in touch with the earliest Communists of the country in Kanpur, a working class city. He was in touch with Satyabhakat, Radha Mohan Gokulji, Shaukat Usmani, etc. So practically Bhagat Singh was part of the Communist movement in India since its very inception, his later activities testifies this fact. Bhagat Singh did not become formally a member of the Communist party as it was still in the formative period. Bhagat Singh had met one of the founders of the Communist movement, Muzzafar Ahmad, who had come to Lahore after his release from jail in the Kanpur conspiracy case in 1924, about which he himself had referred in his autobiographical writing. While Bhagat Singh had no reservations about joining the Communist Party, but they themselves probably were trying to shape their own revolutionary organization HSRA as an elementary form of Communist organization. Bhagat Singh was also clear as is evident from his jail writings, that ultimately HSRA had to take recourse to mass organization of workers, peasants, students and other potentially revolutionary sections of society. Whereas he and his group were of the view that keeping in mind the backwardness among Indian masses, some spectacular revolutionary actions along with sacrifices of young men, to awaken the masses from slumber, were necessary to arouse the upsurge against British colonialism. Sohan Singh Josh had aptly described it in his *Four Meetings with Bhagat Singh*. And after the formation of HSRA in September 1928, some such political developments took place, which did not allow any time to HSRA to transform it as a party nucleus of large mass organizations, though apart from Naujawan Bharat Sabha, Lahore Students Union, Bal Students Union, Bal Bharat Sabha like mass organizations were also formed. This is interesting to know that NBS had helped form Bal Bharat Sabha, an organization of school students between the age of 12 and 16. And no historian has paid attention to this interesting aspect of the freedom struggle. President of Bal Bharat Sabha Amritsar,

Kahan Chand, aged just 11 years was awarded three months rigorous imprisonment. Yash, later a renowned editor of the Urdu daily *Milap* and son of Mahasha Khushal Chand was secretary of Bal Bharat Sabha, whose on record age was ten years and who was being persecuted on three counts including assisting the Lahore City Congress and Naujawan Bharat Sabha. In those days, total numbers of 1192 juveniles under the age of 15, were convicted for political activities. The share of Punjab being 189 and Bengal 739. Apart from Bal Bharat Sabha, Bal Student Union was also active then. In fact this shows the impact of Bhagat Singh in those days on not only youth, even the Lahore City Congress was affected by his magnetic personality.

Lala Lajpat Rai's grandson Baldev Raj was secretary of the Bal Student Union and Dayanat Rai was President. Such was the infectious impact of patriotic feelings generated by Bhagat Singh and his comrades in those days. Alarmed by Bhagat Singh's impact on youth, Bhagat Singh was arrested by the Lahore police in May 1927 on the excuse of his involvement in the October 1926 Dussehra bomb case. He was kept in jail for about six weeks, before being released on the bail bond of sixty thousand rupees, which was withdrawn a few months later. It was during this period, Bhagat Singh planned mass activities, but before such mass activities could be expanded in these areas, the Simon Commission came to India. Naujawan Bharat Sabha in Punjab was more active than even the Congress and in spite of differences with Lala Lajpat Rai, in the background of Lalaji's association with communal elements, which was openly opposed by Bhagat Singh and Naujawan Bharat Sabha and angrily Lala Lajpat Rai had shut the doors of his house for Bhagat Singh, Sukhdev and Bhagwati Charan Vohra, Lalaji was requested to lead the demonstration against the Simon Commission, when he was visiting Lahore on October 30, 1928. Bhagat Singh himself was not present in the demonstration and NBS activists were providing cover to Lalaji and when the clash with British police took place, the S.P. of Lahore city Scott ordered a *lathi* charge and D.S.P. Saunders personally hit blows upon Lalaji, resulting in his death on 17th November, due to this brutal attack. Basanti Devi, widow of the late C.R. Das, exhorted the country youth to avenge the insult heaped on the nation. Bhagat Singh could not miss the occasion even though he and HSRA wanted to renounce violent activities. To protect the honour of the nation, HSRA decided to do away with Scott, who was responsible for ordering this attack. Bhagat Singh and Rajguru were chosen to shoot Scott. Jai Gopal was to identify and Chandershekhar Azad was to provide cover to the whole team. Bhagat Singh was supposed to shoot first, but at the signal given by Jai Gopal, identifying the British officer, Rajguru immediately shot at him, while Bhagat Singh tried to call Azad by saying, 'Panditji he is not Scott'. (Proceedings of the Lahore conspiracy case, Sukhdev's notes on sides), before Bhagat Singh could complete his sentence, Saunders was already shot by Rajguru, who always wished to be in the forefront of every action. Bhagat Singh had no option but to pump three or four more bullets into Saunders' fallen body in order to ensure that he did not survive. The task was complete and even the killing of Saunders, who was equally responsible for Lalaji's death and who was as much a symbol of colonial power as was Scott, revolutionaries owned the act with posters in Lahore by the next morning.

But this action also sealed the fate of Bhagat Singh, who himself was absolutely clear in his own mind that he was going to be executed in this case, whenever he was arrested. So with a razor sharp mind and with crystal clear perception, Bhagat Singh decided to perform as many spectacular revolutionary acts as possible in the short duration of his remaining lifetime. In fact he drew a clear plan of his life and actions and it was the most powerful British colonial authority, which was getting trapped in his drawn out political map of the events to follow— his own martyrdom, but whose time and manner was selected by Bhagat Singh himself and that is a very fascinating story of the greatest symbol of the Indian revolutionary movement, Bhagat Singh.

Many comrades of HSRA were underground for their involvement in the Kakori rail dacoity case, particularly Chandershekhar Azad. After the Saunders' murder, Bhagat Singh, Rajguru, Sukhdev, et cetera. also went underground. Immediately after this case, Bhagat Singh escaped to Calcutta along with Durga Bhabhi. There he remained in touch with Congress session delegates like Sohan Singh Josh and also some Bengali revolutionaries, out of which Jatinder Nath Das agreed to come to Lahore to train other comrades in the bomb making technique. HSRA, at this point was in a fix, while adopting the socialist perspective of Indian liberation, they wanted to focus on organizing workers, peasants, students and youth; on the other hand, Saunders' murder and some earlier cases against them could not allow them to work openly. Neither could they take cover of the Congress Party for open political work, as they had serious and fundamental differences with the Congress Party. If they allowed themselves to be tried in the pending cases against them and after getting cleared, participate in the process of organizing masses, there was very little scope for that. The only option Bhagat Singh could visualize in such a binding situation was to awaken the countrymen by their revolutionary activities but with minimum loss of life and then sacrifice their own lives in such a manner that the whole country became aware of their goals and ideas. Bhagat Singh also wanted to remove the terrorist tag from their organization, as well as from their individual selves. For this they wished to use such platforms, from where their voice could reach millions of people. Bhagat Singh could visualize that what they could not achieve by living longer, they would achieve by sacrificing their lives in the prime of the youth but in a manner in which their sacrifices would not go unnoticed, rather these became the focus of several compatriots. By shooting Saunders in daylight, HSRA moved in this direction in right earnestness. This incident inspired millions of countrymen as Lala Lajpat Rai, one of the foremost leaders of the country and his death caused due to the colonial police's brutal *lathi* charge, made them simmer with anger in their humiliation. By killing Saunders, HSRA and Bhagat Singh came into centre focus of the nation's political scene, though Bhagat Singh made it absolutely clear in one of his court statements that they bore no personal grudge or malice against anyone and 'we hold human life sacred beyond words would sooner lay our lives in the service of humanity than injure anyone else' (*Selected Writings of Shaheed Bhagat Singh*, ed. Shiv Verma, p. 72).

When Jatin Das came to Lahore, bomb factories were established in some rented houses. To stabilize the people's enthusiastic response to Saunders' murder, Bhagat Singh wanted another such equally spectacular action. The British colonial government was bent upon notifying Public Safety Bill and Trade Disputes Bill as law, in spite of stiff opposition from the masses on roads and from members of the

Central Assembly. And they decided to throw harmless bombs to cause a loud noise by their explosion in the Central Assembly. The issue was discussed in the central committee of HSRA in the absence of Sukhdev. Bhagat Singh's proposal to send him for action was rejected as he was bound to be trapped in the Saunders' murder case and the party did not want to lose leadership at such a crucial time. When Sukhdev came to know of the decision, though a close friend of Bhagat Singh, he became upset and angry with him. He taunted him for 'trying to save his life', knowing fully well that he was the best suitable person for the job, as no one else could project the party view as effectively as he could. The central committee met again and Bhagat Singh insisted that not only would he go, he along with his other comrades would get themselves arrested after the act. B.K. Dutt was to accompany him. The party wanted them to escape after the act, but reluctantly agreed to Bhagat Singh's proposals. Along with Jai Dev Kapoor, who was to accompany them to the Central Assembly, but come out before the throwing of bombs, Bhagat Singh observed the entry and exit of the Central Assembly. Dr. Saiffudin Kitchlew, member of the Assembly had recognized him, despite his getting shaved in this period. This action was inspired by the similar act of France's revolutionary Vaillant in the French Parliament to focus attention on the poverty of people, which had the famous one-liner, 'it needs explosion to make the deaf hear'. This is the first sentence of the pamphlet thrown by Bhagat Singh, and B.K. Dutt in the Central Assembly after they had thrown two harmless bombs over the empty benches of the Central Assembly. But the explosion did create a commotion in the Assembly and only a few members like Pandit Motilal Nehru, Madan Mohan Malviya and Jinnah could keep their calm by remaining standing on their seats. Most of the others, including the home secretary ran helter skelter, some even hiding under the benches. And here the two historic slogans came into existence on the Indian political horizon—*Inqlab Zindabad*—(Long Live Revolution) and *Samrajyavad Ka Nash Ho* (Down with Imperialism) and in the course of time, these slogans particularly *Inqlab Zindabad* became part of not only revolutionary groups, but of all other organizations, including even Congress stages. Of course the RSS, a Hindu Maha Sabha like communal organization would never touch this slogan. In fact *Inqlab Zindabad* is a translation of 'Long Live Revolution', an international slogan of the working class movement, it was tried to be translated in Hindi as, *Kranti Chirjivi Ho*, but it did not catch the imagination of people. *Inqlab Zindabad* not only caught the imagination of Hindi-speaking people of India, it spread from Agartala to Madras and from Srinagar to Bombay. Not only that this slogan became an international slogan, it became quite popular in Pakistan, Bangladesh, Nepal and so many other countries as well and Bhagat Singh felt rightly proud that 'in his small life, he had made this slogan reach crores of Indians'. *Inqlab Zindabad*, finally replaced *Bande Matram*, which was the popular slogan of the nationalist movement from 1905 to April 8, 1929, prior to Bhagat Singh and Dutt raising it in the Central Assembly. In any objective analysis of Bhagat Singh 'contribution to the national movement, the most popular slogan of the masses *Inqlab Zindabad*, would always shine with his name'.

This action was planned in a very meticulous manner. Photographs of Bhagat Singh and Dutt were made before the action, copies of the statement issued on the occasion were made in plenty and the press got these in time and on very same day, April 8, 1929. *The Hindustan Times* published the full statement in its special evening edition. British police officers were scared even to arrest them as both men held live pistols in their hands, but while shouting slogans, they put their pistols on the table, indicating to the police that they were ready to be arrested. Police officers moved towards them only after they had kept their pistols aside and arrested them. In the meantime, Jaidev Kapoor had already gone out of the Assembly hall. The purported target of the revolutionary group was achieved and now the next task was to spread the message of revolution to the countrymen. Bhagat Singh had again a well thought out plan. They would not defend them in British courts, rather they would use British courts as platforms to spread their values by making political statements there. They did not hire any lawyer for their defence, but accepted the consultancy with advocates, so nationalist advocate Asaf Ali was available to them for consultancy and Asaf Ali read Bhagat Singh and B.K. Dutt's historic statement in the sessions court on June 6, 1929, where they were being tried in the Delhi bomb case. This statement is a policy document which explains the aims and objectives of the revolutionary movement in most lucid terms:

'We humbly claim to be no more than serious students of the history and the conditions of our country and her aspirations. We despise hypocrisy. Our practical protest was against the institution, which since its birth has eminently helped to display not only its worthlessness, but its far reaching power for injustice. The more we have pondered, the more deeply we have been convinced that it exists only to demonstrate to the world India's humiliation and helplessness and it symbolizes the overriding domination of an irresistible and autocratic rule. Solemn resolutions passed by the house have been contemptuously trampled underfoot on the floor of the so-called Indian Parliament' (same p. 71).

Bhagat Singh and Dutt further clarified their aim, 'we deliberately offered ourselves to bear the penalty for what we had done and to let the imperialist exploiters know that by crushing individuals, they cannot kill ideas. By crushing two insignificant units a nation cannot be crushed' (p. 73). And they dared the colonialist power by putting the question: 'Can ordinances and safety bills snuff out the flames of freedom in India? Conspiracy cases, trumped up or discovered and the incarceration of all young men who cherish the vision of a great ideal, can not check the march of a revolution. But a timely warning if not unheeded, can help to prevent loss of life and general sufferings. We took it upon ourselves to provide this warning and our duty is done' (pp. 73-74).

The main statement ends with these words. Bhagat Singh and Dutt in their statement had explained how thoughtfully they had thrown the harmless bombs in 'vacant spaces', in order not to harm any one, not even the British and the only harm these did was, slight damage to the empty bench and slight abrasions in less than half a dozen cases. And since they were asked in the lower court, 'what he meant by the word revolution', in his statement in his session court addition, he explains the concept of revolution almost in Marxist terminology. They speak of the knowledge of capitalism and establishment of dictatorship of proletariat, for the consummation of the ideal of revolution. And yet they also tell the British colonial power the Marxist epithet that 'peaceful transition is also possible if timely warning is heeded by the power that be' the statement concludes again with the slogan 'Long Live Revolution'.

In fact the concept of revolution had become so all engrossing for Bhagat Singh that all his attention and energy was focused on clarifying it to himself as well as to his comrades and countrymen and the imperialist British power. When Ramanand Chatterjee, the editor of *Modern Review* ridiculed the slogan Long Live Revolution, Bhagat Singh and Dutt rebutted him with the letter which was published in *The Tribune* on December 24, 1929. 'Revolution did not necessarily involve sanguinary strife. It was not a cult of bomb and pistol. They may sometimes be mere means for it achievement. A rebellion is not a revolution. It may ultimately lead to that end' (p. 81).

Bhagat Singh defines revolution as the 'spirit of longing for change for the better' and they wish that the spirit of revolution should always permeate the soul of humanity, so that the reactionary forces may not accumulate strength to check its eternal onward march'.

Shiv Verma in his introduction to the *Selected Writings of Shaheed Bhagat Singh* has drawn attention to 'Ideology and development of the revolutionary movement from Chapekars to Bhagat Singh'. This is a significant analyses of the Indian revolutionary movement. Though there had been sporadic rebellions or revolutionary activities against the British colonialism from 1757 onwards, when they had won the battle of Plassey and started controlling India step by step through the East India Company. There had been tribal revolts in Bihar, Jharkhand like those of Tilka Manjhi, Sido-Kanu and others, even before the first war of independence fought in 1857, after which direct British rule was established.

Incidentally, Veer Savarkar, who wrote a book in Marathi under the same title in 1907 or so, was not the first to call it the first war in place of Ghadar, as described by British colonialism. It was Karl Marx, as early as in 1858, calling it the first war of 'Indian independence', to whom the present followers of Savarkar, that is RSS, VHP, Shiv Sena, BJP, Bajrang Dal, et cetera, hate vehemently. The so-called votaries of nationalism are not prepared to give credit to Marx for giving them the first lesson in nationalism, because that lesson does not lead to 'cultural nationalism' of their variety.

Shiv Verma had traced the entry of revolutionaries in the freedom struggle from the Chapekar brothers in Poona in 1897, who fired the first shots. It was the time when Tilak dominated the national scene, who used to expose the British colonial state machinery's anti-people role in his paper *Kesri*. At that time there was an outbreak of plague in Poona and British officer Rand was too oppressive. On June 22, 1897, Rand and Averest were shot dead by the Chapekar brothers, who went to the gallows. But the distinct feature of these earliest revolutionaries was that they were inspired by strong religious sentiments of Hinduism. The same situation prevailed in Bengal. Bankim Chandra's novel—*Anand Math* published in 1882, containing the nationalist song as war cry of *Sanyasi* revolutionaries called—*Vande Matram*, which had created so much controversy at its non-existent centenary in September 2006. The trend continued with Savarkar in Maharashtra. So during the first phase from 1897 to 1913, Shiv Verma sees as the 'phase of revolutionary movement inspired by Hindu religion'. Anushilan Samiti in Bengal was also in the same line. Khudi Ram Bose and Praful Chaki had given their lives in the cause of revolution in 1908 in Bihar. Khudi Ram Bose was even younger than Sarabha, at the time of his execution. Madan Lal Dhingra, who shot dead Colonel Wyle in London and got executed in 1909, was also inspired by Savarkar. Tilak, Lala Lajpat Rai, Bipan Chandra Pal and Aurobindo Ghosh like the earliest nationalists drew their inspiration from religion. But at the same time there was another trend, which Shiv Verma had not been able to pay due attention, particularly in foreign countries and in Punjab. Shyamji Krishan Verma and Madam Bhikaji Cama, Indian revolutionaries abroad were flying the flag of socialism high, as early as in 1907 or so. Shyamji Krishan Verma through his paper *Indian Sociologist* and Bhikaji Cama through their association with the international socialist movement. In Punjab, Ajit Singh, an uncle of Bhagat Singh and others had formed the 'Bharat Mata Society' and it focused on peasants' exploitation. Punjabi nationalist poet and comrade of Ajit Singh, Banke Dayal's song *Pagri Sambhal Jatta*—take care of your turban, O' peasant, was a war cry in Punjab. This song describes the exploitation of peasants and exhorts him to revolt. This song was first sung in March 1907, and it centenary year also fell in 2007. Banke Dayal was imprisoned for writing this song. Aurobindo's brother, Barinder Kumar Ghosh and Swami

Vivekananda's brother Dr. Bhupender Nath Dutt, had both overstepped narrow religious vision of nationalism and adopted a more advanced and progressive socialist vision of nationalism in their later life.

Shiv Verma had rightly focused upon the Ghadar party formation in America as the beginning of the secular nationalist movement from 1914 onwards. Although the process of its growth was going on from 1909 itself, when Ajit Singh, revolutionary uncle of Bhagat Singh, was forced to leave the country into exile. Lala Hardyal, Tarak Nath Das and G.D. Kumar like revolutionaries were either writing pamphlets or bringing out papers in India and abroad, which had finally led to the formation of the Ghadar party, a later popular name of 'Hindustani Association of the Pacific Coast', under the presidentship of Baba Sohan Singh Bhakna and Lala Hardyal as general secretary. The association came into being on 21st April, and its paper *Ghadar Di Goonj* started from November 1, 1913, with which the party also became popular as Ghadar party and its foundation day was celebrated on 1st November every year. *Ghadar Di Goonj* was started initially in Urdu, but later editions in Punjabi, Hindi, Gujarati, et cetera, also began and its circulation was beyond ten thousand in those days. The party was named the Ghadar party to appropriate the legacy of the 1857 Ghadar movement and British colonialists discredited the word Ghadar which was given a new respectability. Its headquarters in San Francisco was named Yugantar, again to appropriate the Yugantar revolutionary movement of Bengal. The organization and movement had several Punjabis, followed by Bengalis and a few members from UP, CP and the south. The Ghadar party gave a call to liberate India through armed struggle and gave even the date of February 21, 1915, later changed to 19th February. That the movement did not succeed due to various factors, but it revolutionized the traditional revolutionary movements in India, which for the first time, after 1857, was inclusive of people from all religious communities. Not only Kartar Singh Sarabha, the youngest martyr and hero of the movement, there was Vishnu Ganesh Pingley, Rehmatullah like martyrs and Tarak Nath Das, Champak Raman Pillai, D. Chenchiah, Barkatullah like activists from different parts of the country. It had a true all India character and modern secular perception. That is why after being detected in its attempt to overthrow the British colonial regime in1915 it reorganized itself and it took the shape of the first Communist groups in Punjab to which Bhagat Singh was directly related. In fact Bhagat Singh's personality was shaped by the tradition of his uncle Ajit Singh and by the Ghadar party in the true sense.

The Ghadar movement took place prior to the 1917 Soviet revolution, but it was first among the organizations worldwide, which were deeply impressed by it. By 1922 or so, Ghadarite revolutionaries had started reaching the Soviet Union and getting ideological training from the Communist University of Working People of the East, which was established in 1921. Barkatullah, Secretary of the Ghadar party, after Lala Hardyal had left the USA, was in the Soviet Union even prior to Rattan Singh and Santokh Singh, who were most important Ghadarites, had come to the Soviet Union in 1922. Santokh Singh later started *Kirti*, the Punjabi journal from Punjab, with which Bhagat Singh was deeply associated. Apart from Ghadarites, there were many other Indian revolutionaries in the Soviet Union in those days. Bhagat Singh was also in touch with the Kanpur group of communists—Radha Mohan Gokulji, Satyabhakat, Hasarat Mohani and Shaukat Usmani. He had also met Muzaffar Ahmad in Lahore earlier. Satyabhakat even wrote a small book on Bhagat Singh in Hindi, *Krantiveer Bhagat Singh*, after his martyrdom.

Shiv Varma had discussed the growth of Bhagat Singh's thought towards scientific socialism, through his writings and also through his close personal interaction with him in jail and before that. In Bhagat Singh, he had concluded the ideological development of revolutionaries movement in India reaching the perception of the socialist revolution. This has been an objective assessment, yet some later movements also need mention. The Chittagong revolt of 1932 was one such revolutionary movement, which is comparable to the earlier Ghadar movement. Led by legendary Master Surjya Sen, inclusive of both Anushilan and Yugantar factions, the Chittagong revolt had given the call of 'Do and Die', much before Gandhi had given the call of 'Do or Die' in 1942. The Chittagong revolt led to the martyrdom of the young revolutionary girl Preeti Lata Wadedar, apart from other martyrs. Another distinctive feature of surviving

Chittagong revolutionaries was that they also joined the Communist group in jail, while serving their sentence, under the influence of renowned Ghadarite Baba Gurmukh Singh, Ganesh Ghosh and Anant Singh like legendary Chittagong revolutionaries became committed Communists.

In 1940, Udham Singh, inspired by Bhagat Singh shot dead Michael O'Dwyer, responsible for the Jallianwala Bagh massacre and of other oppression in Punjab in 1919 and got hanged in London. 'Quit India' movement of 1942, also had the experience of freeing certain areas of Ballia from British yoke for a few days. Netaji Subhas Chandra Bose's Azad Hind Fouj's march towards Indian freedom and the 1946 Navy revolt are part of the glorious legacy of India's revolutionary movements. But the distinctive feature of all revolutionary movements after Bhagat Singh and HSRA, is that these had been secular and democratic to the core and broadly leftist in thought. Netaji Subhas Chandra Bose was helped out of India by none else than Bhagat Ram Talwar in Kabul, a Ghadarite sympathizer and brother of martyr Harikishan.

Returning to Bhagat Singh's story, there were two priorities in the agenda of Bhagat Singh in jail:

(i) To expose British colonialism through courts by using courts as the platform for the spread of their ideas.
(ii) To expose the brutalities of British colonialism in jail by resorting to hunger strikes in jail and thus drawing public attention.

Bhagat Singh was successful to the hilt in achieving his tasks in both the activities. Not that British authorities were unaware of his plans, but they were just put in the dock by the self-sacrificing spirit of Bhagat Singh and his comrades.

The third agenda of Bhagat Singh was his own ideological development. It is amazing to see a man, about to go to the gallows, immersing himself deep, in the most serious study of the history of world revolutionaries and in most trying circumstances. Bhagat Singh did not have the privilege to go to libraries every day or bookshops, with a purse full of money to buy books at will and then visit the coffee house occasionally to discuss new ideas. He was preparing court statements, in which his serious study of Marxism definitely helped him. He was organizing hunger strikes for months together, he was spending time with his comrades, he was being brutally beaten up in courts by police and then nursing his wounds in jail and along with all these things, he was studying and taking notes from the books he was reading. He was also writing as mentioned by Shiv Verma in his preface.

Mention is made of four manuscripts drafted by Bhagat Singh in jail:

(i) The Ideal of Socialism (ii) Autobiography (iii) History of Revolutionary Movements in India and (iv) At the Door of Death. According to Shiv Verma, these manuscripts were smuggled through Kumari Lajjawati of Jalandhar, who handed them over to Bejoy Kumar Sinha in 1938, after his release from Andaman jail. Sinha passed these on to a friend for safe custody, who destroyed the manuscripts in fear of a police raid at some stage. However the manuscript of Jail Notebook was collected by Kulbir Singh or some other member of Bhagat Singh's family. Kumari Lajjawati, who was secretary of the Bhagat Singh defence committee and Congress activist, frequently visited Lahore jail to discuss legal aspects of the case. In an interview to Nehru Memorial Museum and Library's oral history cell, she mentioned that she brought some papers given by Bhagat Singh, which later she showed to Feroze Chand, editor of *People*, Lala Lajpat Rai's established paper from Lahore. Feroze Chand was told to select, whatever he wanted for publication in the *People*. Feroze Chand selected some papers and returned the remaining to Lajjawati, which she handed over to Bejoy Kumar Sinha in 1938. Feroze Chand published *Why I Am an Atheist*, out of those papers on September 27, 1931 issue, ironically, Bhagat Singh's first birthday after his execution on 23rd March the same year. Prior to that *People* in its issue of 29th March, just after Bhagat Singh's execution, published extracts from the now famous 'The Letter to Young Political Workers.' It seems that Feroze Chand had selected, what had been mentioned by Shiv Verma as, 'At the Door of Death' and some other papers, including Bhagat Singh's letter on death sentence given to the young revolutionary Harikishan, which was also published by *People*. Bhagat Singh's father was keen to acquire or at least see those papers, which was strictly refused by

Lajjawati, purportedly on the instructions of Bhagat Singh himself. The strange part of this whole saga of indifference to the documents, considered so valuable now, is that neither Kumari Lajjawati nor Feroze Chand, not even Bejoy Kumar Sinha, who was given the custodianship of those papers on the instructions of Bhagat Singh himself, took the trouble to look seriously at the papers and at least note down their contents. How Shiv Verma had seen the contents of those papers, is also shrouded in mystery, he might have seen them in jail from Bhagat Singh himself, but whether those were really the proper manuscripts or just notes like Jail Notebook, can't be said with certainty. It does not seem that this mystery will be resolved. This does seem certain that the essentials of Bhagat Singh's thought had come to light and evaluation of his thought process can be made on the basis of retrieved documents, which are quite substantial.

On the surface it appears difficult to write four full-fledged books in such a short time (about two years April 8, 1929 to March 23, 1931), which included the activities mentioned above. Out of the two titles two seem interrelated and autobiographical—the autobiography and *At the Door of Death*—the other two, if these could be shorter pamphlets, then those seem possible, but writing a full-fledged history of the revolutionary movement in India, seems somewhat impossible under those circumstances.

However, Bhagat Singh did plan to write a full-fledged book on 'The Science of the State', for which he had taken detailed notes, which are included in his Jail Notebook, the only original part of it. In this proposed book, Bhagat Singh was trying to trace the growth of the state from primitive communism to the modern socialist state. Had he got the time to write this book, probably it would have been a major contribution to Marxist study of the concept of the state, which can be observed from his notes as well.

The manuscript which survived and issued in reprint by Leftword Books in 2007, the first print being published in 1994, edited by Bhupender Hooja, is a significant document in its own right. It is not a notebook like the prison notebooks of Gramsci or philosophical notebooks of Lenin, not even like Che Guevara's diaries. It is not a diary at all, this notebook is unique in its own way. It includes the notes of the books read by Bhagat Singh in jail, before his execution.

Apart from being significant in its selection, these notes are an objective mirror of development of Bhagat Singh's ideology. These are also reflective of his aesthetic sensibilities, as many quotes are from classic literary pieces of world literature. These quotes show that Bhagat Singh was a revolutionary with rare sensitivity. During his student days and after, his fondness for films had been mentioned by many of his close friends and comrades. Being a fan of Charlie Chaplin films and also films like *Uncle Tom's Cabin* or *Three Musketeers.*

Being a good singer, acting in the college drama team—all these show his involvement with literature and other art forms. That is why the older revolutionary Ram Saran Das asked Bhagat Singh for an introduction to his poetry collection—*Dreamland*, which is now one of his more important documents.

This is also interesting to know that much before Bhagat Singh's Jail Notebook came to be focused upon in India, it was discussed in detail by Soviet ideologist L.V. Mitrokhin in his 1981 book—*Lenin and India*, whose Hindi translation was published in 1990. In this book, one full chapter is devoted to *The Last Days of Bhagat Singh.* In this book references have been made to even earlier documents such as A.V. Raikov's 1971 article 'Bhagat Singh and His Ideological Legacy', Mitrokhin's own, *The Books Read by Bhagat Singh,* included in the 1971 publication, *India on Lenin,* etc. In these Russian publications, assessment of Bhagat Singh's ideological development has been made quite objectively and he had been placed in the tradition of Marxist thought. I myself had seen the manuscript of the Jail Notebook in the Nehru Memorial Museum and Library in 1984 sometime and started writing about it in Hindi journals occasionally, regretting its non-publication. NMML had got its copy from Bhagat Singh's younger brother Kulbir Singh with the condition of 'not publishing it'. It was only in 1992 that the late Bhupendar Hooja, chief editor, *Indian Book Chronicle* from Jaipur, started serializing it in his monthly. My letter of appreciation made Hooja feel more confident about its authenticity and so he published it with his editorial notes in book form in 1994 from Jaipur. Despite some good reviews and being such a significant historical document, the notebook remained somewhat less focused. Ironically translations of the notebook were done in Hindi and other languages, without giving any credit to the painstaking work of annotations done by its elderly, yet energetic editor of the notebook, Bhupender Hooja. Its new edition in 2007 has brought this historical document into proper focus and has drawn the attention of historians, students of Indian revolutionary freedom movement and political activists alike. This document should be read in relation to Bhagat Singh's other significant documents like, 'Why I Am an Atheist', 'Court Statements', 'Letter to Young Political Workers', etc., which by now have acquired the status of classic documents of the revolutionary movement. In fact in the notebook, the quotes taken from books, other than literary sources are sort of references to the significant books of development of democratic political thought, which include books from ancient Greek thought to the latest Marxist classics of that time. In a way the notebook is also a mirror of the ideological development of Bhagat Singh's personality, which concluded with the partially read book of Lenin on March 23, 1931. Punjabi revolutionary poet Paash has paid an apt tribute to Bhagat Singh in his last moments, by saying that 'Indian youth need to read the next page of Lenin's book, folded by Bhagat Singh on the last day of his life'.

Bhagat Singh's story continued in jail through indefinite hunger strikes, along with his comrades, in which their dear comrade Jatin Das gave his life on September 13, 1929, on the 63rd day of his fast unto death. His health was beyond redemption, forcible feeding of milk had burst his lungs and despite appeals and break of fast by his other colleagues a few days earlier, Jatin Das refused to give up his fast, with the clear understanding and declaration that he was consciously giving up his life for the nation. Bhagat Singh and Dutt continued their fast even after Jatin Das's death, breaking it only in the first week of October, making at that time, a record of 115 days fast. Bhagat Singh had another round of hunger strikes against the tribunal hearing Saunders' murder case, when they were brutally beaten up at the orders of presiding Judge Coldstream, the order, from which Indian Judge Agha Haider had disassociated himself on record, for which he was removed from the tribunal.

The political weapon of hunger strike was used by Bhagat Singh and his comrades in a most effective manner. In fact it needs to be emphasized that the moral strength of observing self-sacrificing hunger strike has always been effective in all societies and it still carries that a strength. The difference between a suicide bomber and hunger striker is that a suicide bomber, while giving his life for the cause, dear to him, takes away the lives of others as well and as such loses the sympathy of people, whereas a hunger striker, harming only his or her health or even sacrificing his or her life, pricks the conscience of the nation. Bhagat Singh and his comrades were aware of this fact and they used it to the hilt, erasing the impression of being killers or terror creators. This also shows the political maturity of Bhagat Singh. The weapon of hunger strike is quite effective even today, provided it carries the moral strength of the cause and the person undertaking this step.

Bhagat Singh and his comrades boycotted the trial of Saunders' murder and the way the tribunal handed over the death sentence to Bhagat Singh, Rajguru and Sukhdev, is thoroughly exposed in A.G. Noorani's book *The Trial of Bhagat Singh*. It was nothing but murder, committed by British colonialists of Indian revolutionaries, through judicial drama and Bhagat Singh had befittingly written to the Governor of Punjab on 20th March, three days before their execution, to treat them as 'war prisoners' as they were waging war against British imperialism and as such 'they should be shot dead' rather than being hanged. But the British imperial power proved to be so cowardly that they could not even maintain their own timing of hanging, that is 6 to 7 a.m., against all international norms, they hanged Bhagat Singh, Rajguru and Sukhdev at 7 p.m. on 23rd March itself, the day a huge rally was held at Lahore by Naujawan Bharat Sabha, which apprehended that execution would take place on the 24th morning. Scared of a huge gathering at Lahore Central Jail of people, British colonial officials executed them at 7 p.m. on the 23rd itself. But the news could not be withheld from the people of Lahore. The rally was about to end, when the news of executions came and people rushed to the gates of the jail. Scared British officials cut the warm bodies of martyrs in pieces and after filling these in sacks, took them away from the back gates of the jail towards Sutlej riverbank near Ferozepur. It was a whole night exercise, British officials getting some *Granthis* and *Pandits* from Ferozepur town, to perform so-called religious rituals. Whereas they were not even shown the bodies, which were burnt in kerosene in an alarming hurry in a jungle, near Ganda Singhwalla village. People from Ferozepur and Lahore followed in the night itself, searching for the place and before the dawn of 24th March, they were able to locate the soft place, out of which some unburnt and half burnt bones, smell of kerosene and stains of blood came out. People in anguish and anger collected these items and reached Lahore. The proper cremation of three martyrs was done on the banks of river Ravi, where earlier Lala Lajpat Rai was cremated. The Congress party in Punjab at that time, formed a fact finding committee to enquire into the mistreatment to dead bodies of the martyrs. Newspapers in those days, particularly *Bhavishya* from Allahabad, had highlighted committees hearing, but the report was either not released or remain dumped in Congress papers. While the Kanpur riots report of Congress, after the execution of martyrs had drawn national attention and its reprint has been published by the National Book Trust, it is strange that no one ever even refers to the Congress party's fact finding report about supreme martyrs bodies disposal by British colonial authorities, Kanpur riots, which started after the execution of Bhagat Singh and his comrades, unfortunately assumed communal colour and tragically took the life of Congress leader, nationalist journalist and admirer of Bhagat Singh—Ganesh Shankar Vidyarthi.

The condition of the martyrs memorial was similar. The fact is that Naujawan Bharat Sabha had formed a memorial committee to build a suitable memorial for the martyrs, which was sabotaged by the Congress party through the father of Bhagat Singh, S. Kishan Singh, with the promise that the Congress party would build a national memorial for the martyrs. That later a memorial near Ferozepur called Hussainiwala was built, had no relevance at that time to the national movement. Lahore was the hub of the national movement, it was the place where Bhagat Singh and his comrades had spent their lives in political action, it was there, they were executed and it was there, where they were properly cremated, where earlier Lala Lajpat Rai had been cremated. The most logical thing would have been to build a memorial in memory of Lala Lajpat Rai, Bhagat Singh, Sukhdev and Rajguru on the banks of river Ravi, which would be a source of inspiration for the youth of Punjab, which could even be a deterrent to the division of Punjab.

At looking back more than 80 years, one can only wonder that how come no memorial was built to these martyrs in Lahore or birth places of Bhagat Singh and Sukhdev in Lyallpur, now called Faislabad in Pakistan. Even today it is desirable that Pakistani and Indian democratic people should erect a suitable memorial at Lahore, as well as at Faislabad, in memory of Bhagat Singh. He is the one and perhaps only symbol, which evokes respect among Pakistani people as well.

Bhagat Singh is the common thread between now divided Punjabis — a symbol of resistance against colonialism and imperialism. He can still become a common symbol of resistance against American neo imperialism as well. There are some other interesting aspects of the Bhagat Singh saga of Indian history. Bhagat Singh had an excellent rapport with national leaders—be it Subhas Chandra Bose, Jawaharlal Nehru, Lala Lajpat Rai, Madan Mohan Malviya or others. Despite a difference in approach they remained in interaction, while Chandershekhar Azad's meeting with Nehru at Allahabad as described by Nehru himself was not that pleasant. Nehru did not seem much impressed by Azad, but Nehru did pay one thousand rupees to help revolutionaries to go to Russia, which could not materialize, due to Azad's death. Subhas Chandra Bose and Nehru were both greatly appreciative of Bhagat Singh's personality. Congress leaders and revolutionary youth often worked at crossroads, owing to their different perceptions. Seeing Lala Lajpat Rai going wayward with communal forces, Bhagat Singh and his comrades attacked him openly. Yet they did not break with him, same Lala Lajpat Rai's grandson was the secretary of Bal Students Union inspired by Bhagat Singh, Motilal Nehru, Madan Mohan Malviya, Dewan Chaman Lal all condemned bomb throwing by Bhagat Singh in the Central Assembly in rather strong words. Gandhi declared it even as 'a mad act of two young men', Bhagat Singh described Dewan Chaman Lal as a 'psuedo socialist' in his famous session court statement and Tej Bahadur Sapru, as no different from the British, if the system remains the same. Yet the same Pt. Motilal Nehru, Diwan Chaman Lal, Madan Mohan Malviya, even Tej Bahadur Sapru, apart from Jawaharlal Nehru, Subhas Chandra Bose and Jinnah, who stood for these revolutionary youth in courts, or when they were observing hunger strikes, they went to every possible extent to save their lives. Advocates like Asaf Ali, Kailash Nath Katju, Chandra Bhan Gupta, Mohan Lal Saxena, all stood by the youth. It was a spirit of nationalism, which bound these national leaders and revolutionary youth. They criticized each other bitterly, yet together at the time of crisis, particularly against British oppression of the Indian people. Something which needs to be learnt by present-day national leaders and youth.

Another aspect of Bhagat Singh and the revolutionary movement was total opposition to the caste system and communalism. Dalit movements of today, if after Ambedkar, accept any other national hero, as their genuine supporter, it is Bhagat Singh. Bhagat Singh's writings and his conduct earned him the love and support of the Dalit masses. In jail, before going to the gallows, Bhagat Singh was not only reading Lenin, he asked for food from *Bebe*, the name given to Dalit jail employee Bogha affectionately by Bhagat Singh, with the logic that either the mother cleanses the defecation of her children or the scavenger of grown up people. So Bhagat Singh treated the scavenger of the jail like his mother, despite his resistance to do so. And when Bhagat Singh, Sukhdev and Rajguru were going to the gallows, laughing and singing, it was warder Charat Singh and other prisoners, who were crying and also shouting *Inqlab Zindabad*, after Bhagat Singh.

And this is also to be underlined that none of the communal organizations of Hindus, Muslims or Sikhs had spoken a word in favour or defence of these revolutionaries. This also needs to be noted that it is only the left movement in the country, which has truly tried to uphold and imbibe the spirit of the revolutionary movement of our country, while the right forces inside and outside Parliament, have always tried to make noises about appropriating the legacy of this movement, whether on the issue of NCERT books or the so-called *Vande Matram* controversy. In fact rightist forces during and after the freedom struggle had always tried to divide the Indian people on narrow communal lines and always played the role of agents of imperialist forces, old or new. So the left forces of the country are the inheritors of the legacy of the revolutionary freedom struggle, though ironically they were dubbed as 'traitors' for not supporting the 1942 'Quit India' movement, by the agents of imperialism.

In this whole saga, two persons and an institution knew the exact ending of the whole scenario—Gandhi and Bhagat Singh, both knew that nothing can stop execution of revolutionaries. Gandhi because of his own convictions and Bhagat Singh due to his own, equally or perhaps much stronger convictions. The instititution of British colonialism of course knew its finale, as it was bent on finishing these young men, particularly Bhagat Singh, in whose personality it observed the traits of a growing Indian Lenin. The British could afford to deal with the Gandhian Congress party, shedding its political power, but protecting its economic interests. It could not afford to have Bhagat Singh, who, if he remained alive, would have seen the complete overthrow of the system of imperialist and capitalist exploitation. In a way Bhagat Singh had his way vis-à-vis British colonial power. With a group of less than hundred individuals, all over the country, it could unnerve and rattle the most powerful empire on earth, could chalk out its own path to martyrdom, as it must, according to his perception, stir up millions and millions of people, which was to be admitted by none else than Pattabhi Sitaramaya, the Congress historian and Gandhi's candidate against Subhas Chandra Bose in the Tripuri Congress, that Bhagat Singh is no less popular than Mahatma Gandhi. This was not a small achievement for a young man of less than 24 years, with just six or seven years of active political career behind him. After the pronouncement of death sentence, Jaidev Kapoor asked Bhagat Singh 'if he regretted dying so young?' Bhagat Singh first laughed at the question, then replied seriously—'Stepping up on the path of revolution, I had thought that if I could spread the slogan of '*Inqlab Zindabad*' throughout the country, by giving away my life, I would feel that I have received the full value of my life. Today sitting behind the bars of execution barracks, I hear the sound of slogan from crores of people. I believe that this slogan of mine would attack imperialism as the driving force of the freedom struggle till the end. What more value can be of such a small life?'

And Shiv Verma had mentioned an incident of the jail in July 1930, when Bhagat Singh had come to Lahore Burail jail from central jail to meet them on the excuse of discussing their court case. Jokingly they pronounced judgments on one another, excepting Rajguru and Bhagat Singh, knowing they were the ones, who would be hanged. And then Bhagat Singh said that we were afraid to face the reality as the sentence would be 'To be hanged by the neck till we are dead'.

'He was in form that day, he was speaking in low pitch, that was his style. Showing off was not his habit, that was perhaps his strength also.' Then he quotes Bhagat Singh's own words:

'This is the highest award for patriots and I am proud that I am going to get it. They may kill me, but they can not kill my ideas. They may crush my body, but they will not be able to crush my spirits. My ideas will haunt the British like a curse till they are forced to run away from here.' Speaking with his full passion, he continued, 'Bhagat Singh dead will be more dangerous to the British enslavers than Bhagat Singh alive. After I am hanged the fragrance of my revolutionary ideas will permeate the atmosphere of this beautiful land of ours. It will intoxicate the youth and make him made for freedom and revolution, and that would bring the doom of British imperialists nearer. This is my firm conviction, I am anxiously waiting for the day when I will receive the highest award for my services to the country, my love for my people.' (p. 41)

And Shiv Verma concludes his introduction to the writings of Bhagat Singh with these words—'Bhagat Singh was correct, the spirit never dies and it did not die then either'. (p. 42)

And I would conclude that the spirit of Bhagat Singh needs to be lived much more than in 1931. I would recommend the study of Bhagat Singh's Jail Notebook and other writings with Bhagat Singh's own words, which he wrote as an introduction to the poetry collection of fellow revolutionary Ram Saran Das–*Dream Land*:

'Please do not read it to follow blindly and take for granted what is written in it. Read it, criticize it, think over it, try to formulate your own ideas with its help.' Shiv Verma (p. 123).

2

Remembering Bhagat Singh: 75 Years of Martyrdom*

One of the founders of the Communist movement and party in India Muzaffar Ahmad wrote in Bangla about his meeting with Bhagat Singh in 1926. Naujawan Bharat Sabha was formed that year, and a year before, the Communist party came into existence at Kanpur. Abdul Majid of Peshawar and Muzaffar Ahmad had been imprisoned following the Kanpur Bolshevik conspiracy case, and Bhagat Singh had come to pay his respects to Muzaffar Ahmed at the house of his fellow-prisoner and comrade, Abdul Majid. Naujawan Bharat Sabha was a mass organization of youth formed by Bhagat Singh to expose the exploitative character of Bristish colonialism through mass meetings. Thus from the very beginning of Bhagat Singh's active political life, his inclination towards the Communist movement is quite obvious. It is not without reason that the eminent historian Bipan Chandra wrote in an introduction to Bhagat Singh's 'Why I Am an Atheist' in the 1970s: 'During 1925 to 1928, Bhagat Singh read voraciously, devouring in particular books on the Russian Revolution and the Soviet Union, even though getting hold of such books was in itself at the time a revolutionary and difficult task . He also tried to inculcate the reading and thinking habit among his fellow revolutionaries and younger comrades.[1] Already by the end of 1928, he and his comrades had accepted socialism as the final objective of their activities and changed

* Earlier published in *Analytical Monthly Review.*

the name of their organization from Hindustan Republican Association to Hindustan Socialist Republican Association'. Adding the word 'socialism' was quite significant and the motivation to add it originated from Bhagat Singh. And it was not a vague kind of socialism which Bhagat Singh carried in his mind. He accepted socialism as a concept by going through books on Marxism and the experiences of the Soviet Union. Books on both the themes were hard to get in those days as rightly observed by Bipan Chandra.

And when Bhagat Singh landed in jail after throwing bombs in the Delhi Assembly on April 8, 1929, along with B.K. Dutt, his reading became even more organized and mature, even though he had to spend a lot of his time fighting against the atrocities of the jail authorities by resorting to hunger strikes for weeks together, and preparing to present a revolutionary viewpoint in the course of the trial of the cases against him and his comrads: the Lahore conspiracy case, which resulted in his, Sukhdev's and Rajguru's execution and the Delhi Assembly bomb case, in which he and B.K. Dutt were convicted and transported for life, before the sentencing in the Lahore conspiracy case. During the trial, which continued for many weeks, Bhagat Singh and his comrades were subjected to all kinds of police torture and cruelty. Yet the full might of British colonialism which was arrogant enough to claim that 'the sun never sets on the British empire', could not crush the spirit of Bhagat Singh and his comrades. Sri Rajyam Sinha, widow of Bejoy Kumar Sinha, in her reminiscences of her husband, a comrade of Bhagat Singh, 'A Revolutionary's Quest for Sacrifices', gives graphic details of the police torture the revolutionaries, particularly upon Bhagat Singh, were subjected to, inside and outside the court. The revolutionaries had refused to come handcuffed to the court. The court had agreed to it, but did not honour its word and according to Bejoy Kumar Sinha's notes, 'obviously a scuffle began and hell was let loose. Their prestige pricked, the police was hell bent on teaching the accused the lesson of their life. A special Pathan force was requisitioned and merciless beating began. Bhagat Singh was singled out for this. Eight ferocious Pathans pounced on him and with their regulation boots kicked him viciously and beat him with *lathis* ruthlessly. Mr. Roberts, a European officer, pointed out to Sardar Bhagat Singh and said, 'This is the man; give him more beating.' They were dragged on the ground and carried like logs of wood and thrown on the benches. All this happened right in the presence of the visitors in the court compound . The Magistrate too was watching all this apparently thinking that he had no jurisdiction, as he was not presiding over the court. Sheo (Shiv) Verma (who later joined the Communist Party of India [Marxist]) and Ajoy Kumar Ghose (who rose to the position of General Secretary of the Communist Party of India later) fell unconscious. Bhagat Singh then raised his voice and told the court, 'I want to congratulate you on this. Sheo Verma is lying unconscious and if he dies, you will be responsible for this.'[3] One is reminded of the Abu Ghraib and Guantanamo prisons while reading this account.

Three days later, on October 28, 1929, 'The police authorities submitted a report with the concurrence of the jail authorities that it was possible to beat them and even kill them but it was not possible to bring them to the court handcuffed.'

Bhagat Singh, just 22 years old at that time, by virtue of his towering personality, terrorized the British colonial power. The British were not worried when Bhagat Singh was part of a 'terrorist group' for a brief period: they were confident they could deal with terrorism. But they were terror-stricken when HRA turned into HSRA, Bhagat Singh became its chief ideologue and by his statements and mature political conduct in jail and court, got the masses of the country rallying behind them. Bhagat Singh and comrades resorted to frequent hunger strikes for human and political rights for political prisoners. During one of these hunger strikes Jatin Das, a very dear comrade, sacrificed his life on September 13, 1929 in Lahore jail. Crores of Indian people gathered at all railway stations, en route when his mortal remains were taken by train from Lahore to Calcutta. The popularity of Bhagat Singh and his comrades among the Indian masses rose to a level that matched the popularity of Mahatma Gandhi himself. A statement to this effect was made by none else than B. Pattabhi Sitarammaya, who wrote the history of the Congress Party. It is also well known that at the Kanpur session of the Congress Party, held immediately after the execution of Bhagat Singh and his comrades black roses were shown to Mahatma Gandhi by Congress workers, in a spontaneous reaction to the hangings.

Bhagat Singh read much more voraciously inside the jail, despite being certain that he was going to be hanged for his political actions. Even minutes before being taken to the gallows, he was reading a book by Lenin, got through his advocate. The Punjabi revolutionary poet Paash, who was himself martyred by Khalistani terrorists on March 23, 1988, on his hero's martyrdom day, paid an apt tribute to Bhagat Singh in one of his prose pieces saying, 'Indian youth have to read the next page of Lenin's book, left unread by Bhagat Singh at his death'.[4]

Letters written from the jail by Bhagat Singh invariably include lists of books he wanted his visitors to bring him from Dwarka Dass Library, in Lahore. These books were primarily on Marxism, economics, history and creative literature. Thus, in a letter to Jaidev Gupta, his friend, on July 24, 1930, Bhagat Singh asks for the following books to be sent to him through his younger brother, Kulbir — (i) *Militarism* (Karl Liebcnecht) (ii) *Why Men Fight* (Bertrand Russell) (iii) *The Soviets at Work* (Lenin) (iv) *The Collapse of the Second International* (Lenin) (v) *Leftwing Communism* (Lenin) (vi) *Mutual Aid* (P. Kropotkin) (vii) *Field, Factories and Workshops* (P. Kropotbin) (viii) *Civil War in France* (Marx and Engels) (ix) *Land Revolution in Russia* (Lenin) (x) *The Punjab Peasant in Prosperity and Debt* (M. Darling) (xi) *Historical Materialism* (Bukharin) (xii) *The Spy* (Upton Sinclair).

Bhagat Singh had command of four languages, without much formal training or education. He wrote in Punjabi, Hindi, Urdu and English . His Jail Notebook includes notes jotted down from the 108 authors and 43 books he read. The books included—Karl Marx, *On Religion*, Engels, *Socialism: Utopian and Scientific* and *Origin of Family, Private Property and the State*, Thomas Paine's, *Rights of Man*, Jean Jacques Rousseau's *Emile and Social Contract*, Rene Descartes, *Discourse on Matter*, Machiavelli's, *The Prince*, Spinoza's, *Tractates: Politics*, Micheal O'Dwyer's, *India As I Know It*. The authors referred to, with their quotations from unnamed books include Lord Byron, Omar Khayyam, Mark Twain, John Stuart Mill, Henrik Ibsen, Thomas Jefferson, William Wordsworth, Alfred Tennyson, Charles Fourier, Rabindranath Tagore, Karl Kautsky, Leon Trotsky, Thomas Carlyle, Fyodor Dostoyevsky, Edmund Burke, Socrates, Plato, Aristotle, Epicures, Seneca, Francis Bacon, John Locke, John Milton, Mahatma Gandhi, Madan Mohan Malviya, Bipan Chandra Pal, Valentine

Chirol. The notes also refer to two reports—The Montagu Chemsford Report and the Simon Report. Isn't this list an encyclopaedia in its range? Do even the most well read students of contemporary universities, have such a range of interest at the age of 23, even with the internet making all human knowledge available to them at the click of a mouse? (The only original comments, along with the notes on books, in the Jail Notebook are on the subject, The Science of State. Bhagat Singh was probably planning a book on the history of political developments in human society, from primitive communism to modern socialism.)

How was all this possible? It was because of Bhagat Singh's sincerity and commitment, his total devotion to the country and its people. Can we find such examples, in India or abroad? The only name that comes close is that of Che Guevara, who was as committed and as devoted to his cause as Bhagat Singh was, and who faced death with as much courage, ignoring the comforts of being a minister in the newly liberated Cuba. Che Guevara took to the jungles of Bolivia, to fight US imperialism and to liberate the whole of Latin America. He was a true internationalist revolutionary, crossing the boundaries of nationalism in a most healthy and positive manner. Che Guevara was much more advanced in thought than Bhagat Singh, as the conditions the two men lived in were different. By Che Guevara's time, revolution had won at many places, and revolutionary ideology and literature had also reached far beyond the boundaries of nations. Yet the quality of spirit, the commitment to revolution and the level of sincerity, brings these young revolutionaries close to each other, as close as Marx and Engels were to each other. Che Guevara and Bhagat Singh, in spite of the many years, geographical space separating them are the most unified symbols of revolutionary struggle against imperialism and capitalist exploitation of mankind. Both fought against these forces ferociously and both sacrificed their life with the fullest awareness that they were dying for a cause much dearer to them than their own life.

At the last meeting with Jaidev, his comrade and co-accused in the Lahore conspiracy case, before his execution, Bhagat Singh said, 'If by sacrificing my life, I am able to spread the slogan *Inqlab Zindabad* all over the country, I shall consider myself to be fully rewarded. Today

I can very well hear crores of my countrymen shouting the slogan even while I am confined behind the thick walls of my death cell ... I trust this slogan will continue to inspire our liberation struggle against imperialism.'[5]

Bhagat Singh clarified his concept of revolution in a statement to the court during the Delhi Assembly bomb case trial, 'By 'revolution' we mean the present order of things, which is based on manifest injustice, must change.' Bhagat Singh and his comrades wanted to build a system 'in which the sovereignty of the proletariat should be recognized and world federation should redeem humanity from the bondage of capitalism and the misery of imperial wars'. [6]

In a letter to the Punjab Governor dated March 20, 1931, three days before his execution, Bhagat Singh wrote, 'Let us declare that the state of war does exist and shall exist as so long as the Indian toiling masses and the natural resources are being exploited by a handful of parasites. They may be purely British capitalist or mixed British and Indian or even purely Indian. They may be carrying on their insidious exploitation through mixed or even a purely Indian bureaucratic apparatus. All these things make no difference. No matter, if your government tries and succeeds in winning over the leaders of the Indian society through petty concessions and compromises and thereby cause a temporary demoralization in the main body of forces. No matter, if once again in the Indian movement, the revolutionary party, finds itself deserted in the thick of war.'

He further asserts, 'The war shall continue. It shall be waged ever with new vigour, greater audacity and unflinching determination till the Socialist Republic is established and the present social order is completely replaced by a new social order, based on social prosperity and thus every sort of exploitation is put an end to and humanity is ushered into the era of genuine and permanent peace'.

'The days of capitalist and imperialist exploitation are numbered. The war neither began with us nor is it going to end with our lives. It is the inevitable consequence of historical events and the existing environments. Our humble sacrifices shall only be a link in the chain that has very accurately been beautified by the unparalleled sacrifice of Mr. Das and the most tragic but noblest sacrifice of comrade Bhagwati Charan and the glorious death of our warrior, Azad. [7]

Netaji Subhas Chandra Bose at a large public gathering in Delhi on the same day, 20th March, said 'Bhagat Singh is today not a person, but a symbol. He symbolizes the spirit of revolt, which has taken possession of the country.'

And the *Free Press Journal* in its issue of March 24, 1931 wrote, 'S. Bhagat Singh, Rajguru and Sukhdev live no longer. In their death lies their victory, let there be no mistaking it. The bureaucracy has annihilated the mortal frame. The nation has assimilated the immortal spirit. Thus shall Bhagat Singh, Rajguru and Sukhdev live eternally to the dismay of the bureaucracy ... To the nation, S. Bhagat Singh and colleagues will always remain the symbols of martyrdom in the cause of freedom.'[8]

Reading Bhagat Singh's Jail Notebook and court statements, it seems as if we are going through today's reality. Replace the word 'British' with 'American' and the stark reality is much darker than in 1931. Bhagat Singh was very clear about the Indian leadership as such and today's Indian rulers fit into the category of those 'pure Indians', who are being won through 'petty concessions' by American imperialism, but in the words of Bhagat Singh, 'The war shall continue', which neither began with them and which has not ended with their lives.

The lives of Bhagat Singh and Che Guevara have been sacrificed in the fight against imperialism, but these are not lives lost. These are lives which haunt imperialism, even decades after their death. Che Guevara could haunt America in today's Boliva and Chile, and in the same way Bhagat Singh will keep haunting the Bushs and Blairs and the other new avtars of the colonialism of the 1930s.

Bipan Chandra has rightly said that Bhagat Singh had 'clearly emerged as a revolutionary fully committed to Marxism and capable of applying it with the full complexity of its method', adding that even in embracing death, he applied these methods correctly. Bipan Chandra also says that 'it is one of the greatest tragedies of our people that this giant of a brain was brought to a stop so early by the colonial authorities.'[9] Yes, it is the tragedy of our people, but it is the nature of colonialism and imperialism to cause such tragedies, be it in India or Vietnam, in Iraq, Palestine or Latin America. But people do avenge these by more ferocious struggles against imperialism, if not today, then tomorrow.

3

Correspondence of Bhagat Singh

As we know in 2007, 107 documents of Bhagat Singh, apart from his Jail Notebook and Hindi translation of Dan Breen's *My Fight for Irish Freedom* have come to light. These include five letters published for the first time in March, 2007 by this author.[1] Out of these 107 documents, 45 fall in the category of correspondence—letters, telegrams and notices/leaflets. Bhagat Singh's correspondence is available from 1918, when he had not completed even 11 years of age. There are three notices and four telegrams and 38 letters among these 45 documents. The letters can be broadly divided into two types: 15 letters of a personal nature, addressed to family members and friends; and 23 letters of a political nature, addressed to his father, friends, British officials, judges, editors of journals, etc. There are however, personal references in the political letters, and reference to the political context in the personal letters.

The first five available letters of Bhagat Singh were written between 1918 and 1921, that is from the age of 11 years to 14 years. Another set of ten personal letters were written from the jail during 1930-31, when he was a little over 22 years old. The first set of five personal letters belongs to an absolutely innocent phase of Bhagat Singh's life, and the second set of ten personal letters, belongs to a mature and intellectually very fertile period of his life.

The first political letter written by Bhagat Singh in 1923, at the age of 16, was addressed to his father. The remaining 20 plus letters were written between 1927 and 1931, including one written just a day before his execution. This is the most mature period of Bhagat

Singh's personality, from the age of 20 to 23 plus. These political letters will not be discussed in detail here, as they need more space and attention.

The notices first, though just three in number, carry great significance. The first of these notices was pasted on the walls of Lahore, sometime during the night on December 18, 1928. The notice was drafted on 18 December itself by Bhagat Singh, though it was issued in the name of Balraj, Commander-in-chief of HSRA, Hindustan Socialist Republican Army; the military wing of Hindustan Socialist Republican Association, (also known as HSRA). Balraj was the pseudonym of Chandershekhar Azad. Both wings of the Hindustan Republican Association, HRA, were rechristened HSRA in September, 1928, at Ferozeshah Kotla grounds in Delhi.

This notice was pasted in context of the killing of J.P. Saunders, Deputy Superintendent of Police, Lahore on December 17,1928 in broad daylight, in front of the office of the Superitendent of Police, SSP office in Lahore city. A few weeks earlier, on October 30, 1928, Saunders had mercilessly beaten up Lala Lajpat Rai, when he was leading a huge procession against the Simon Commission. Lala Lajpat Rai died on 17th November, and, exhorted by Basanti Devi, the widow of C.R. Das, the famous nationalist, HRSA decided to avenge this 'national humiliation'. Exactly a month later, Saunders was killed and the notice appeared on the walls of Lahore. This notice was in Bhagat Singh's own handwriting, and was later produced as an exhibit in the court, during the Saunders' murder trial. The notice declares in bold letters—'J.P. Saunders is killed; Lala Lajpat Rai is avenged.' The text of the notice reads—'Really, it is horrible to imagine that so lowly and violent a hand of an ordinary police official, J.P. Saunders could ever dare to touch in such an insulting way the body of our leader, so old, so revered and so loved by 300 million people of Hindustan and thus cause his death. The youth and manhood of India were challenged by blows hurled down on the head of India's nationhood.'

The subheading of the notice is 'Beware ye tyrants; Beware.' The notice warns the British not to 'injure the feelings of a downtrodden and oppressed country. Think twice before perpetrating such a diabolic deed.'

The other subheading is 'Long Live Revolution'. In this section, the text reads—'Sorry for the death of a man. But in this man has died the representative of an institution, which is so cruel, lowly and so base that it must be abolished. In this man has died an agent of the British authority in India, the most tyrannical of governments in the world.'

The last paragraph of the notice reads—'Sorry for the bloodshed of a human being; but the sacrifice of individuals at the altar of the revolution that will bring freedom to all and make the exploitation of man by man impossible, is inevitable, *Inqlab Zindabad*.'[2]

One can see the socialist philosophy of HSRA, adopted three months earlier, taking shape in this notice. The British colonial government is seen as 'the most tyrannical government of the world' and Saunders is identified not as an individual, but as a 'representative of an institution', the institution of colonialism and exploitation. 'Death of a man' is regretted, but in the death of this man, the death of the colonial system is hailed.

Another notice about the same incident, issued on 23rd December, also carries the name of Balraj, but was actually written by Bhagat Singh. Here again, the action against Saunders is justified on the grounds that 'this was an avenge for the biggest national insult' in the form of an attack on the grand old man of India, Lala Lajpat Rai. It is also justified on the grounds that it was as per 'the rule (rule 10-b&c) of HSRA'. The slogan *Inqlab Zindabad* (Long Live Revolution) is repeated in this notice as well.[3] It seems that HSRA had given serious thought to the adoption of the slogans *Inqlab Zindabad* and 'Death to Imperialism' (*Samrajyavad Murdabad*), which reverberated four months later, in the Central Assembly, Delhi. For Bhagat Singh, the political purpose of the slogans was to arouse people's emotions. Earlier, the slogan of *Vande Matram* was used to do it. Now they thought that an advanced slogan was necessary to raise people's consciousness. That is how all the three notices issued by HSRA under the name of Balraj, and scripted by Bhagat Singh, prominently focused on these slogans. The slogans adopted from the 1917 Bolshevik Revolution of Russia, suited Indian conditions perfectly, and caught the imagination of the people in no time.

The third, more elaborately political, notice/leaflet was printed and thrown into the Central Assembly on April 8, 1929, by Bhagat

Singh and B.K. Dutt, after exploding harmless bombs there. This notice/handbill quoted the French Revolutionary Vaillant's words to justify the act, *It takes a loud voice to make the deaf hear*. The leaflet refers to the repressive measures adopted by the British colonial regime, in the form of the Public Safety and Trade Disputes Bill. The Press Sedition Bill was reserved for the next session. The leaflet refers to HSRA as a serious and responsible organization, which had decided to stop 'this humiliating farce' and let 'the alien bureaucratic exploiters' do what they wished to, but to make them 'come before the public eye in their naked form.'

The leaflet also refers to 'the callous murder of Lala Lajpat Rai' and declares that 'it is easy to kill individuals but not ideas. Great empires crumbled but the ideas survived. Bourbons and Czars fell while the revolution marched ahead triumphantly.' These are clear references to the French Revolution of 1789 and the Bolshevik Revolution of 1917. By far this is the clearest political statement by Bhagat Singh and his associates about the power of ideas to arouse people for revolution. It is a clear break from the earlier emotive and quasi-religious approach of Indian revolutionaries to arouse people against 'foreign rulers'.

Emphasis on 'the sanctity of human life' has again been asserted in the concluding paragraph of the leaflet, but the need to sacrifice individuals has also been underlined. 'The sacrifice of individuals at the altar of the great revolution that will bring freedom to all, rendering the exploitation of man by man impossible is inevitable.'[4]

The leaflet concludes with the slogan—*Inqlab Zindabad*. All three notices/handbills issued by HSRA, and drafted by Bhagat Singh, show that the revolutionary movement in India had taken the clear ideological position of Lenin's anti-imperialist stance.

There is yet another document, which can, in effect, be considered a fourth notice. This was a note written by Bhagat Singh on June 17, 1929, as life convict no. 117 of the Mianwali jail. It is addressed to the Inspector General (jails) Punjab, Lahore and announces that/ 'he is 'on hunger strike from 15th June' and he has 'lost six pounds of weight.' By asserting himself as a 'political prisoner', Bhagat Singh lists his demands for 'better food, bathing facilities, availability of books/newspapers', et cetera.[5] This notice shows that a mature political personality was developing in Bhagat Singh.

Three brief telegrams also confirm the ideological positions taken by HSRA in these notices.

On January 24, 1930, Bhagat Singh and the other accused in the Lahore conspiracy case greeted Third International Moscow on 'Lenin Day'. They came to court wearing red scarfs around their necks and shouted slogans like 'Socialism Zindabad' and *Samrajyavad Murdabad*, and sent telegrams to the Magistrate. The content of the telegrams was published in *The Tribune* of January 26, 1930.[6]

They sent another telegram to Hindustani Samiti, in Berlin, on April 5, 1930, condoling the death of the Indian revolutionary, Shyamji Krishan Verma.[7] The third telegram was sent to the accused in the Kakori case, who were on hunger strike in Bareilly jail. They were Sachinder Nath Bakhshi, Rajkumar Sinha, Mukundi Lal and Manmath Nath Gupta. They were requested to end their hunger strike in view of the notification issued for classification of prisoners jail.[8]

The other telegram was one sent by Bhagat Singh to the Home Secretary, Government of India, on January 24, 1930, drawing his attention to the fact that though they had ended their hunger strike in view of the assurances given to them regarding the treatment of political prisoners in jail, the Congress leaders of the jail reform committee were not being allowed to meet them. It also mentions that undertrial prisoners of the Lahore conspiracy case were badly beaten up on the orders of police officials, on October 23 and 24, 1929.[9]

Among Bhagat Singh's personal letters, out of the five written during the early phase of his life, three are addressed to his grandfather, Arjan Singh and two are addressed to his aunt Hukam Kaur, the widow of his uncle Swaran Singh. These letters were written between the ages of 11 and 14 years.

The first of these letters is dated July 22, 1918, when Bhagat Singh was a student of the sixth class. It is addressed to his grandfather, who had come to visit his ancestral village, Khatkar Kalan, at that time. The letter, written in Urdu, refers to the marks scored by Bhagat Singh in his class tests. There is another letter to his grandfather, exactly a year later on July 27, 1919, again in Urdu, and again referring to his performance in tests. The third letter to his grandfather refers to 'the preparations of railwaymen for strike, likely to begin next week'. Dated November 14, 1921, this letter in Urdu shows the influence of the non-cooperation movement being at its peak in those days, on Bhagat Singh.[10]

The first of Bhagat Singh's letter to his aunt, Hukam Kaur is dated October 24, 1921, and mentions a painting, or picture, of his uncle, Swaran Singh. The letter is written in Punjabi, in the Gurmukhi script. The second letter to the aunt is written on November 15, 1921, three weeks later; this letter is also in Punjabi, though the spellings of words are incorrect.[11] Bhagat Singh learnt Punjabi through his own efforts, influenced by the Nankana Sahib *morcha* of those days. In schools, Urdu was the medium of instruction and he chose Sanskrit as an optional language. Punjabi was not taught at school. In 1921, peacefully protesting Sikhs were massacred at Nankana Sahib, where Mahant Narain Das misused the gurudwara. Bhagat Singh, influenced by the protest movement, himself took to wearing the black turban worn by the protesting Sikhs. He welcomed the marchers when they reached his village, but one of his uncles Dilbagh Singh, reported him to the police.

The second set of personal letters were written during a more mature phase of his life. Of these ten letters, all written from the jail, four are addressed to his close personal friend, Jaidev Gupta, who was a sympathizer of the revolutionary movement, but not part of its organization. Three letters are addressed to his younger brother, Kulbir Singh, who was around 17 years old at that time. Kulbir used to meet Bhagat Singh in jail frequently. A letter each is addressed to B.K. Dutt, his sister, Promila, and his younger brother, Kultar Singh, who was just 12 years old at that time. Kultar was attached to his elder brother and remained so till the end of his life in 2005.

The letter to Kultar is very touching. Seeing tears in his eyes, Bhagat Singh wrote this letter to him on March 3, 1931 from Central Jail, Lahore. As we can see, Bhagat Singh wrote his last personal letters to his brothers. Kultar and Kulbir, on the same day, March 3, 1931, both in Urdu. Bhagat Singh writes to Kultar that he was 'pained to see tears in his eyes' and couldn't bear to see them. He advises his brothers affectionately to take care of their health and education. The letter to Kultar quotes the famous Urdu *ghazal, Use yeh fiqr hai hardam naya tarze wafa kya hai...*[12]

Though not as emotional as with Kultar, Bhagat Singh addresses Kulbir also as 'my very dear *aziz* brother'. He tells him that 'life is very hard and the world very cruel'. Saying a final goodbye, Bhagat Singh refers to an accompanying Hindi letter, to be given to the sister of 'K'. This letter might have been addressed to B.K. Dutt's sister, to whom he had written earlier also, but it is yet to be recovered. There are two more letters addressed to Kulbir, dated September 16 and 25, 1930. In one of these, he refers to a ban on meetings between prisoners and relatives, and in the other, asks Kulbir why he brought their mother to the jail despite the ban. He tells Kulbir to collect his books, papers, etc., from the jail as the judgment was likely to be pronounced shortly. He advises his brother to face difficulties and sufferings in life boldly as 'thousands of other people are facing these'. He also tries to prepare his brother for the total ban on meetings that he believed was likely.[13]

Bhagat Singh's letter to B.K. Dutt, written in October, 1930, is often referred to by historians. Here he is in his best form, 'I will climb the gallows gladly and show the world as to how bravely the revolutionaries can sacrifice themselves for the cause.' In this letter, he refers to the 'sufferings faced by the surviving revolutionaries'. He has some advice for such surviving revolutionaries, 'Those revolutionaries who have by chance escaped the gallows should live and show the world that they can not only embrace the gallows for the ideal but also bear the worst type of tortures in the dark dingy prison cells.' He adds, 'Revolutionaries not only die for their ideals but can face every calamity.'[14]

The integrity of Bhagat Singh's revolutionary personality is revealed in some of these letters. Traits of his revolutionary personality were visible in the Latin American revolutionary, Che Guevara, 30 years later.

In his letter to Promila, sister of B.K. Dutt, the emotional side of Bhagat Singh's personality comes to the fore when he tells her that separation (from B.K. Dutt) is unbearable for him, as Dutt is a friend dearer to him than real brothers. And as in all other letters, he advises her 'to be calm' and face everything 'with courage'.[15]

The four letters written to Jaidev Gupta have their own

significance. He is more open with Jaidev than with anyone else. He can ask for shoes to books from Jaidev. He wants to learn Persian, as is revealed from one of these letters to Jaidev written on June 3, 1930. The letter, containing a list of a dozen books to be sent for him from the Dwarka Das Library, is quite well known. In another letter, written in February, 1930, Bhagat Singh asks for *rasgullas* and oranges, and a tin of Craven cigarettes, as 'Dutt's condition is bad without cigarettes'. He also asks for 'some interesting novels, published recently', as the book he was then reading was 'quite dry'.[16] In yet another letter, Bhagat Singh expresses his unhappiness at the jail authorities not allowing Jaidev to meet him.

There is an image of Bhagat Singh, with a pistol in one hand, and throwing bombs into the Assembly with the other, popularized by the print and electronic media for long. The reality is exactly the opposite. Any authentic image of Bhagat Singh can be created with holding a book or carrying a book in the long pocket of his shabby *kurta pyjama*, and not with pistols and bombs in his hands. The image of Bhagat Singh in western attire appears only after the killing of Saunders in December, 1928. Every one of his close comrades and friends has referred to his habit of voracious reading. Books on Bhagat Singh, and his own writings, most of them published in the 1970s bring this fact out clearly. Yet the media, including films like *Rang De Basanti*, perpetuate the image of the gun-wielding Bhagat Singh.

Bhagat Singh's political letters are not discussed here in detail, as these need more space and attention. These letters carry references to personal aspects of his life, just as a few of his personal letters reflect traits of his political personality. Some of these letters are written to people very close to him, but the dominant theme in them is political. The first such letter is addressed to his father, Kishan Singh, in 1923, and was written when Bhagat Singh was only 16 years old. In this letter, he bids 'goodbye to home', as he begins his life devoted to 'the service of the country'. Bhagat Singh's political letters, written between 1923, and March 22, 1931, when he wrote his last letter to his comrades, a day before his execution, are of great significance not just to historians but to anyone who tries to understand his ideology and political personality.

Three of these letters are addressed to his father: the one mentioned above, another one on April 20, 1929, and the third one on October 4, 1930. This last letter is a very harsh one, in which Bhagat Singh censures his father for his unnecessary intervention in his case. Two letters are addressed to his close comrade, Sukhdev and are both written in 1929, during incarceration in jail. They discuss themes like 'suicide' and 'individual love' in the life of revolutionaries. Eleven letters are addressed to British authorities, the police, jail and court officials, and deal with political struggle in jails and courts. There are two letters addressed to editors of journals. One is addressed to the editor of *Mahathi* (Hindi), on February 27, 1928, and the other is addressed to *Modern Review*, on December 12, 1929, from jail. The letter dealing with political trials, with reference to Harikishan Sarhadi's trial, was published in *The Tribune* after his execution. There is also a letter, written in October, 1929, and addressed to his friend Amar Chand, who was then living abroad. Then there is a letter written from the jail to the Lahore Students Union Conference, on October 19, 1929. Before writing his last letters to his comrades on March 22, 1931, he wrote to the Governor of Punjab, on March 20, 1931, three days prior to his execution. This letter can be seen as a classical political letter: it calls for his 'right to be shot dead', as a 'prisoner of war' instead of 'being hanged', as Indian people and British colonialism were 'engaged in a war' and Bhagat Singh and his comrades claimed to be 'the soldiers of that war from the Indian side.' This right was denied to Bhagat Singh as the British colonial government was not morally strong, but the letter acquired historic significance.

The study of Bhagat Singh's correspondence is an interesting, unexplored and significant area of research in context of the Indian revolutionary movement. Hopefully, the revolutionary movement will derive sufficient inspiration from this brief exposure to a fascinating set of documents.

REFERENCES

1. Chaman Lal (Editor), *Shaheed Bhagat Singh: Dastavejon Ke Aaine Mein*, Publications Division, Government of India, 2007
2. Shiv Verma (Editor), *Selected Writings of Shaheed Bhagat Singh*, National Book Centre, New Delhi, 1986 (First Edition), pp. 62-63.

3. Chaman Lal (Editor), *Shaheed Bhagat Singh: Dastavejon Ke Aaine Mein*, Publications Division, Government of India, 2007, pp. 30-31.
4. Shiv Verma (Editor), *Selected Writings of Shaheed Bhagat Singh*, National Book Centre, New Delhi, 1986 (First Edition), pp. 67-68.
5. Chaman Lal (Editor), *Shaheed Bhagat Singh: Dastavejon Ke Aaine Mein*, Publications Division, Government of India, 2007, pp. 30-36.
6. Shiv Verma (Editor), *Selected Writings of Shaheed Bhagat Singh*, National Book Centre, New Delhi, 1986 (First Edition), p. 82.
7. Chaman Lal (Editor), *Shaheed Bhagat Singh: Dastavejon Ke Aaine Mein*, Publications Division, Government of India, 2007, p. 47.
8. Ibid., p. 47.
9. Shiv Verma (Editor), *Selected Writings of Shaheed Bhagat Singh*, National Book Centre, New Delhi, 1986 (First Edition), pp. 77-78.
10. Chaman Lal (Editor), *Shaheed Bhagat Singh: Dastavejon Ke Aaine Mein*, Publications Division, Government of India, 2007, pp. 23-25.
11. Chaman Lal (Editor), *Shaheed Bhagat Singh: Dastavejon Ke Aaine Mein*, Publications Division, Government of India, 2007, pp. 25-26.
12. Ibid., p. 74
13. Ibid., pp. 71-73
14. Shiv Verma (Editor), *Selected Writings of Shaheed Bhagat Singh*, National Book Centre, New Delhi, 1986 (First Edition), p. 115.
15. Chaman Lal (Editor), *Shaheed Bhagat Singh: Dastavejon Ke Aaine Mein*, Publications Division, Government of India, 2007, p. 71.
16. Ibid., pp. 68-70 .

* This paper was presented at the national seminar on Bhagat Singh, organized by the Institute of Punjab Studies, Mohali and ICHR, New Delhi, at Panjab University, Chandigarh, on September 27-29, 2007. It was published later in *The Tribune* with minor changes.

4

Political Correspondence of Bhagat Singh

Though Bhagat Singh lived for just 23 years and a few months, and spent not more than eight years as a political activist, he left a rich store of correspondence. Letters of Bhagat Singh are available from the time he was just 11 years old when he used to write to his family members from his school. The period of his political correspondence roughly starts from the year 1923, with a letter addressed to his father. This is a well known letter, written when Bhagat Singh left home for Kanpur 'to serve the nation.' The letter, written originally in Urdu, is reproduced below:

Respected Father,

Namaste,

My life has already been committed to a noble cause—the cause of freedom of India. For that reasons, comforts and worldly desires have no attraction in my life. You must remember that at the time of my sacred thread ceremony (Yagyopavit), when I was quite young, Bapuji (grandfather) had declared that I was being pledged for the service of the country. I am therefore honouring the pledge of that time, I hope you will excuse me.

Yours obediently
Bhagat Singh. [1]

Though a simple and short letter, it helps us understand Bhagat Singh's mental make up and his political commitment. From an early phase of his life, Bhagat Singh was clear that his life was dedicated to the nation, and so he was never tempted by such things that could be considered normal for his age—good clothing, good food, and living in comfort, given the rich financial background of his family. He started living in hardship by his own choice. He worked as a newspaper vendor in Kanpur, worked for *Pratap*, the Hindi paper edited by Ganesh Shankar Vidyarthi, and worked during the floods around Kanpur engaged in relief activities. His grandfather pledged him for the service of the country, and he took that pledge seriously, more seriously than his family did. No one in the family perhaps wanted to see him die, even while serving the nation, yet Bhagat Singh never faltered when the cause of freedom needed his life.

From 1923 to March 22, 1931, a day before his martyrdom, Bhagat Singh wrote a number of letters to members of his family, friends, and editors of publications and many official letters to British officials—judicial as well as administrative. Two more letters addressed to his father are available—one written in April, 1929, after his arrest in the Delhi Assembly bomb case, and another written on October 4, 1930, which is again a historic document. Bhagat Singh's father was a Congress activist; for that matter, his whole family was part of the freedom struggle, as is clear from Bhagat Singh's first available letter to his father. His grandfather Arjan Singh himself was a nationalist, and all his three sons—Kishan Singh, Ajit Singh and Swaran Singh were freedom fighters. Swaran Singh died at the age of 23, the age at which Bhagat Singh was to die later. He died of tuberculosis, contracted in jail. Ajit Singh remained exiled for 38 years, and returned only to die, on August 15, 1947, the day India attained independence. Kishan Singh, along with two brothers, served many jail terms; so did the two younger brothers of Bhagat Singh later, Kulbir Singh and Kultar Singh.

In his second letter to his father, Bhagat Singh writes to his father about being shifted to the Delhi jail, after being kept in police remand from 8th April till 22nd April. He informs his father that 'the drama' of a trial will be over within a month. He also tells his father that he does not need a lawyer; however he needs legal 'consultation'. He also asks for a few books to be sent to him. From this letter one comes to know about Bhagat Singh's strategy regarding 'political trials', which he elaborated later in many of his letters and other writings. Bhagat Singh was clear that 'political actions' by revolutionaries should not be 'denied' in the courts; on the contrary, 'these should be accepted', and the philosophy of such actions should be propounded 'in the courts' by the revolutionaries. The third letter to his father, written on 4th October with much anguish, makes this strategy more clear, when Bhagat Singh censures his father, quite harshly, for his 'unwanted interference' in the case, in order to 'save' the life of his son. Bhagat Singh's father had given a petition to the special tribunal, conducting the Saunders' murder trial, that his son was 'innocent and he had nothing to do with Saunders' murder'. Bhagat Singh writes that he was 'astounded' to know about this petition, and that 'it has upset the whole equilibrium of my mind.' He adds very strongly: 'In the political field, my views always differed with those of yours, I have always acted independently without having cared for your approval or disapproval.'

Bhagat Singh reminds his father that though he (his father) always wanted him, to fight his case seriously and defend himself properly, he, Bhagat Singh, always opposed it. Then he tells his father, 'We have been pursuing a definite policy in this trial'. He then explains their policy—'I have always been of the opinion that all political workers should be indifferent and should never bother about the legal courts and should boldly bear the heaviest possible sentence inflicted upon them. They may defend themselves but always from political considerations and never from a personal point of view. Our policy in this trial has always been consistent with this principle; whether we were successful in that or not is not for me to judge.'

In this letter, the maturity of Bhagat Singh's political thinking can be seen at its peak. He tells his father 'My life is not so precious, at least to me, as you may probably think it to be. It is not at all worth buying at the cost of my principles. There are other comrades of mine whose case is as serious as that of mine. We have adopted a common policy and we shall stand to the last, no matter how dearly we have to pay individually for it.' After explaining his policy about the case, Bhagat Singh performs a most difficult duty—that of censuring his father, and he does not shirk from this unpleasant but politically necessary duty.

'Father, I am quite perplexed, I fear I might overlook the ordinary principles of etiquette and my language may become a little harsh while criticizing or rather censuring this move on your part. Let me be candid, I feel as though I have been stabbed in the back. Had any other person done it, I would have considered it to be nothing short of treachery. But in your case, let me say that it has been a weakness—a weakness of the worst type.

This was the time when everybody's mettle was being tested. Let me say, Father, you have failed. I know you are as sincere a patriot as one can be. I know you have devoted your life to the cause of Indian independence. But why, at this moment, have you shown such a weakness? I cannot understand.'[2]

This was not just a private letter; Bhagat Singh insisted that this letter must be published at the earliest, and so it was in *The Tribune*. Probably, this move by Kishan Singh made Bhagat Singh so apprehensive that he instructed Kumari Lajjawati, Secretary, Bhagat Singh, Defence Committee, while handing over the bag containing his papers, before his pending execution, 'to hand over these papers only to Bejoy Kumar Sinha', who was his close friend at an ideological level. Sinha was then undergoing imprisonment in the Andamans. According to Lajjawati, Bhagat Singh had specifically instructed her 'not to hand over these papers to his father'. And Lajjawati followed these instructions and refused even 'to show' the papers to Kishan Singh, when he wanted them.[3] Lajjawati gave this bag to Lala Firoze Chand, editor of *People*, the weekly established by Lala Lajpat Rai, and asked him to take whatever papers he felt could be published. Lala Firoze Chand took out some papers, which were later published in *People*. These included—'Letter to Young Political Workers' (fragments), written on March 29, 1931. 'On Political Trials' (June 9, 1931), and 'Why I Am an Atheist' (September 27, 1931). Lajjawati claims she handed over the remaining papers to B.K. Sinha in 1938, after his release from the Andamans. How they were lost, is a somewhat controversial and unconfirmed story.

Bhagat Singh's letters to Sukhdev are equally significant for expressing his philosophical views about life, particularly about the topics of 'love' and 'suicide'. But the reference point here again is political consideration. Bhagat Singh was initially not chosen by the revolutionary group to carry out the act of throwing bombs into the Delhi Assembly, because of his indispensability for the party, even though Bhagat Singh himself had pleaded to be nominated for the job. Sukhdev was not present at that meeting, and after his return he charged Bhagat Singh of having a soft spot for some unnamed woman and considering himself to be too important to risk his life. At Bhagat Singh's insistence, the meeting of the group was called again, and Bhagat Singh was chosen to go to the Assembly. Bhagat Singh also got the approval of the group to 'not escape' and use the platform of the courts to propound their political views. To rebut Sukhdev's accusations, Bhagat Singh wrote a letter to him on April 5, 1929, which was delivered by Shiv Verma to Sukhdev on 6th April, two days before the throwing of bombs in the Delhi Assembly. While expressing his anguish at being misunderstood by 'my brother, my own brother', Bhagat Singh dwells upon the features of his own personality. He says emphatically, 'I am full of ambition and hope, and full of the charm of life. But I can renounce all at the time of need, and that is the real sacrifice.' Bhagat Singh also refers to the over idealistic bent of mind of a radical activist, while referring to the natural feeling of love. 'We in spite of all radical ideas that we cherish, have not been able to do away with the over idealistic Arya Samajist conception of morality. We may talk glibly about all the radical things that can possibly be conceived, but in practical life we begin to tremble at the very outset. This I will request you to do away with.'[4]

In another letter to Sukhdev, Bhagat Singh responds to Sukhdev expressing his desire 'to commit suicide', if he got the 'sentence of transportation for life'. He wished only for 'death' or 'release', Sukhdev said. Bhagat Singh gives him a very sharp reply. Sukhdev was earlier not able to withstand police tactics and had made a 'statement', after his arrest in April, 1929, as when Bhagat Singh and Dutt, also in police custody, had both refused to give any statement to the police after their arrest in the Delhi bomb case. Again, when all the other comrades involved in the Lahore conspiracy case continued their hunger strike in support of Bhagat Singh and B.K. Dutt's hunger strike, and Jatin Das even gave his life, Sukhdev could not sustain the hunger strike for long. Bhagat Singh reminds Sukhdev of their earlier conversation about 'suicide', when they had not been arrested, when

Sukhdev thought suicide to be *horrible and heinous.* At that time, Bhagat Singh has said that 'in some situations suicide may be justifiable'. Bhagat Singh now takes the view that 'suicide is a heinous crime. It is an act of complete cowardice. Leave alone revolutionaries, no individual can ever justify such an act.' Bhagat Singh debates with Sukhdev about the role of 'suffering'. Sukhdev thinks that suffering cannot serve the country, and that is why he did not endure the suffering of a hunger strike. Here Bhagat Singh defends the role of hunger strike in order to improve the miserable condition of political prisoners in jail. He asks a question in this context: Could the death of comrade Jatinder Nath Das be called suicide? Bhagat Singh then emphatically answers the question—'No. Striving and sacrificing one's life for a superior ideal can never be called suicide.' He underlines the fact that due to their hunger strike they won the rights for better treatment of political prisoners. 'Ultimately, our sufferings bore fruit. Big movements started in the whole country. We were successful in our aim. Death in the struggle of this kind is an ideal death.'

Bhagat Singh tells Sukhdev that getting hanged in this case 'will also be beautiful, but committing suicide, to cut short life just to avoid some pain, is cowardice.' Bhagat Singh discusses Russian literature at length in this context, since it was a topic they had been discussing during their earlier life outside the jail. Bhagat Singh speaks about the role of a jail in understanding the realities of life:

'I want to tell you that in jail, and in jail alone, can a person get an occasion to study empirically the great social subjects of crime and sin, I have read some literature on this and only the jail is the proper place for the self-study of all these topics. The best part of the self study for one is to suffer oneself.'

One can write a thesis on the basis of just this one letter, which is a clear expression of his philosophical, political and cultural ideas. Bhagat Singh tells Sukhdev that they were not doing something very unusual in life. They were just 'a product of the needs of our times', as was Marx. And here he gives the most mature Marxist understanding of Marx, which Marx himself had given earlier:

'I shall even say that Marx, the father of communism, did not actually originate this idea. The Industrial Revolution of Europe itself produced men of this kind. Marx was one among them. Of course,

Marx was also instrumental to an extent in gearing up the wheels of his time in a particular way.

I (and you too) did not give birth to the idea of socialism and communism in this country; this is the consequence of the effects of our time and situation upon ourselves. Of course, we did a bit to propagate these ideas and therefore I say that since we have already taken a tough task upon ourselves, we should continue to advance it. The people will not be guided by our committing suicide to escape the difficulties; on the contrary, this will be quite a reactionary step.'

One can see a committed theoretician of the Marxist revolution taking shape in Bhagat Singh at the age of 23, when this letter was written. He asserts his materialistic thinking, their atheist approach towards god, hell, heaven, etc. and declares that he is hundred per cent certain about the capital punishment being awarded to him: 'I do not expect a bit of moderation or amnesty. Even if there is amnesty, it will not be for all, and even that amnesty will be for others only, not for us; it will be extremely restricted and burdened with various conditions. For us, neither can there be any amnesty nor will it ever happen. Even then, I wish that release calls for us should be made collectively and globally. Along with that, I also wish that when the movement reaches its climax, we should be hanged.' Bhagat Singh declares his unflinching faith in the revolution, in the face of his certain death: 'A revolution can be only achieved through sustained striving, sufferings and sacrifices. And it shall be achieved.' To Sukhdev and his kind of persons in revolutionary movements, his biting lesson is:'You will kindly excuse me for saying that had you acted according to this belief right at the time of imprisonment (that is, had you committed suicide by taking poison), you would have served the revolutionary cause, but at this moment, even the thought of such an act is harmful to our cause.'[5] Here one is reminded of the young Bengali woman revolutionary of Chittagong fame, Preetilata Waddedar, who had consumed a capsule of cyanide, after throwing a bomb in the British Club, on September 24, 1932 and was martyred. Her death would never be considered suicide by revolutionary movements.

Bhagat Singh sent a message to the second Punjab Students Conference, held at Lahore, on October 19, 1929, under the presidentship of Subhas Chandra Bose. Here the very first line of his message shows how Bhagat Singh was trying to remove the tag of 'bombs and pistols'attached to their movement. He says: 'Today, we cannot ask the youth to take to pistols and bombs.' The youth will have to spread this revolutionary message to the far corners of the country. They have to awaken crores of slum-dwellers of the industrial areas and villagers living in worn out cottages, so that we will be independent and the exploitation of man by man will become an impossibility.'[6]

In a letter addressed to Ramanand Chatterjee, the editor of *Modern Review*, who ridiculed the slogan of *Inqlab Zindabad,* Bhagat Singh reasserts, 'Revolution did not necessarily involve sanguinary strife. It was not a cult of the bomb and pistol. They may sometimes be mere means for its achievements.'[7]

Bhagat Singh wrote two letters in the context of Harikishan's trial. Harikishan had shot at the Governor of Punjab during the convocation of Punjab University, Lahore, on December 23, 1930. The Governor survived, but an official died in this attack. Harikishan was just a young boy of 18 years and was bound to be hanged in this case; however the way the lawyers conducted his case made Bhagat Singh quite unhappy. While one of the letters is untraceable the second one was found among Bhagat Singh's papers, and was published in the *People*, on June 9, 1931, after Harikishan was hanged on May 31, 1931. Bhagat Singh defends his earlier line of facing such trials by boldly accepting the deed and facing the consequences, which will make the public sympathize with the cause. He comes down heavily on the lawyers in the context of this case and castigates them, 'Lawyers should not be so unscrupulous as to exploit the lives and even deaths of young people who come to sacrifice themselves for so noble a cause as the emancipation of suffering humanity. Why should a lawyer demand such an incredible fee as has been paid in the above case?' Bhagat Singh was particularly unhappy the way Harikishan was shown as not being so bold, whereas Bhagat Singh knew that they 'are trying to belittle the beauty of the marvellous character of our young comrade.'[8]

Two more of Bhagat Singh's letters need special mention here, while the official correspondence of Bhagat Singh with British judicial and jail officials again needs to be deferred for another paper. Bhagat Singh wrote to the Governor of Punjab on behalf of all three condemned prisoners of the Lahore conspiracy case on March 20, 1931, three days before the execution. In the letter, they plead 'to be shot dead as war prisoners' as India and British colonialism were 'at war' and they were 'soldiers on the Indian side'. The letter contains a historic statement, 'The days of capitalist and imperialist exploitation are numbered. The war neither began with us nor is it going to end with our lives. It is an inevitable consequence of the historic events and the exciting environments. Our humble sacrifice shall only be a link in the chain that has accurately been beautified by the unparalleled sacrifice of Mr. Das and the most tragic but the noblest of sacrifices of comrade Bhagwati Charan and the glorious death of our dear warrior, Azad.'[9]

The last letter or rather last words authored by him on 22nd March, just a day before his final journey, are addressed to his comrades and rightly so. He lived and died amongst them. It is interesting to know that his last words were written in Urdu. These words were written neither in English, which he mastered in the last part of his life, nor in Punjabi, his mother tongue, whose Gurmukhi script he learnt through conscious choice. Incidentally, his last letters to his younger brothers, Kulbir and Kultar, penned on 3rd March, were also in Urdu. Urdu is the first and last language of his expression, perhaps he expressed himself most comfortably in that language, which he learnt at school, since it was the medium of instruction in schools in those days. Bhagat Singh was at complete peace with himself, fully content with the life he lived in the last moments, and he expresses it in these words, 'I am proud of myself these days and I am anxiously waiting for the final test, I wish the day may come nearer soon.' Bhagat Singh prolonged his trial to the extent possible by various means at his disposal, most of these created most imaginatively, with the full awareness that he was eventually getting the capital punishment, because of his political agenda—to expose the British judicial and administrative system so thoroughly that the Indian people become aware of the true form of the colonial regime. And when his agenda was completed, he was ready to face death most boldly, just as Che Guevara faced in Bolivia, 36 years later, challenging the American army man to shoot him. Only one thing pricked Bhagat Singh: 'My heart nurtured some ambitions for doing something for humanity and for my country. I have not been able to fulfil even one thousandth part of these ambitions. If I live, I might perhaps get a chance to fulfil them. If ever it came to my mind that I should not die, it came from this end only.'[10]

One should mark here that the word 'humanity' comes before the word 'country'. On March 23, 1931, Bhagat Singh had become a truly international martyr for the cause of humanity, and not just an Indian martyr for the cause of the country. His political consciousness had grown to the level of aiming for 'human liberation' and not just 'Indian liberation'. One should understand Bhagat Singh from this perspective.

REFERENCES

All quotations except 3 are from Shiv Verma's, *Selected Writings of Shaheed Bhagat Singh*.

1. Shiv Verma (Editor), *Selected Writings of Shaheed Bhagat Singh*, National Book Centre, New Delhi, 1986, first edition, p. 55.
2. Ibid., pp. 112-14.
3. Interview with Lajjawati by Nehru Memorial Museum and Library
4. Shiv Verma (Editor), *Selected Writings of Shaheed Bhagat Singh*, National Book Centre, New Delhi, 1986, first edition, p. 55.
5. Ibid., pp. 106-11.
6. Ibid., p. 79.
7. Ibid., pp. 80-81.
8. Ibid., pp. 124-27.
9. Ibid., pp. 154-56.
10. Ibid., p. 157.

* Paper presented at a seminar on 'Bhagat Singh and His Legend', organized by the World Punjabi Centre at Punjabi University, Patiala on October 22, 2007, and later published in *Mainstream*.

5

Rare Documents*

Memorial programmes on Bhagat Singh have gained momentum since, 2006, on completion of 75 years of his martyardom. Several publications have been brought out since then, in Hindi, Punjabi, English and many other Indian languages, and the activity continues uninterrupted. A proposal to set up a Bhagat Singh Chair at Jawaharlal Nehru University, New Delhi, has been accepted by the National Programme Implementation Committee. Mooted by this author, the proposal was endorsed by Prof. Bipan Chandra, Prof. Prabhat Patnaik and Prof. G.S. Bhalla. It was supported by many eminent scholars and political leaders like Prakash Karat, A.B. Bardhan and Shashi Bhushan. As part of the memorial programmes all over the country, this author was invited to deliver lectures on Bhagat Singh's intellectual contribution to and role in the freedom movement. These fifty plus lectures were delivered at far flung places like Arrah (Bihar), Patna, Indore (MP), Rohtak (Haryana), Ranchi (Jharkhand), Mumbai, Benaras and Thanjavur (Tamil Nadu) between September 2006 and continue till date.

By 2007, the birth centenary of Bhagat Singh, and coincidentally, also the 150th anniversary of the first war of Independence of 1857 were observed. An emotion of patriotism had emerged afresh in the country, more so in the wake of US neo imperialism becoming more aggressive and dangerous than the old British imperialism. The whole country is reliving the nationalistic tradition and in the political

* Earlier published in *Mainstream* and *The Tribune.*

renaissance taking place, the image of Bhagat Singh is emerging as the supreme ideological symbol of anti-imperialist resistance particularly through the efforts of leftist organizations. At the international level too, people engaged in struggles against neo imperialism are looking to Bhagat Singh as a symbol of resistance, along with Che Guevara.

Some rare documents acquired by this author during this period, highlight Bhagat Singh's national and international significance. One of these documents is an editorial in the Tamil weekly *Kudi Arasu* in the March 22-29, 1931 issue, immediately after the execution of Bhagat Singh and others. This editorial, written by Periyar E.V. Ramasamy Naicter, was translated into English and published in *Modern Rationalist* in November, 2006, by followers of Periyar at my request, after more than 75 years of its first publication. It was Periyar, who got Bhagat Singh's essay, 'Why I Am an Athiest', translated in to Tamil, as early as 1934, by comrade P. Jeevanandan, and published as a booklet. This booklet continues to be popular in Tamil Nadu, and many editions of it have come out. This was perhaps the first ever translation of this historic document in any Indian or non-Indian language; it preceded even the Punjabi translation. There were many instances of creative writing in Tamil, after the execution of Bhagat Singh, which were proscribed by the British authorities in those days.

Internationally reports of the execution of Bhagat Singh and disturbances in the country that followed it, were published in the pro-communist *Daily Worker* from New York. It is almost strange that the news of Bhagat Singh's execution was published in *The Tribune* of Lahore and *Daily Worker* of New York on the same day, March 25, 1931, in that age of slow communication channels. *The Tribune* could not publish this report on 24th March, as the news of the execution on 23rd March, at 7 p.m., remained suppressed even in Lahore, where the executions took place. On March 27, 1931. *The Daily Worker* also carried a report on Kanpur that followed riots on the executions.

Five unpublished letters of Bhagat Singh were also found during this period. Copies of four of these letters were acquired from the Nehru Memorial Museum and Library (Teen Murti), New Delhi. The fifth letter was recovered from the exhibits of the Lahore conspiracy case. The copies of all these letters were gifted to this author by Malwinderjit Singh Waraich, a dedicated writer and activist focusing on the revolutionary movements in India's struggle for freedom. Three of these letters are in English, one in Punjabi, and one in Urdu.

From these documents, one can better understand Bhagat Singh's ideological perspective and the significance of his contribution to India's freedom struggle.

(Letter not produced here)

6

Knowing Bhagat Singh Through His Own Documents: Rare Documents from Supreme Court Digital Records*

When the Supreme Court established its Museum to display the history of the judicial system in India, it also began displaying records of historic trials as well and the first ever historic trial was put on exhibition and rightly so, was the 'Trial of Bhagat Singh'. It was inaugurated by then Chief Justice of India, K.G. Balakrishnan on September 28, 2007, on the occasion of birth centenary celebrations of the most significant martyr and popular hero of not only India, but of the whole South Asian youth. Supreme Court Museum curator Noorul Hooda and National Archives' Rajmani Srivastava worked hard to collect various documents, items like bombshells, pictures, publications, et cetera.There was so much matter collected that not all of it could be displayed during the exhibition period. Later the Supreme Court recorded the items of exhibition in digital form in 2008 and out of that collection some of the rare writings of Bhagat Singh came to light for the first time since 1931, when Bhagat Singh, Rajguru and Sukhdev were executed on March 23, 1931 at Lahore central jail. How the three young patriots were put to judicial murder, this has been brought to fore by one of the most eminent legal scholars of the country A.G. Noorani in his book of the same title as of the exhibition, *The Trial of Bhagat Singh; Politics of Justice.*

* Earlier published in *The Hindu* on August 15, 2011.

The most significant part of Bhagat Singh's life is that of his jail period, from his arrest on April 8, 1929 from the Central Assembly, Delhi, where he and B.K. Dutt offered themselves to be arrested after throwing harmless bombs in the Assembly to 'make the deaf hear'. They faced two trials, first the Delhi bomb case trial, which started on May 7, 1929, in Delhi and was committed to Sessions Judge under charges 307 I.P.C. and Explosives Act, who started the trial in the first week of June. Bhagat Singh and B.K. Dutt made a historic statement on June 6, 1929. Dutt was represented by eminent nationalist counsel Asaf Ali, Bhagat Singh fought his own case with the help of a legal adviser. On June 12, 1929, just in less than a week-long trial, both were convicted and transported for life. From June 6, 1929 statement to his last letter to his comrades on March 22, 1931, a day before his execution, Bhagat Singh read and wrote so much that one can just wonder at his explosion of talent at the age of 21 years plus. He wrote letters to family/friends, jail and court officials, wrote major articles like 'Why I Am an Atheist', 'Letter to Young Political Workers', 'Jail Notebook', et cetera. On June 14, 1929, after conviction in the Delhi bomb case, Bhagat Singh was transferred to Mianwali and B.K. Dutt to Lahore jail. It started a chain of prolonged struggle throughout the jail period. It began with a hunger strike from June 15, 1929 itself by both Bhagat Singh and B.K. Dutt to demand Political Prisoner status. Bhagat Singh was also shifted to Lahore jail after some time and he and Dutt were kept away from others accused of Lahore conspiracy case like Sukhdev, et cetera. The trial of Lahore conspiracy case dealing with Saunders' murder began on July 10, 1929, when Bhagat Singh was brought to court on a stretcher due to his and Dutt's hunger strike since 15th June. Others accused of Saunders' murder case in the Lahore conspiracy came to know about this hunger strike on that very day and almost all of them joined the hunger strike. This historic hunger strike by Bhagat Singh and his comrades resulted in the martyrdom of Jitin Das on September 13, 1929. Though Bhagat Singh and other comrades ended hunger their strike on 2nd September, after assurances from the Congress Party team and British officials about acceptance of their demands, but resumed it on 4th September, again, as British officials went back on their word. It finally ended on 4th October, after 112 days, though, 'political prisoner' status was still not given, but some other demands were acceded to. During Special Magistrate Rai Sahib Pt. Kishan Chand conducted trial of the Lahore conspiracy case, on October 21, 1929, an incident occurred in the court, when provoked by approver Jai Gopal, a sliper was thrown at him by the youngest accused of the case, Prem Dutt. Despite disassociation of others accused of the act, Magistrate order handcuffing of the accused and that led to brutal beating of Bhagat Singh, Shiv Verma, B.K. Dutt, Bejoy Kumar Sinha, Ajoy Ghosh, Prem Dutt and many others, after they refused to be handcuffed. They were brutally treated inside the jail and at court gate in front of the Magistrate. Ajoy Ghosh and Shiv Verma had become unconscious due to the brutalities of the police and Bhagat Singh was specially targeted by British officer Mr. Roberts. The details of these brutalities have been well recorded by Bejoy Kumar Sinha. In February 1930, Bhagat Singh resumed his hunger strike for 15 more days, as the British officials did not fulfil the acceded demands earlier. Meanwhile the prestige of revolutionaries due to their hunger strikes and court statements soared to new heights and British prestige was down to the lowest ebbs. From the Central Assembly and media in India to the world over this case was drawing attention. While dismissing appeals by Bhagat Singh and B.K. Dutt against the Delhi bomb case judgement, the Punjab High Court, Lahore acknowledged Bhagat Singh to be a 'Sincere Revolutionary'!

The British colonial regime led by Viceroy Lord Irwin took the unprecedented step of issuing the Lahore conspiracy case ordinance on May 1, 1930, by which the proceedings being conducted by Special Magistrate Lahore were transferred to a three judge Special Tribunal established to conduct and complete the proceedings within the fixed period and the judgement of the tribunal was not allowed to be challenged in the High Court or superior courts. Only the Privy Council in London could hear an appeal against it. This ordinance was never approved from Central Assembly or by British Parliament and lapsed immediately after its given life without any legal or constitutional sanctity. Its only purpose was to hang Bhagat Singh in the shortest time, which it did by delivering judgement on October 7, 1930 of sentencing Bhagat Singh, Sukhdev and Rajguru to the gallows. It began its proceedings from May 5, 1930 and all accused of the Lahore conspiracy case refused to attend its proceedings after May 12, 1930, when they raised slogans and sang revolutionary songs, brutalities repeated on them, as were done during October 1929, in front of the Special Magistrate. This time Ajoy Ghosh, Kundan Lal and Prem Dutt became unconscious. Perhaps this is the only political trial of the world, where the accused remained absent during the whole proceedings and remained even unrepresented by their legal counsel also. Advocates engaged to defend the accused were insulted by tribunal and subsequently accused themselves directed them not to defend them in their absence. These details can be seen in A.G. Noorani's book, *The Trial of Bhagat Singh*, but what remained suppressed all these years were many letters/petitions of Bhagat Singh made to either jail authorities or to the special tribunal or to the Punjab High Court, Lahore during 1929 to August 1930. These letters reveal another hunger strike in July end 1930, by Bhagat Singh, about which he himself informs High Court that it was against jail rules. There could still be more documents, which might come out. The printing of complete proceedings of Delhi Assembly bomb case and Pt. Sri Kishan, Special Magistrate Court proceedings can bring more facts to light. Punjab Archives in Lahore still holds 135 files of the Bhagat Singh case, which are not being allowed to be consulted even to Pakistani scholars, though Kuldip Nayar is trying to get access to these through his influence in Pakistan. In 2006, during the 75th martyrdom anniversary of Bhagat Singh, Rajguru and Sukhdev; Rana Bhagwan Das, acting Chief Justice of Pakistan Supreme Court handed over four volumes of exhibits of the Lahore conspiracy case to Punjab and Haryana High Court, Chandigarh, which also revealed some new documents. While the source of documents in Supreme Court records is not clearly mentioned, but undoubtedly these are part of trial proceedings at both levels. These letters are self- explicit in their content and with the background given above, can be understood in the context of the freedom struggle. These letters show Bhagat Singh's amazing command over the English language apart from Urdu, Hindi and Punjabi, and his beautiful handwriting as well, and legal terminology. Historian V.N. Datta doubted Bhagat Singh's command over English, in his book, *Gandhi and Bhagat Singh* as Bhagat Singh being an undergraduate and ascribed it to Pt. Nehru or Asaf Ali. For legal professionals, judges, lawyers also these letters present a wonderful experience, how a 21 year plus undergraduate youth could have such maturity in such complex matters of legal defence, but Bhagat Singh's very talent and competence scared the British colonial regime to no end and they became more determined to get rid of him by hook or by crook, which according to judicial experts proved to be 'crook' only. Bhagat Singh's unpublished letters also throw further light on this British judicial 'crook'.

In the Supreme Court digital records nearly 20 documents of Bhagat Singh's own writings have been stored. But some of these like the June 6, 1929 statement, Ideal of Indian Revolution, et cetera. have already been published. Here only 12 letters/petitions unpublished till now are being published for the first time on completion of 80 years of the martyrdom of Bhagat Singh, Rajguru and Sukhdev and this writer acknowledges gratefully Hon'ble Supreme Court's permission to do so. Ten documents are in complete form, while two letters/documents, one, relating to October 21, 1929 court incident and another petition of about early 1930 have the first page only, the second and likely final page in these two documents are not in the digital records. Letters are being reproduced in facsimile form also to see the beautiful handwriting of the great revolutionary.

(Original scanned letters in Annexure 2)

7

April 8, 1929: A Day to Remember*

A historic event took place on April 8, 1929, in the political history of India, referring to which L.K. Advani committed a blunder, when he referred to Bhagat Singh's execution as related to this event. A great deal is being written about Advani's sense of history with reference to his book *My Life: My Country*, but it is necessary to recollect the significance of the event referred, by way of narrating the facts from historic records and reminiscences of fellow revolutionaries of Bhagat Singh.

It was at 12.30 p.m. on April 8, 1929, when Sh. Vithalbhai Patel (elder brother of Vallabhbhai Patel, the first Deputy Prime Minister of India), President (Speaker in today's terms) of Central Assembly (present day Lok Sabha) rose to give his ruling on the result of voting on the Trade Disputes Bill, which was heatedly discussed in the assembly, along with another bill—'Public Safety Bill'. Both bills had created much resentment in the country and people were agitated over these bills' repressive provisions. In fact the British government was defeated on the Public Safety Bill in the select committee meeting of the Central Assembly, when the bill was defeated 62 to 61, with the help of the Assembly President's casting vote. However the British government was able to get the Trade Disputes Bill through, and before its result could be announced there was an explosion in the assembly and suddenly the hall was filled with smoke and slogans rose in loud

* Earlier published in *The Mainstream.*

voices by two young men from the visitors' gallery. The three slogans raised many times over were—'*Inqlab Zindabad*', 'Down With Imperialism' and 'Workers of the World Unite'. Another explosion took place a few minutes later and hurriedly the hall and visitors gallery were emptied, except for a few people standing. In the Assembly, those who remained on their seats were—Pt. Motilal Nehru, Mohammad Ali Jinnah and Madan Mohan Malviya, apart from the Home Secretary, Government of India—James Crerar. In the visitors' gallery, who could be seen, were—Devdas Gandhi, Mahadev Desai, Asaf Ali, Vallabhbhai Patel, Brij Lal Nehru and Sir Sobha Singh. John Simon of Simon Commission fame was also present in the visitors' gallery. Hindi writer and editor of *Phansi Ank* of *Chand* from Allahabad, Chatur Sen Shastri was also there with family, whom Bhagat Singh himself had brought into the assembly. Chaman Lal, a reporter of the *Hindustan Times* and sympathizer of revolutionaries was also there to cover the proceedings. Though both bombs were thrown by Bhagat Singh, B.K. Dutt took the responsibility of throwing one bomb, because he did not want to be acquitted and stay 'away from Bhagat Singh'. He wanted to be with Bhagat Singh through thick and thin. This was mentioned by Asaf Ali in an interview many years later.

After a few minutes of slogan shouting and throwing of pink leaflets by these young men, Sergeant Terry and Inspector Johnson moved towards these young men, one of whom was 'playing with his pistol' in hand (Bhagat Singh). Police officers were scared to go close to them, but the young men made no attempt to escape and kept the pistol on the side table, seeing the terror on police officers' faces. The two were arrested and they were in their khaki shirts and shorts, with one of them wearing his felt hat. The man with the hat was Bhagat Singh and the other young man was his comrade, Batukeshwar Dutt. Jaidev Kapoor, the third accomplice in the action, left the assembly hall minutes earlier and burnt the passes acquired from one assembly member. Bhagat Singh, B.K. Dutt and Jaidev Kapoor had been visiting the assembly premises in the days prior. CID reports have a record of their visit to assembly premises on April 6, 1929. Even Chandershekhar Azad had visited the premises to have a first hand assessment of it, being the commander of HSRA. The leaflets thrown in the assembly carried the signature of Balraj, the party name of Chandershekhar

Azad, though the leaflet was drafted by Bhagat Singh himself. It started with a quotation from French revolutionary Vaillant—'It needs explosions to make the deaf hear'. The statement, he made while taking similar action inside the French parliament about four decades earlier and for which he was also executed. The Hindustan Socialist Republican Association (HSRA), formed on September 8 and 9, 1928 at Ferozeshah Kotla grounds Delhi, had planned this action after killing Saunders, a police officer responsible for killing of great nationalist leader Lala Lajpat Rai. Lala Lajpat Rai died on 17th November, because of *lathis* blown upon his body by Saunders on October 30, 1928 at Lahore, when he was leading a procession against the Simon Commission.

According to court and police records only six persons had been shown with minor injuries. These were—George Schuster (Seat No. 4-B), P.R. Rao, Shankar Rao, Bomanji Dalal, S.N. Roy and Rai Bahadur Dubey. Medical reports later confirmed 'trivial injuries'. Furniture, including some tables was damaged. The affected seats were 87-88-89 and 146-147-148. Bhagat Singh bought his felt hat from Calcutta in December, 1928 and the pistol wDubeyas given to him by veteran Anushilan revolutionary Pratul Das in Dacca. Before entering the assembly on 8th April, he gave a watch to Jaidev Kapoor, which was given to him by Shachinder Nath Sanyal, who got it from Ras Behari Bose earlier. This historic watch is in Hardoi now. Bhagat Singh also exchanged his new shoes with the old ones worn by Jaidev Kapoor.

Bhagat Singh and Dutt stayed in a house in Sita Ram Bazar, Delhi during February-March and at Nai Sarak house in the first week of April to plan and execute this action. On 7th April night, Sukhdev took Bhagwati Charan Vohra, Durga Bhabhi and Susheela Didi from Lahore to Delhi to see Bhagat Singh 'for the last time'. They reached Kudsiya Gardens in Delhi on 8th April morning, where they treated Bhagat Singh to his favourite *rasgullas* and oranges. Susheela Didi applied a blood dot on his forehead and Bhagat Singh left for the Assembly around 10.30 a.m. from there. After they were arrested and being taken by the police to the police station, Bhagwati Charan Vohra, Durga Bhabhi and their three-year-old son Shachi saw Bhagat Singh and shouted 'Lambu Chacha'. Durga Bhabhi put her hand on his mouth.

On 3rd or 4th April, Bhagat Singh and Dutt got photographed from Ramnath, a photographer at Kashmere Gate, Delhi, the photograph with felt hat wearing Bhagat Singh became historic and got engraved on the minds of Indian people and abroad. Jaidev Kapoor and Shiv Verma had to perform other duties. Bhagat Singh had typed leaflets thrown in the assembly and made 10-15 copies of it. This statement and photograph was immediately delivered to reporters. Durga Das, representing *Statesman* those days took care to telegraph the statement to his London office, rather than Calcutta and that trick worked. Chaman Lal collected the copy of the leaflet from the assembly premises and the *Hindustan Times* came out with the special evening edition that very evening. The statement got international coverage as well. The *Hindustan Times* was an eyesore for the British government those days because of its strong support for the freedom struggle and between 8th April to 12th June, when the sentence to 'transportation for life' was pronounced by Sessions Judge Middelton to Bhagat Singh and Dutt, in this case, there are many CID reports referring to the *Hindustan Times* pro-nationalist role in those days. One Ghosh, an assistant editor of *Hindustan Times* in those days is also referred to as a sympathizer to revolutionaries cause. Many police officers have also been suspected of 'leaking' information to the *Hindustan Times* about the investigation in the case. Suspicion had been on *Hindustan Times* staff for hosting Bhagat Singh and Dutt in Delhi.

On 13th May, in a police raid on Saharanpur house, the police recovered three negatives and some photographs of Bhagat Singh and Dutt, which were identified by Ramnath photographer in an identification parade held later. CID reports records the publication of these photographs in *Bande Matram*, of Lahore in the 12th April issue, though these were being sold in Lahore from 11th April. According to CID reports photographs may have been printed on 10th April but the CID records also confirm the *Hindustan Times* had published 'excellent photographs' and the statement of HSRA earlier.

The FIR of the incident was filed by Lala Hans Raj Saheb, duty constable Karampur under Section 3 and 4 of the 'Explosives Act 1908' against Bhagat Singh and Dutt. Kishan Singh, father of Bhagat

Singh was allowed to meet him on May 3, 1929 only, when it was known that Kultar Singh, ten-year-old brother of Bhagat Singh and fifth class student was also arrested by the police. Bhagat Singh was not in favour of defence, however Asaf Ali represented B.K. Dutt, Bhagat Singh fought his own case, in consultation with Asaf Ali. The trial started on May 7, 1929. The famous statement by Bhagat Singh and Dutt, was read in sessions court on June 6, 1929. This historic statement was drafted by Bhagat Singh, whose language only was polished by Asaf Ali. Some portions of the statement were expunged from records by the judge on 9th June. The judgment was delivered on June 12, 1929, convicting them both and sentencing them to 'transportation for life'. An appeal was filed against this judgment in Delhi High Court. Justice E. Ford and Justice Addison dismissed the appeal no. 748 on January 13, 1930 and upheld the sentence. However the judges acknowledged Bhagat Singh as a 'sincere revolutionary' in their judgment.

Bhagat Singh and Dutt were sent to Mianwali and Lahore jail respectively on June 15, 1929. Bhagat Singh and Dutt both began their hunger strike for the facilities they enjoyed in Delhi jail. Later when the Lahore conspiracy case proceedings began from July 10, 1929, Bhagat Singh was also shifted to Lahore jail to be with the others accused. He was brought on a stretcher, being on hunger strike, for 25 days. The others accused of the Lahore conspiracy case also joined the hunger strike from 13th July, which later resulted in the martyrdom of Jatin Das on 13th September. Bhagat Singh was sentenced to death in the Lahore conspiracy case on October 7, 1930. Appeals up to the Privy Council were exhausted by the end of February, 1931. Bhagat Singh, Rajguru and Sukhdev were executed on March 23, 1931 at Lahore central jail.

B.K. Dutt lived in Patna after release and died in a Delhi hospital in 1965.

8

Hunger Strikes by Revolutionary Freedom Fighters: Bhagat Singh and Jatin Das*

In India, a hunger strike or fast has become a mixed phenomenon. On one side the fast/hunger strike is used as an effective political weapon to raise the consciousness of masses, as has been done throughout world history, but on the other side, it is being treated as a media fad to create sensational news, but overshadowing its true spirit and seriousness.

Incidentally, a fast or hunger strike is not India's or the Gandhian movement's contribution to the world or the Indian political scenario, though it has been effectively used in India. The real progenitors of fast/hunger strike as a political weapon are Irish revolutionaries. It was during 1916-1920 that the world was shaken by Irish revolutionaries soul shaking fast unto deaths. In India this spirit was imbibed by the revolutionary movement first and then only the Gandhian movement appropriated it as a political weapon to arouse people's consciousness for the burning issues.

In India, during the freedom struggle Jatindar Nath Das, popularly known as Jatin Das, sacrificed his life after a 63 days fast, while Bhagat Singh observed a total of five months plus fast/hunger strike in three of his known/unknown struggles for political rights inside the jail from April 8, 1929 to March 23, 1931, the day of his martyrdom.

* Earlier published in *Hard News*.

They were inspired by Irish revolutionaries' sacrifices through hunger strikes, particularly Terence MacSwiney's sacrifice after many days of fast inside jail. Wikipedia page gives a glimpse of Irish revolutionaries' sacrifices through hunger strikes as under.

In October 1920, the Lord Mayor of Cork, Terence MacSwiney, died on hunger strike in Brixton prison. Two other Cork IRA men, Joe Murphy and Michael Fitzgerald, also died on hunger strike in this protest along with Monaghan native, Conor McElvaney who lasted 79 days before death. The *Guinness Book of Records* lists the world record in hunger strike (without forced feeding) as 94 days, which was set from August 11 to November 12, 1920 by John and Peter Crowley, Thomas Donovan, Michael Burke, Michael O'Reilly, Christopher Upton, John Power, Joseph Kenny and Seán Hennessy at the prison of Cork. Arthur Griffith called off the strikes after the deaths of MacSwiney, Murphy and Fitzgerald.

Bhagat Singh and Batukeshwar Dutt started their first hunger strike from June 15, 1929, when they were transported for life in the Delhi Assembly bomb case and were shifted from Mianwali and Lahore jails respectively. They decided to start an indefinite hunger strike from the very first day of their arrival in the respective jails of Punjab, when they were not shown the courtesy of being 'political prisoners', as they were treated with respect during their Delhi jail stay from April 8, 1929 to June 14, 1929. Bhagat Singh even protested against segregating him and B.K. Dutt from each other, since trial of the Lahore conspiracy case, dealing with murder of Saunders was going to begin very shortly, in which Bhagat Singh was treated as one of the most focused accused. He wrote to I.G. Prisons, Punjab about this transfer on June 17, 1929. And on the same day, he also informed him of him being on hunger strike and raised certain demands; the most important one was to be treated as a *political prisoner*. On June 18, 1929, Superintendent Mianwali jail sought some clarifications from Bhagat Singh on his letter to I.G. Punjab and Bhagat Singh replied on June 19, 1929. Later when Bhagat Singh was also sent to Lahore jail, he and B.K. Dutt sent a joint letter to Home Member of the Government of India in this regard. All these three letters have historic significance in context of their struggle for the right of political prisoners in jail.

After a few days, Bhagat Singh was transferred to Lahore jail, but their hunger strike remained unknown to their own comrades, since they were lodged in different jails. On July 10, 1929, when all 16 accused arrested out of 25, against whom F.I.R. was lodged, appeared before the magistrate, they were shocked to see Bhagat Singh being brought to the court on a stretcher, since his condition was bad. From 10th July, all the others accused in this case also joined the hunger strike. Jatin Das warned his comrades about the pains and tortures of the hunger strike and mentioned that he would not back out of it, even if others left. Only he had the earlier experience of a hunger strike as he participated in it as the non-cooperation movement prisoner in Calcutta. And Jatin Das's warning proved true, even Sukhdev like revolutionaries could not sustain it for very long, only Bhagat Singh and a few other comrades could continue it. Baba Sohan Singh Bhakna, Ghadar party convict and nearing release, also joined the hunger strike, despite his old age and Bhagat Singh's efforts to dissuade him from not joining and he paid for it by getting his jail remission cancelled, thus spending more time in prison. This hunger strike is one of the most significant hunger strikes of a political nature in the world. The British colonial regime tried their best to break the strike by all kinds of means, mostly oppressive and some deceitful. The Congress Party got involved as after July 10, 1929, media started reporting about the conditions of hunger strikers every day and they were becoming popular among Indians every day. Jail enquiry committees, jail reform committees, et cetera, were formed, but the government yielded nothing. At one time, British officials accepted that they would implement some recommendations and Congress Party leaders assured revolutionaries of their demands being acceded. At this assurance on September 2, 1929, revolutionaries except Jatin Das suspended their hunger strike. Jatin Das's condition now was irretrievable and he did not want to let the British colonial regime escape the responsibility of killing him inside the jail. Bhagat Singh also resumed his hunger strike within two days, as British officials refused to release Jatin Das unconditionally, knowing full well that he was going to die. Jatin Das died in the hunger strike after 63 days on September 13, 1929. Jinnah made a historic speech in the Central Assembly in support of hunger striking revolutionaries on September

12 and 14, 1929, a day before and a day after the martyrdom of Jatin Das, as his speech could not be completed in a single day. It was the Irish hunger strike martyr Terence MacSwiney's sister, who remained in solidarity during the Bhagat Singh, Jatin Das hunger strike and sent a message on Jatin Das's martyrdom like her own brother's earlier. Bhagat Singh continued his hunger strike till 4th October, making a record those days of 112 days fast in jail. Though British officials yielded a bit, but for agreed demands, Bhagat Singh had to observe 15 days hunger strike again in February, 1930. Bhagat Singh resorted to hunger strike again in July-August, 1930, against jail rules and he informed Special Tribunal Lahore, whose proceedings they boycotted throughout the trial and also Punjab High court, where he filed a petition against denial of interviews by jail authorities. The fact about Bhagat Singh's third hunger strike in July-August, 1930 remained suppressed till now and it has come to light only from some of his letters displayed in the Supreme Court exhibition in September, 2007.

Despite Bhagat Singh and his comrades' valiant fight inside the jail for securing rights for 'political prisoners' as special category, they were not given this status, neither after transfer of power in 1947, this right has been acceded by different governments in India, despite thousands of opposition workers being imprisoned in the 1975-77 emergency. In fact, despite first Indian Prime Minister Pandit Jawaharlal Nehru's own strong dislike of British colonial laws like the Indian Sedition Act, the whole Indian Police Act (IPC) and Criminal Procedure Act (CRPC) and many more British colonial laws are still intact in India, Pakistan and Bangladesh. I wonder why social movements launched by Jayaprakash Narayan, whose name has now been dumped by media in favour of Anna Hazare, or the latest one by Anna Hazare have ever demanded the removal of colonial period laws from statue books of 'Free' India! It just proves the point made by Bhagat Singh in one of his writings that–what difference it makes to Indian people if in place of Lord Reading or Lord Irwin, Purshottamdas Thakkar or Tej Bahadur Sapru rules India, as long as the living conditions of people remain the same. So the new rulers of India and Pakistan retained most of the anti-people oppressive colonial laws like Sedition Law on statue books after 1947 and till date no movement has been launched to get these laws abolished or only the new breed of Bhagat Singhs have to perform the remaining task of getting rid of colonial vestiges, being used in much worse form of mixing this with feudal oppressive tendencies of the Indian political and bureaucratic class.

In post 1947 India, Potti Sriramulu, a freedom fighter himself gave up his life for the creation of Andhra Pradesh through hunger strike and Darshan Singh Pheruman did the same for the creation of Punjabi suba or present-day Punjab. I doubt if anyone using the weapon of fast/hunger strike has got the same spirit and sincerity as Irish revolutionaries, Bhagat Singh, Jatin Das, even Mahatma Gandhi, Poti Sriramulu or Darshan Singh Pheruman like freedom fighters had. The question also arises why Irom Sharmila's ten-year-old hunger strike does not appeal to our middle class and media, because this is against colonial type laws. And what is the difference between D.K. Barooah's call during emergency that 'Indira is India and India is Indira' and between retired IPS officer Kiran Bedi's call, 'Anna is India and India is Anna'?

Bhagat Singh and B.K. Dutt's letter to Home Member, Government of India–June 24, 1929.

Central Jail
Lahore
June 24, 1929

We, Bhagat Singh and B.K. Dutt, were sentenced to life transportation in the Assembly bomb case, Delhi . As long as we were under trial prisoners in Delhi Jail, we were accorded a very good treatment from that jail to the Mianwali and Lahore central jails respectively, we wrote an application to the higher authorities asking for better diet and a few other facilities, and refused to take the jail diet.

Our demands were as follows:

We, as political prisoners, should be given better diet and the standard of our diet should at least be the same as that of the European prisoners. (It is not the sameness of dietary that we demand, but the sameness of standard of diet.)

We shall not be forced to do any hard and undignified labour at all.

All books, other than those proscribed, along with writing materials, should be allowed to us without any restriction.

At least one standard daily paper should be supplied to every political prisoner.

Political prisoners should have a special ward of their own in every jail, provided with all necessities as those of the Europeans. And all the political prisoners in one jail must be kept together in that ward.

Toilet necessities should be supplied.

Better clothing.

We have explained above the demands that we made. They are the most reasonable demands. The jail authorities told us one day that the higher authorities have refused to comply with our demands.

Apart from that, they handle us very roughly while feeding us artificially, and Bhagat Singh was lying quite senseless on the 10th July, 1929, for about 15 minutes, after the forcible feeding, which we requested to be stopped without any further delay.

In addition, we may be permitted to refer to the recommendations made in the U.P. Jail Committee by Pt. Jagat Narain and K.B. Hafiz Hidayat Hussain. They have recommended the political prisoners to be treated as 'Better Class Prisoners'.

We request you to kindly consider our demands at your earliest convenience.

By 'Political Prisoners', we mean all those people who are convicted for offences against the State, for instance, the people who were convicted in the Lahore conspiracy cases, 1915-17, the Kakori conspiracy cases and Sedition cases in general.

Yours

Bhagat Singh

B.K. Dutt

(From *Selected Writings of Bhagat Singh* edited by Shiv Verma)

DR. ALAM AND DR. GOPI CHAND RESIGN.

The Tribune.

VOL. XLIX. NO. 211. LAHORE, SUNDAY, SEPTEMBER 15, 1929. Price : One Anna.

JATINDRANATH DAS PASSES AWAY.

[T]housands Attend Funeral Procession.

[PE]OPLE SHOWER FLOWERS AND COINS.

Calcutta Corporation Adjourns.

[P]T. MOTILAL NEHRU WILL MOVE ADJOURNMENT OF ASSEMBLY

[H]E DIED FIGHTING FOR BETTER TREATMENT OF POLITICAL PRISONERS.

Mr. Jatindranath Das lying dead in Borstal Jail

Mr. Jatindranath Das passed away at 1-5 p.m. on Friday.

"I am not a Bengali. I am an Indian."
Jatin's Parting Words

HARTAL IN LAHORE.

[From Our Special Representative.]

"I kissed my shoulder on which was placed Jatin's bier, imagining that it was rendered holy," said Dr. Alam giving an account of how the procession started from the Jail Gate.

> He has bravely laid down his life for what he believed to be the cause of the country.
> PT MOTILAL NEHRU.

"I AM NOT A BENGALEE."

Mr. Das breathed his last at 1-5 p. m.

A few minutes prior to his death, he said that he had changed his mind. "I do not [illegible] that my obsequies should be performed at the Kali Bari in the [illegible] Bengali fashion. I am not a Bengali; I am an Indian," were his parting words. And in deference to his last wishes, the original plan of carrying his dead body to the Kali Bari was given up.

> The cause for which Mr. Das died will triumph, although for the present Government may think think wrongly, that they have won.
> MR. SEN GUPTA.

(See Page 2)

Calcutta Corporation Adjourns.

Mayor Pays Tribute to Jatin Das.

Calcutta, Sep. 13.

"Today Mr. Jatindra Nath Das becomes a great hero for all Bengalees and for all Indians to worship, and the cause for which he gave his life is certainly going to triumph, although for the present the Goverment may think wrongly, that they have won said Mr. J. M. Sengupta, Mayor, adjourning the Corporation meeting this evening as a mark of respect to the memory of Mr. Das.

Mayor continued, "Mr. Das was arrested in Calcutta a little over two months ago and was taken to the Punjab on a charge which was in all conscience a very serious one. Now that he had gone it is possible for those who had known him well to say that he was perfectly innocent of the charges brought against him by the Government. Whatever opinions people might have with regard to the charges there cannot be but one opinion amongst Indians, and particularly of people of Bengal, that Mr. Jatindra Nath, an unknown hero, was fighting for a cause which had nothing to do with the offences he was charged with.

Mr. Das was fighting for the better treatment of political prisoners, a cause for which in other parts of the world people in the past have fought and died. In all civilised countries, political prisoners do take upon themselves the right to vindicate their position. The same thing happened with regard to Macswiney and it was the same thing with regard to Mr. Jatindra Nath Das. It would be well if youngmen of the country would follow in the footsteps and show to the world, as other great men have shown in the past that however much the Government of the country might imprison our body our soul is beyond the control of foreign Government."

A condolence motion expressing sorrow and sending condolence to the bereaved family was adopted, the whole house standing in silence.—*Free Press.*

SWARAJISTS AND LADY SCHUSTER'S PARTY

Simla, Sep. 13.

The Congress Party leader, Pandit Moti Lal Nehru, issued an emergent whip, advising members of the Party not to attend Lady Schuster's garden party this afternoon. This whip says:

"The attendance of the members of the Party at Lady Schuster's garden party this afternoon was permitted on her assurance that it was not an official function and was being held in order to enable her to meet her friends of the Assembly before her approaching departure for England. News has just been received that Mr. Jatin Das, one of the hunger-strikers of the Lahore case, died at 1 p. m. He has bravely laid down his life for what he believed to be the cause of the country. As a mark of respect for the memory of that great soul, I direct that no member of the Congress Party will attend Lady Schuster's party this afternoon. I am writing to Lady Schuster on behalf of the Party, and members need not take the trouble to write separately."

CONFERENCE AT PT. MOTILAL'S HOUS[E]

Commotion in Simla.

VICEROY'S EXECUTIVE COUNC[IL] MEETS TO DISCUSS SITUATION.

(From Our Special Correspondent.)

Simla, Sep. 13.

There is considerable commotion [in] Simla since 3 o'clock this afternoon [in] consequence of the death of Mr. Jatind[ra] Nath Das.

The Executive Council of t[he] Governor-General held an emerge[ncy] meeting at Viceregal lodge a[nd] discussed the situation that has arise[n] and the prospect of a censure motio[n] by Pandit Motilal Nehru tomorrow [in] the Assembly.

The form of this motion underwe[nt] considerable changes every hou[r] as the result of conversations [at] Pt. Motilal's residence. At on[e] time the formula was considered [illegible] doubtful of admission because as [it] then stood it related to the administration of Jails which is a provincial subject but the defect in the language was suddenly removed an[d] new text drafted.

Pandit Malaviya and Mr. Jayakar wer[e] consulted and their party will suppor[t] the motion.

Mr. Jinnah's attitude, it was diffi[cult] to ascertain as he was at Lady Schuster's garden party till the afternoon. But he has given a definite pledge to support the motion and it is expected his followers, who number ten, wi[ll] also join him. Thus the Governme[nt] of India will be censured for allowing scandalous treatment to the undertrial prisoners in the jails which forced them to resort to hunger-strike and has already resulted i[n] the death of Mr. Jatin Das afte[r] sixty-one days' fast.

ELECTRIC ATMOSPHERE.

The atmosphere on the eve o[f] further discussion on the Hunger Strike Bill is indeed electric and the executive Council anticipating [illegible] time, is discussing all aspects of the situation and how best to wriggle out of it. There are three courses open to them. firstly that as five accused in the Lahore Case have terminated hunger-strike and hunger-strike is now confined to Sardar Bhagat Singh and Mr. Dutt, they may withdraw the Bill. Secondly, they may agree to Mr. Kelkar's dilatory motion for circulation to elicit public and legal opinion. The third course is to proceed with the Bill. Should the last be the case then attempts would be made to induce Mr. Kelkar to withdraw his motion and Mr. K. C. Roy to withdraw his amendment for a select committee and thus throw out the Bill by taking advantage of the atmosphere.

I understand that neither Mr. Kelkar nor Mr. Roy will refuse to adopt this course should that be deemed necessary. Any way the fate of the Hunger-Strike Bill from Government point of view is very uncertain as the whole attempt of the Government to [illegible] this legislation on the Statute [illegible] at any cost by resort even to certification if necessary has been [illegible] in the melting pot by the death of Mr. Jatin Das. The Government's decision of this evening is not known at the time of wiring.

Jatin Das's dying photo in Jail—The Tribune, Lahore, September 15, 1929

Subhas Bose after Jatin Das's martyrdom

Jatin Das's father performing his last rites in Calcutta

9

Trial, Jail Notebook and Changing Images*

When Bhagat Singh, a young man of 23 years was hanged along with Rajguru and Sukhdev in Lahore jail on March 23, 1931, the whole country was shaken. At that time, Bhagat Singh was more popular than Mahatma Gandhi. The image of Bhagat Singh on the popular mind was that of a brave patriot, who kissed the gallows smilingly for the honour and freedom of the country, but it clouded the real personality of Bhagat Singh. These clouds started clearing in 1970 when Prof. Bipan Chandra, an eminent historian while introducing the new edition of Bhagat Singh's article, 'Why I Am Athiest', revested the sharp thinker in him. Many writings of Bhagat Singh were in print earlier also, but since the publication of *Documents of Bhagat Singh and His Associates* (in Hindi) edited by Jagmohan Singh and Chaman Lal in 1986 and *A Martyr's Jail Notebook* edited by Bhupender Hooja in 1994, every aspect of Bhagat Singh's personality came out clearly. Though friends of Bhagat Singh like Ajoy Ghosh, Shiv Verma, et cetera, of the Communist Party, wrote about Bhagat Singh's revolutionary intellectual personality. Prof. Bipan Chandra presented Bhagat Singh as an original thinker in the context of the Socialist movement in India going beyond his traditional image of a brave patriot. Prof. Sumit Sarkar and Prof. Irfan Habib have underlined that the freedom struggle fought under the leadership of Bhagat Singh was a revolutionary struggle, which was parallel to the struggle under

* Earlier published in *Frontier*.

the leadership of Mahatma Gandhi. The revolutionary struggle by Bhagat Singh and his associates was not aimed just at getting freedom from British colonialism. This struggle was to liberate India from colonialism as well as from local feudalism and to establish a politico-social system in India, in which no man could exploit other men, whether white or black, local or foreigner, in which no Indian could be exploited either socially, economically, politically, religiously or culturally. This was a revolutionary struggle to build an expolitationless classless society. In Hindi, Hans Raj Rehbar, Manmath Nath Gupta, in their books focused on this aspect of Bhagat Singh's personality. In English also a number of books appeared. A.G. Noorani's book, *The Trial of Bhagat Singh* published in 1996, and Kuldip Nayar's *Martyr Bhagat Singh: Experiments with Revolution* deserve mention. Now, it has been proved beyond doubt that Bhagat Singh was inspired by Marxist philosophy. He was not only a revolutionary organizer and activist, he was a thinker and writer of very high calibre. Bhagat Singh was an image incarnate of indomitable and unbelievable moral courage. From April 8, 1929 to March 23, 1931, a period of about two years, which Bhagat Singh spent in jail, testifies the above statement. The kind of reading Bhagat Singh did during his jail stay, in view of tough torturing conditions in jail, is not only fantastic, it is almost impossible. Bhagat Singh's study in jail was not just a pastime, he wrote more than a hundred pages in notes and comments contemplating upon this study and even made plans of writing a few books. This has been revealed after his *Jail Notebook* was published in 1994.

Though Bhagat Singh and his co-workers had deep differences with the leaders of the national movement like Lala Lajpat Rai and Mahatma Gandhi, yet they respected the elders. Revolutionaries viewed Lala Lajpat Rai as being influenced by communal thinking, yet when British colonialism martyred Lala Lajpat Rai by brutal showering of *latins*, these revolutionaries avenged his death by shooting dead ASP Saunders, considered responsible for Lalaji's death. Lala Lajpat Rai died on November 17, 1928, while protesting against Simon Commission in Lahore and Saundars was killed within a month in broad daylight in Lahore, by Bhagat Singh and his associates. There were posters all over the country that Lalaji's death was avenged. Though the common Indians wholeheartedly appreciated that act of the revolutionaries, and they became heroes among people, yet the national leaders condemned their act.

The country's political scenario around 1928 was as follows:

(i) The Indian National Congress was the central organization leading the freedom struggle of the country. INC included landlords and capitalists; also it included people committed to liberal democratic views and some communalists. Mahatma Gandhi, was the most respected. He was a nationalist, but not socialist. People like Jawaharlal Nehru, Subhas Chandra Bose and Jayaprakash Narayan were socialists and were intellectually influenced by the Bolshevik Revolution of Russia of 1917. Nationalists like Sardar Patel were also representatives of landlords and capitalist interests.

(ii) Organizations like the Muslim League, RSS and Hindu Maha Sabha were dividing Indians on Hindu or Mulism communal perceptions and these were spreading the poison of communalism. These organizations generally got patronization from British colonialism and big landlord capitalist classes.

(iii) The third force on the political scene was that of those who wanted the revolutionary transformation of Indian society. In this third force, there were communist groups, revolutionary organization of Bhagat Singh, and the leaders of Dalit power like Dr. B.R. Ambedkar and E.V. Ramasamy Naicker (Periyar). But there was no unity and only Bhagat Singh received the support among Indian masses. Bhagat Singh emerged like a parallel political personality to Mahatma Gandhi.

British colonialists were worried about the political views and the unimaginable strong moral personality of Bhagat Singh. Mahatma Gandhi was also acquianted with Bhagat Singh's personality and his views and it was very clear to him that there are two clear paths of struggle against British colonialism. One was the path of Mahatma Gandhi and another was the path of Bhagat Singh. After the publication of Mahatma Gandhi's and Bhagat Singh's entire writings, now the picture of the national movement of the time is clear. One path was reformist, the transition from white to black rule, without changing the system. The second path was revolutionary for building a new Indian society based on social equality. It was also clear by 1930 or so, that, Bhagat Singh and his comrades had renounced terrorism. Bhagat Singh himself condemned terrorism in his writings and in his court statements. But Bhagat Singh had renounced only terrorism and not revolution. Rather he had become a stronger revolutionary. That is why, he wrote his article, 'Why I Am an Atheist' around 1930 and sent his 'Draft Revolutionary Programme' to the students and youth of Lahore from jail.

The Trial of Bhagat Singh: Politics of Justice by A.G. Noorani smashes many other myths. It was a common refrain that the British nation respects justice and that whatever happened during British rule, even police terror or torture was regulated by certain legal process. During British rule, the accused were killed by hanging and not in false encounters as in free India. There was a complete judicial process to hang the accused, etc. By giving details of Bhagat Singh's trial, Noorani has established that the so-called judicial process adopted by British rule was completely hypocritical, deceptive and completely fraudulent. The process was in reality murder of the whole judicial process.

Bhagat Singh had escaped from Lahore on December 17, 1918, after eliminating Saunders with the help of Durga Bhabhi and had he not been arrested on April 8, 1929, after throwing bombs in Central Assembly (Parliament of today), Delhi, along with B.K. Dutt, he could have saved himself from the gallows. But Bhagat Singh was made of different stuff. He had voluntarily chosen the path of martyrdom. That is why, he did not engage any advocate for his defence ; he asked only for legal counsel and till the end, he fought his own cases with the help of legal counsel. Bhagat Singh was very clear about his aim. He believed that political prisoners should advance their political goals while fighting the cases. The political goal should be dearer than their own lives. Believing in this principle, Bhagat Singh exposed the hollowness of the British political and judicial system. He knew the outcome most clearly since he was to sacrifice his life. At the time of his arrest in 1929, Bhagat Singh was just a few months more than 21 years, but possessed, a rare ideological clarity and commitment. He was accused in two cases, he was sentenced to death not in the Central

Assembly bomb case, but he and his 24 close associates were committed to trial in the Saunders' murder case. This case under the title of the Lahore conspiracy case was first referred to the special court of Rai Sahib Pandit Sri Kishan, where the complaint was filed on July 10, 1929. These were 13 assessed in all, of which seven became approvers, nine were absconding and 16 were produced in the court. They were accused of Saunders' murder, conspiracy of revolution, inciting the rebellion against the state, etc. This case got the attention of the Central Assembly and Mohammad Ali Jinnah spoke about this case in the Assembly on September 12 and 14, 1929. He focused on the brutal police tortures on these men and the dishonesty of the British Government. In jail and in courts these young patriots were subjected to continuous inhuman tortures, which included brutal beatings. These revolutionaries stayed on hunger strike for months and one of the accused Jatindra Nath Das, even lost his life due to the hunger strike. Yet the British colonial rule, making a mockery of its so-called rule of law and judicial process, issued an ordinance under the signature of the then Viceroy, and Governor General Lord Irwin on May 1, 1930 from the summer capital Shimla. Under this ordinance, a three judge special tribunal was established to hear the Lahore conspiracy case. There was to be no appeal against the verdict and the sentences would not require confirmation by the High Court. This ordinance would last only for six months and for a further term, approval from the Central Assembly was a must. Lord Irwin had made a foolproof arrangement to get Bhagat Singh sentenced to death within six months. The ordinance, had armed the tribunal to conduct the trial even without the presence of the accused in court. All kinds of accusations could be made and any kind of evidence be recorded against any accused, who might not even be present in court. The Lahore High Court Bar Association and many leading lawyers protested against this ordinance, but of no avail. The tribunal started the trial on and from 5th May, and by the end of June, Justice Agha Haider was replaced as he had an inclination to give a fair trial to the accused. This tribunal, the murderers of the whole judicial process sentenced Bhagat Singh, Rajguru and Sukhdev to death on October 7, 1930, 23 days before its term was to expire. The British Government in India had proposed to record the evidence of more than six hundred persons, yet to hang Bhagat Singh within the stipulated period, the evidences of more than two hundred people were dropped. Later in England, D.N. Pritt pleaded before the Privy Council against this sentence based as it was on this patently illegal ordinance, but his sound pleas fell on deaf ears, which included Indian Judge Dinshah Mullah as well. So in this way the British colonial raj, thumping the drum of its so-called rule of law and judicial process, after a totally fraudulent trial hanged three young patriots on March 23, 1931.

Bhagat Singh was absolutely free from illusion. He knew that they could be sentenced to death. He was anguished, when his father S. Kishan Singh made an appeal against the judgement. Bhagat Singh made a representation to the British Governor General claiming themselves as war prisoners, who were waging a war on British colonialism and made the demand that they should be shot dead by army detachment. Bhagat Singh, Rajguru and Sukhdev were hanged at 7.33 in the evening and even their dead bodies were cremated in the most uncivilized and undignified manner near Ferozpur. The half-burnt body parts were collected by Bibi Amar Kaur, sister of Bhagat Singh and other relatives, friends and followers from Hussainiwala near Ferozpur city.

Though Bhagat Singh had become a people's hero throughout the whole country, yet even after his martyrdom, Mahatma Gandhi condemned his heroic act done for the honour of the country. In his negotiations with Lord Irwin, not to mention getting the death sentence to Bhagat Singh and other accused, he even went on to advise the British administrators how to deal with the post hanging situation in the country. Now all these documents are published and kept in the National Archives. Netaji Subhas Chandra Bose and Jawaharlal Nehru kept admiring these young men, but none of them offered any help. Though in the Assembly bomb case, none of the members received any serious injuries and Bhagat Singh and Dutt had made their intention clear by saying, 'Explosions are necessary to make the deaf hear', yet all members except Madan Mohan Malviya, condemned these young men and even passed a resolution of condemnation in the Assembly. Now when some members of Parliament are raising the demand to install a picture of Bhagat Singh in Parliament, then justifiably one should raise the demand that the resolution passed in the Central Assembly, on April 8, 1929, condemning Bhagat Singh and B.K. Dutt be withdrawn, cancelled and expunged from the proceedings. Strangely Bhagat Singh's thoughts irritate even *swadeshiwala* Atal Bihari Vajpayee, which he expressed during the release of Kuldip Nayar's book, *The Martyr Bhagat Singh: Experiments in Revolution*. Kuldip Nayar observed that he cannot change history. But today the whole emphasis of cultural nationalism is to change Indian history. People who need Bhagat Singh, is the real third force of the country meaning Dalits, workers and youth. But this force is yet to get united and organized.

10

Jinnah and His Defence of Bhagat Singh*

The storm created by the then BJP President L.K. Advani's comments on Jinnah, is dying out now, but the controversy has brought into focus the role of different political personalities during the Indian freedom struggle. Historians of modern India and journalists keep commenting on, or evaluating the role of political characters of the national freedom struggle, but it is important that this debate should not be based on the sensation created by a statement of a political leader; rather it should be based on facts and events and it should be conducted objectively, in a completely dispassionate manner. It should not end as 'a storm in a teacup'.

In this context, the most significant fact is that most leaders of the Indian freedom struggle had contradictions in their personality, whether it was Mahatma Gandhi, Netaji Subhas Chandra Bose or Mohammad Ali Jinnah or any other leader. Political leaders of free India are no less free from contradictions including L.K. Advani, who, on one occasion, to create communal tension, goes on a *rathyatra* and expresses joy at the demolition of the Babri Mosque on December 6, 1992 and on another occasion describes December 6, 1992 as 'the saddest day of my life'. Even the so-called secular Congress is no different: the party decribes the Gujarat massacre of Muslims in 2002 as a fascist spectre, but it conveniently forgets the thousands of Sikhs crushed under the weight of the 'big tree' that fell in 1984.

Mahatma Gandhi used to say, 'Pakistan will be built on my dead

---

* Earlier published in *The Tribune*.

body'. The creation of Pakistan did not cause his death, but an extreme form of Hindutva did. Ironically Gandhi was trying to resolve the caste and religious contradictions of the Indian society within the frame work of a 'tolerant and liberal Hinduism'; Netaji Subhas Chandra Bose got stuck in the whirlwind of world politics, where on one side were the British imperialists, from whom he wanted to liberate India, but on the other, were the fascist Hitler/Mussolini/Tojo, on whom he was depending for help. Vinayak Damodar Savarkar, who was once the role model for revolutionary nationalists like Madan Lal Dhingra, because of his book on the 1857 Revolt, turned out to be a spokesman of extreme Hindutva and an apologist for the British imperialists. He also became an accused in the Gandhi murder case. Though he was acquitted by the court, his image as a communal personality remained. In fact it was his extreme Hindutva ideology that led to the counter ideology of extreme Muslim separatism propagated by Jinnah.

What is the root cause of all these contradictions? For any political personality, to gain political power is the ultimate goal and the highest ambition of his life. This reality is not limited to India or Asia, this is true of any country of the world. That is why sensing an opportunity to gain political power in 1947, when Britain had declared its intention to transfer power by June 1948, neither Gandhi-Nehru-Patel nor Jinnah could resist the temptation of making early moves, whereas the one year period was meant for an orderly and bloodless transition, in view of the high tensions of the communal divide between the Hindu and Muslim communities. Without making any administrative and political preparations, power was transferred in a great hurry in August, 1947, during the monsoon, the worst season for a large-scale migration of people; resulting in the massacre of six lakh innocent lives, displacement of more than one crore people, and the rape and maiming of lakhs of women. Had this whole operation been planned in a patient and orderly manner, it would have exposed the incurable disease of Jinnah and may be by the passage of some more time, the division of the country could have been avoided. But British imperialism in order to weaken the newly independent nations and for creating a permanent tension in the area, conspired to divide the country through an early transfer of power. Under the circumstances, Nehru's address to the Central Assembly became a 'historic' event for India and Jinnah's address, quoted by Advani, became a 'historic' event for Pakistan.

Facts have been brought to light about Jinnah's personal conduct, which was never that of a communal or fundamentalist Muslim or Mullah. Coming from an upper middle class family, and as a successful barrister, Jinnah was sufficiently liberal in thought and gentle in behaviour. He never performed 'namaz' and took 'drinks'. That is why Sarojini Naidu, the poetess, called him, an 'apostle of Hindu-Muslim unity'. Birender Kumar Barnwal, in his book in Hindi, *Jinnah: A Relook*, has narrated in detail Jinnah's love for the Parsi girl, Rattan Bai, who left her family to marry him and remained truly devoted to him. In fact, her death in 1929 and Savarkar's Hindutva turn made Jinnah a broken and bitter man and in the late 1930s he turned towards Muslim separatist politics. But one should be aware of the author's interesting facets of Jinnah's personality, before to this turn. Jinnah was close to the Bal Gangadhar Tilak brand of politics before his turnaround.

On September 12 and 14, 1929, in the Central Assembly. Jinnah made a long speech in the context of the hunger strike of Bhagat Singh and his comrades and the British imperialist design to hang these patriots with the sham of a trial conducted 'in the absence of the accused'. This was at a time, when even many Congressmen had condemned Bhagat Singh and B.K. Dutt for throwing bombs in the Assembly, on April 8, 1929, for which act they were 'transported for life', in May 1929. When they went on a hunger strike in the jail in protest against the misbehaviour of the jail staff, and to demand the status of political prisoners the British came up with an amendment in the criminal procedure code waiving the requirement of the presence of the accused or their pleader in the court, and after a sham trial convicted them in a hurried manner.

The Tribune's special correspondent for Shimla reported that while participating in the debate in the Central Assembly on the British bill, on September 12, 1929, Jinnah said, 'The man who goes on hunger strike has a soul. He is moved by the soul and he believes in the justice of his cause'. *The Tribune* report mentioned, 'Mr. Jinnah created a profound impression by the excellent form in which he argued the case. Mr. Jinnah was proceeding in this strain winning applause after applause from the spellbound house.' *The Tribune*, on July 14, 1929, published the full statement of Bhagat Singh and Batukeshwar Dutt, as read out by Diwan Chaman Lal in the house.

Jinnah questioned the British Government, while discussing the amendment proposed by Home member James Crerar, 'Do you wish to prosecute them or persecute them?'

Crerar condemned not only Bhagat Singh and Dutt, but also the accused in the Lahore conspiracy case (1915-1917) and the Kakori case (1925).

Jinnah challenged the law member of the Assembly to go on a fast, to understand the impact of fasting on the human body. He said, 'It is not everybody who can go on starving himself to death. Try it for a little while and you will see.'

He rebutted Crerar by giving the example of Mr. Cosgrave, Prime Minister of Ireland, who was under death sentence, a fortnight before being invited to form a government. Jinnah observed that in so many countries, not only youth, but even grey bearded persons had committed 'serious offences, moved by patriotic impulses.'

Continuing with his arguments, Jinnah asked, what these youth were after all demanding from the government by going on a hunger strike. 'Do they want spring mattresses? Do they want dressing tables? Do they want a set of toilet requisites? No, Sir, they asked for bare necessities and a little better treatment. I ask you in all decency, why cannot you concede this small thing?'

Jinnah's speech began on 12th September and was concluded on 14th September. He put the British Government on the mat by his brilliant expose of British design: 'Don't you think that, instead of trying to proceed with an iron hand and pursuing a policy of repression against your own subjects, it would be better if you realized the root cause of the resentment and of the struggle that the people are carrying on?'

Jinnah even warned the government in this context, 'Money of the taxpayer will (must) not be wasted in prosecuting men, nay citizens, who are fighting and struggling for the freedom of their country.'

According to A. G. Noorani, Jinnah had high esteem for Bhagat Singh and his comrades. Jinnah also said that if this amendment was passed then the trial would be just 'a travesty of justice'.

Jinnah was supported my Motilal Nehru, Jaykar, Rafi Ahmed Kidwai, etc. The amendment was carried through by 55 votes against 47. Jinnah had voted against it. Even in his February 1929 speech in the Assembly, Jinnah had condoled the death of Lala Lajpat Rai, with whom he had cordial relations. Also he pleaded for the release of Sikh leaders jailed in connection with the Sikh Gurdwara Act protests, and opposed the detention of many nationalists like Vallabhbhai Patel, Annie Besant, the Ali Brothers and Hasarat Mohani.

Bhagat Singh, Rajguru and Sukhdev were tried under the amended act, and after a sham trial, were hanged on March 23, 1931, 'a travesty of justice', in the words of Jinnah.

The question arises, we have looked at the fiery nationalist role of Jinnah before 1930, that with such rational (and national) views, why he turned to fundamentalist communal separatist politics?

Searching for the answer, let us look at some examples from modern world politics, Mao, 'Political power grows out of barrel of a gun'. Deng, 'It hardly matters whether a cat is black or white, it should catch mice.' 1967–United Front Governments in eight states comprising Jan Sangh, Akalis, Socialists and Communists; 1977—Janta Party Government consisting of Jan Sangh and Socialists, supported by CPM; 1989–V.P. Singh Government, supported by BJP on one hand and by left on the other.

A few other instances of short cut communal politics in free India, Amrinder Singh resigning from Congress and Parliament in 1984 against the Blue Star Operation, then getting ready to lead the Akali Government in 1986, courtesy Governor S.S. Ray, just losing the chance in the nick of time, signing Khalistani declaration submitted to UN Secretary General Boutres M. Ghali along with brother-in-law Simranjit Singh Mann, again joining Congress and leading Punjab Government in 2002, threatening Mann of arrest for raising Khalistani demand now. The case is the same of Savarkar, Advani, Vajpayee. To garner the majority Hindu vote bank, the politics of blind prejudices against minorities. By riding the Ram Rath in 1990 to power in Delhi in 1998; allowing Gujarat massacre of Muslims by the Modi Government in 2002; now under American pressure, singing the song of Indo-Pak friendship and to gain political power again, to lure Muslim votes–Jinnah drama. Jinnah also did the same, but in reverse order, first liberal then fundamentalist, the same was with Savarkar. But Advani and Vajpayee are first fundamentalists, then trying to be 'liberal'. Is not repeating history called – A Farce?

11

Gandhi and Bhagat Singh: The Historian's Perplexity, and a Thorn in the Neck of the National Movement*

A review of the book, *Gandhi and Bhagat Singh* by V.N. Datta, Rupa & Co., New Delhi, 2008.

When Bhagat Singh, Rajguru and Sukhdev were sentenced to death in the second Lahore conspiracy case, on October 7, 1930 by a controversial three-member special tribunal established by the British colonial government, saving the lives of these patriots turned into a national issue. And who could save these precious lives? In public perception, it was Mahatma Gandhi, who was considered the tallest national leader of India at that time. Since then this question has never been answered and erupts every now and then: Why did Gandhi not save the lives of these young men? Could he have saved their lives at all? This issue has been discussed often enough. *Mainstream* published a series of articles, both in favour of and against Gandhi, but without any convincing conclusion. Academics remained more or less aloof from this contentious issue, but with well known historian V.N. Datta's latest publication, *Gandhi and Bhagat Singh*, the debate has also entered the academic world.

V.N. Datta has referred to earlier debates on the issue and has come out with his own views, which are of course in favour of Gandhi

* An abridged version earlier published in *Economic & Political Weekly*.

to a large extent. Perhaps, the basic question is whether this issue deserves so much energy, space and time. Before probing the different aspects of this contentious question, one should look at the background against which this question was raised, debated and later ignored. Bhagat Singh and his revolutionary group, after changing the name of their organization to 'Hindustan Socialist Republican Association' from the earlier 'Hindustan Republican Association' (September 8-9, 1928) went into quick political action, but they were trapped in the quagmire of British repressive action on the Indian masses, and had to act against their own ideological perspective of building a socialist movement by organizing the masses, and thus creating an alternative to the Indian National Congress in the freedom struggle. The group requested Lala Lajpat Rai, a tall national leader, to lead the mass protest against the visit of the Simon Commission to Lahore on October 30, 1928, in spite of their differences with him on communal issue. Lalaji fell to the brutal *lathi* blows of the colonial police while leading the mass demonstration and succumbed to his injuries on November 17, 1928. Two famous statements were made on that occasion, one, by Lala Lajpat Rai himself on the same evening, that is, October 30, 1928, while addressing a mass rally against the brutality of the British police officers, namely Scott and Saunders, respectively, Superintendent and Deputy Superintendent of Police at Lahore at that time. Lala Lajpat Rai proclaimed at the highly charged mass rally that 'every blow on his body will prove to be the last nail in the coffin of the British colonial rule in India.' The other, equally charged reaction came after the death of Lala Lajpat Rai, from Basanti Devi, the widow of the most respected national leader, C.R. Das. She asked whether 'the youth of this country have lost their sense of shame' and whether 'our young men will avenge the death of our tallest national leader at the hands of a lowly British police officer.' Known to be the most sensitive to the dignity of Indian nationhood, Bhagat Singh's revolutionary group had no option under the circumstances but to avenge the death of Lala Lajpat Rai, who was the symbol of Indian nationalism at that time, despite their bitter differences with him. On December 17, 1928, exactly a month after the death of Lala Lajpat Rai, Saunders was shot dead by Rajguru and Bhagat Singh, with the cover given to them by Chandra Shekhar Azad. Though they all escaped from Lahore in a very daring manner and could even lie low for sometime, Bhagat Singh's sharp intellect and growing political maturity did not allow him to remain idle for long. He decided to act according to certain decisions he had taken. Bhagat Singh could see that in spite of the consensus on the need to have a socialist revolution in India through insurrection, like in Russia in 1917, he and his group were not equal to that great task. He knew that their days were numbered and they must perform such spectacular actions which could awaken the slumbering masses of India. He wanted the socialist ideas of his revolutionary group to reach every nook and corner of the country, and they had to sacrifice their lives to awaken the masses. Bhagat Singh was more than absolutely clear that sacrifice of some of the important leaders of the group was inevitable, and because of his involvement in the Saunders' murder, he had to be one of those leaders, who had to fulfil this responsibility towards the nation and its people. It was with such a clear understanding that the second spectacular act of throwing harmless bombs in the Central Assembly, Delhi (to make the deaf hear), to protest against anti-people laws like the 'Public Safety Bill' and the 'Trade Disputes Bill' was planned and carried out meticulously. The decision not to escape, and to use the courts as a platform to propagate their ideas was also taken with political maturity. To sing national songs and raise slogans in the court, and get brutally beaten up publicly at the hands of British police in response, was also part of that political design. Even to use the weapon of hunger strike and observe a record hunger strike of 115 days, bearing the loss of their dear comrade Jatin Das on the 63rd day, was to rouse the masses. And they did succeed in their aim.

Bhagat Singh delayed the Lahore conspiracy case proceedings. much to the chagrin of British colonial rulers, but he never wanted to save his life. He agreed to appeal to the Privy Council for this purpose but with the clear understanding that the 'execution must not stop'. His wish was that 'they should be executed at a time when the people rose en masse demanding their release'. That is exactly what happened. Bhagat Singh was executed exactly when the whole nation had woken up and he became a household name. The execution proved Gandhi's apprehension, as expressed to Irwin, true, that 'their execution will make them national martyrs'. Martyrs they did become, defeating the designs of both Gandhi and the British Crown, to marginalize them on the Indian political scene.

Gandhi and Bhagat Singh is an enlarged and revised version of a long keynote address delivered by Prof. V.N. Datta at the international conference held on 'Bhagat Singh and His Times', at Panjab University, Chandigarh, in September, 2007, by the Indian Council for Historical Research and the Institute of Punjab Studies. In a short preface, the author argues that 'the question of Bhagat Singh's life and death has to be seen from a broader perspective, especially within the framework of the British Imperial system operating in the country, which is generally ignored'. The author also questions the view of some of the historians that 'Bhagat Singh was a convinced and confirmed Marxist, Socialist and Leninite'. The author takes this view to be one dimensional. Prof. Datta also poses the question, 'What was his (Bhagat Singh's) legacy? What was his achievement?' The author counterpoises Gandhi's view that Bhagat Singh's mode of militant nationalism was 'most injurious to the cause of Indian independence'. Prof. Datta also states that 'Sukhdev was the real brain and organizer of the entire programme' and 'his role has been ignored'; further 'Sukhdev still awaits a historian!'. For a small book of about 125 pages, these questions and observations are too complex. The book, divided into eight chapters, includes in its appendices, the notice issued by HSRA after the killing of J.P. Saunders, the leaflets thrown in the Central Assembly after the bombs, the Governor General's statement after the Gandhi-Irwin pact and the Karachi Congress resolution of March 31, 1931 on 'Fundamental Rights and Economic Changes'. Apart from a useful index and bibliography, a chronology of Bhagat Singh's life has been included in the book.

In the first chapter, the author refers to the debate that took place mostly in the pages of the left-oriented weekly, *Mainstream*, on Gandhi's role in this whole episode. While Ashok Celley, D.P. Das and A.G. Noorani took a strong stand that Gandhi had not sincerely tried to save the lives of these young revolutionaries. Anil Nauriya and Prem Bhasin counter these views by supporting the view that Gandhi did his best to save their lives. K.K. Khullar and Kuldip Nayar are quoted as supporting Gandhi for making the required efforts, while G.S. Deol and Manmathnath Gupta, apart from A.G. Noorani, have been referred to as those castigating Gandhi in this context. S. Irfan Habib, it is mentioned, is somewhat ambivalent on this issue. Some British historians like Roy Jenkins, Andrew Roberts and Allan Campbell Johnson have been shown as describing the events of the Gandhi-Irwin negotiations in a matter of fact manner. The major article in this regard was written by D.P. Das, which was published under the title 'Gandhi and Bhagat Singh' in the Independence Day issue of *Mainstream,* in 1970 D.P. Das had based his arguments on the documents of the British bureaucracy from the national archives. He had also referred to Lord Irwin's autobiography, in which he mentions his dialogue with Gandhi on this issue. This article created ripples, as for the first time Gandhi's stand was questioned in a very serious manner. A.G. Noorani later added this article to his book, *The Trial of Bhagat Singh*, in the form of an appendix, and he himself supported all the arguments of Das with his own painstaking research. Ashok Celly argued that Gandhi never tolerated any other view in the national movement apart from his own. He referred to the expulsion of Subhas Chandra Bose from the Congress Party, despite Bose being the democratically elected President, as he had defeated Gandhi's candidate in the elections. D.G. Tendulkar and Pattabhi Sitarammaya are mentioned as espousing Gandhi's moral dilemma in this regard as a votary of non-violence; he could not defend an act of violence by the young men. The INA General, Mohan Singh, and author G.S. Deol were unhappy with Gandhi's passivity in this matter. All this debate centred round one issue: why did Gandhi not make it a precondition for the Gandhi-Irwin negotiations that the lives of these young men would be spared and the death sentence would be commuted to life sentence? The Privy Council by this time had rejected the appeal on these executions, and now only the Viceroy could commute the sentence and all the appeals were being made to him. Since the Congress Party, as the main driving force of the national movement, was expected to take the lead in this regard, pressure was being built on it from inside and outside to take a clear stand and further make the commutation of the sentence a condition of any agreement with the British Government. Not only Gandhi, who was the undisputed and most powerful leader of the Congress Party, even the Congress working committee did not make that a precondition for the negotiations with the British Government. Subhas Chandra Bose was then a member of the Congress Party. Popular leaders of the party, like Jawaharlal Nehru, were admirers of Bhagat Singh; yet they were all so helpless before Gandhi that no one could force the issue. Their admiration for the revolutionaries remained on paper and confined to speeches.

Prof. Datta has thrown some light on Gandhi's attitude towards revolutionary or militant approaches in the national freedom movement in the third chapter of the book. In 1909, Madan Lal Dhingra, son of a rich, pro-British family from Amritsar, came for higher studies to London, and influenced by Veer Savarkar's militant views, killed Curzon Wyllie, and was executed in London itself, after a quick trial. Gandhi was in London in those days, and he condemned the killing of Wyllie in the strongest possible words. Gandhi has also referred to this case in his tract. *Hind Swaraj*, which many people think is the key to Gandhian thought on Indian independence. Originally published in Gujarati, in 1909, the English edition of this books was banned for some time, when it came out in 1910. Gandhi also condemned the act of a bomb being hurled on Lord Hardinge, on December 23, 1912, during his ceremonial entry into Delhi, after the capital of the country was shifted to the city from Calcutta. Gandhi, in South Africa at that time, declared it to be 'a catastrophe'. Incidentally, Madan Lal Dhingra, and the four people executed in the Lord Hardinge bomb case, Master Amir Chand, Balmukund, Awadh Behari and Basant Kumar Biswas, were highly praised by Bhagat Singh in his writings on the national movement. Gandhi, relying on his South African experience, had made non-violence as his creed for the national movement, and created a political term *satyagraha*, literally meaning 'insisting on the truth', as a new weapon in the country's fight for independence. Gandhi had again strongly condemned the act of a bomb being thrown at the Viceroy's train, on December 23, 1929, by Bhagat Singh's comrades. The killing of Saunders and the throwing of bombs in the Central Assembly were also condemned as strongly as the other actions of the revolutionaries by Gandhi and some other leaders of the Congress Party. Gandhi had described the bomb throwing in the Central Assembly as 'the criminal act of two mad youths'.

In this long chapter on Gandhi's attitude towards the revolutionaries, Prof. Datta has referred to some other interesting aspects of the national movement, such as the commercial interests involved, or, perhaps, one should say the national bourgeoisie interests involved. Everyone knows: that Gandhi was very close to business magnate, G.D. Birla; in fact much of the funds for the Congress Party came from business houses, and the largest share from the Birla family. Prof. Datta has quoted another eminent historian of the national movement, Sumit Sarkar, as saying, that 'G.D. Birla, Walchand Hirachand and Purshottamdas Thakkar thought that the further continuance of the anti-British struggle would adversely affect their commercial interests.' (page 39) This is the same Purshottamdas Thakkar, Bhagat Singh had referred to in his famous quote suggesting it would make no difference to the people if Sir Tej Bahadur Sapru or Purshottamdas Thakkar took the place of Lord Reading or Lord Irwin, so long as the system did not change. Prof. Datta has quoted Gandhi's letter to the Viceroy, written on March 23, 1931, a day on which he observed silence. This is cited as the strongest defence for Gandhi in support of his 'efforts' to save the lives of the young revolutionaries. Instead, the letter, which contains a reference to the revolutionary group that was far from the truth, presents a moral indictment of Gandhian principles. Gandhi says, in his letter that 'the revolutionary party has assured me that, in the event of these lives being spared, that party will stay its hands. Suspension of the sentence, pending cessation of revolutionary murders, becomes, in my opinion, a preemptory duty.' (p. 42)

It is a double moral reflection on Gandhi's 'truthful' personality. Every political personality of those days, and the British administration as well, knew fully well that come what may, Bhagat Singh and his comrades would never give any assurance on renouncing violence under pressure or to 'save lives'. Such was their moral stature. Though it was a fact that Bhagat Singh and his group had decided to keep away from political violence and work towards organizing the masses, they would never convey it to their sworn enemy, the British colonial rulers. Aruna Asaf Ali vouches for this in this very chapter of Prof. Datta's book. Here Bhagat Singh's truthfulness had higher credibility than Gandhi's. Nationalist leader, and Bhagat Singh's counsel, Asaf

Ali was trying his best to get a statement from Bhagat Singh, which would imply that the revolutionaries were shunning terrorism as a political method, but he was not granted permission by the British rulers. Gandhi's letter to the Viceroy, written on the morning of 23rd March, can also be seen as a ritualistic exercise, as the British administration had sent a secret circular to the jail authorities to execute the prisoners on the evening of the 23rd itself, though it was widely believed that executions would take place the next morning, as per the tradition of execution being carried out in the morning.

In fact, Prof. Datta has not quoted the relevant passage from Lord Irwin's autobiography, which has been quoted by D.P. Das in his *Mainstream* article, where Irwin says that during their discussion of the Bhagat Singh issue Gandhi had asked him if he would mind if he (Gandhi) publicly claimed that he put a lot of pressure on the Viceroy on this issue. Irwin had replied that he wouldn't mind that. So 'the best efforts' made by Gandhi 'to save the lives of Bhagat Singh' and comrades, were planned with the full knowledge of the British administration. Prof. Datta has not referred to other relevant facts in this regard. Durga Bhabhi, widow of the revolutionary Bhagwati Charan Vohra, and herself an accused in the attack on the British Governor in Bombay, had met Gandhi in this regard. Gandhi knew her well, and thought she had come to seek his intervention in her own case. She lived underground those days and had warrants against her. Gandhi told her 'to surrender', and the rest he would take care of. But when Durga Bhabhi told Gandhi that she had come to appeal to him to 'save the lives of Bhagat Singh, Sukhdev and Rajguru'. Gandhi told her point blank that he could not do anything in cases related to political violence, and refused to intervene. Chandershekhar Azad was desperate to save Bhagat Singh, as he thought the revolutionary group needed his ideological leadership most urgently. Azad had a meeting with Jawaharlal Nehru, in Anand Bhawan, Allahabad, which Nehru refers to in his 'autobiography'. Nehru was sympathetic, but wanted the revolutionaries to go to Moscow to get training in Marxism, and he actually contributed some money for this purpose; but the project never materialized. Jawaharlal Nehru was actually supporting the 'Bhagat Singh Defence Committee' as well, whose Secretary, Kumari Lajjawati, was a Congress activist. Massive meetings and rallies all over Punjab and elsewhere were taken out under the aegis of this committee. There was a signature campaign all over India to save the lives of the young patriots. A record of at least two lakh signatures is preserved even today in the National Archives, at Delhi. More than forty thousand signatures appear on just one petition from Kanpur. None of these facts finds mention in Prof. Datta's book, when the issue of the value of Bhagat Singh's life is being discussed. Nor is the fact that Gandhi did not take into account this popular sentiment towards Bhagat Singh mentioned, in the book. Pattabhi Sitarammaya has himself recorded this sentiment in 'The History of the Congress Party' when he says, that Bhagat Singh was no less popular than Mahatma Gandhi in those days. Even today, media surveys indicate Bhagat Singh has a very high rate of approval among the people—as high as 64 per cent in a survey conducted by the newspaper, *The Hindu*. A survey commissioned by *India Today* finds Bhagat Singh at the top of the people's approval scale, while Gandhi is found much lower. The Indian people rightly think that Bhagat Singh sacrificed his life to defend the nation's dignity, which was seriously compromised by the death of Lala Lajpat Rai caused by the brutal police charge on him. While the national leaders of the Congress Party exhorted revolutionary youth to 'avenge' this humiliation of Indian nationhood at that time, clever and politically astute leaders like Gandhi diverted the focus from 'national dignity' to 'political violence'.

The revolutionaries trusted Motilal Nehru more in this matter, and when he died on February 6, 1931, they felt they had lost a 'sincere sympathizer' of their cause. This chapter quotes Robert Bernays as saying in his book *The Naked Faquir*, that Sarojini Naidu had told him that 'Bhagat Singh ought to be punished for his crimes, but not by death. After all he is only a rebel.' (47) In this chapter there is also an interesting quote from the internationally renowned Urdu poet, Faiz Ahmad Faiz, that the slogan *Inqlab Zindabad* had replaced *Bande Matram* in those days. Faiz's daughter, Salima Hashmi, had confided to this author that, from his room in the hostel of the Government College, Lahore Faiz had heard the pistol shots that killed Saunders on December 17, 1928. The college is a little away from where Saunders was killed that day.

Lord Irwin, who was a 'liberal' member of the Conservative Party, is introduced in the next chapter. After holding many senior positions, he came to India as Viceroy, in 1926, and served for five years. Days before he relinquished his charge, the 'liberal Viceroy' got Bhagat Singh, Sukhdev and Rajguru executed. In this chapter, the author quotes from the editorial in *The People* of March 22, 1931, which refers to British civil servants' machinations in Punjab, including their threat to 'resign', if these revolutionaries were not hanged. (p. 64) Prof. Datta refers to the bomb thrown at the Viceroy's train and also to the Punjab Governor being shot by young Harikishan during a convocation at Panjab University, Lahore, while these references are all very relevant to the theme of the book the conclusions drawn are somewhat intriguing. The author concludes, 'Bhagat Singh had killed a British police officer and the punishment for murder was hanging. In the imperial calculations Bhagat Singh was a cold-blooded butcher who had committed the murder of a fellow human being. From the British perspective, he was a rebel, a seditionist, a challenger, and wrecker of their system, which they were zealously determined to guard against anarchists like him. Irwin realized that British life in India was unsafe so long as political militancy was not crushed. Of course, he could not ignore the strong feelings of the British bureaucracy in India, and of the Home Government. (pp. 66-67)

One can understand the British colonial viewpoint in this regard, but that does not justify or clarify the nationalist response to that view, which, to say the least, was pitiably inadequate. Even the historian seems to be reconciled to this perspective that the whole issue revolved around whether Bhagat Singh could live under those circumstances or not. To this reviewer, this is a most inadequate explanation. It was Bhagat Singh who more than anyone else, including the British bureaucracy, Gandhi, and Irwin, knew clearly that 'he cannot live in those prevailing circumstances', and he made this clear in his last letter to his comrades, a day before his execution. It can be said in fact, that he almost chose the path to the gallows himself. The injustice done to him, however, by the nationalist leaders and historians, was to obfuscate his viewpoint in this whole debate.

The author has devoted a whole chapter to Bhagat Singh's self education, where he describes Bhagat Singh's personality with great admiration. He quotes Motilal and Jawaharlal Nehru to show their admiration as well. The author narrates Bhagat Singh's life story, particularly the story of his college days, but he commits a blunder while referring to his first arrest by the Punjab police. He writes, 'Bhagat Singh was arrested in connection with the Dussehra bomb outrage in 1926, and was locked up in a small cell on December 17, 1928.' (p. 27) Actually Bhagat Singh was arrested in this case on May 29, 1927 at Lahore and released on bail on July 4, 1927, a full five weeks after his arrest. This is his only arrest by the police before his final arrest on April 8, 1929. Actually December 17, 1928, was the day, on which Saunders was shot dead. But to be fair to the author, this could be a 'printer's devil'. In the chapter on the trial, the author quotes A.G. Noorani, who believed that 'Bhagat Singh's trial was a farce, politically motivated, and the procedures adopted in his prosecution were devious and a 'negation of justice'. (p. 69) But the author's own narration of this trial does not support Noorani's contention strongly. The author praises Bhagat Singh's court statement for its 'elegance, lucidity, cadenced language, the sobriety and seriousness of its theme, the breadth of outlook and loftiness of thought', et cetera, but credits it strangely to Jawaharlal Nehru, despite stating that Asaf Ali had admitted only to 'polishing' Bhagat Singh's language. No source had been referred to substantiate this claim, and the author relies solely on his own assessment that the statement has 'the striking features of Nehru's own prose writings' (p. 74). This shows our academia's view of our supreme revolutionary hero; no one wants to recognize his intellectual potential, and that is why his transition to Marxist thought is also questioned, despite his own writings offering the best proof of that.

In this chapter, the author also raises the issue why no eminent lawyer defended Bhagat Singh and his associates in the Lahore conspiracy case. The author surmises that 'lawyers wished to keep themselves out of a British police officer's murder case because they thought that as Bhagat Singh's counsel they might incur the ire of the British bureaucracy and judiciary from which they were accustomed to seeking favours'. (p. 75) One does not know whether to laugh or cry at such observations. The fact of the matter is that the best lawyers of Lahore, and from the whole country, were prepared to offer their services, and they treated this as a national cause. Lawyers like Asaf

Ali, Kailashnath Katju, Chanderbhan Gupta, Mohan Lal Saxena and the Nehrus, Motilal and Jawaharlal, had all remained concerned about this trial. It was the revolutionaries own decision to engage lawyers selectively. By a conscious decision they divided themselves into three groups. One group completely ignored the court proceedings; they did not engage any lawyer and practically boycotted the court proceedings to show 'the hollowness of the British judicial system'. Another group, which included Bhagat Singh, engaged a lawyer only to counsel them, they represented themselves in the court after consulting their counsel on legal points. The third group properly engaged lawyers. The interesting fact is that the fees of revolutionaries' lawyers were paid by the British, according to their own laws in this regard. And the lawyers who were engaged, Lala Duni Chand, Amolak Ram Kapoor, Pran Nath Mehta, were among the best in the country.

Prof. Datta's observation on Sukhdev that he was the real brain behind the revolutionary acts, comes from the fact that this case was registered as 'Sukhdev vs. the Crown'. Sukhdev in fact had made a statement to the police when he was arrested, that considerably damaged the reputation of the group. But as Sukhdev refused to become an approver, the statement he gave, we must conclude, was obtained through the 'standard police tactics' of misleading the accused through plain lies. Sukhdev in jail, broke his hunger strike midway, even as his comrades bravely suffered the repercussions of prolonged fasting. Sukhdev did not have the consistency, patience, far-sightedness or suffering capacity of a true revolutionary leader, though he was one of the intellectuals of the group, and was quite well read. The saving grace in his case was that he went along with his comrades and accepted the death sentence cheerfully, though he was not part of the conspiracy or actual execution of the murder of Saunders. One of the travesties of justice in this case was the death sentence awarded to Sukhdev.

In a short chapter on the Karachi Congress held immediately after the execution of Bhagat Singh and his comrades, the author has thrown light on Gandhi's capacity to face criticism without yielding from his position. Gandhi told the press emphatically that 'the commutation of the death sentence for these young men was not a part of the truce with the British'. He faced a black flag demonstration and was presented black flowers in Karachi, amid the slogans, 'Go back Gandhi' and 'Down with Gandhism'. He was even described as the 'ally of the British exploiters in India'. (p. 84) Prof. Datta also highlights the fact that writers like Prem Chand and Rabindranath Tagore had kept quiet on these executions. Gandhi declared in his speech at this Congress that 'the way of violence cannot bring *swaraj*; it can lead only to disaster.' (p. 85) But the revolutionaries were not fighting for *swaraj*, they wanted to overthrow the system of exploitation and build socialism in due course, which of course would have been disastrous for the Birlas, Lalchandanis and Thakurs of the country, who funded and supported Gandhi. The author mentions the resolution of condolence passed at the Congress, as per the wishes of Gandhi, but does not mention the resolution on the revolutionary approach to the freedom movement, which was very narrowly defeated. In a full-fledged book on the Karachi Congress, which was banned by the British, Jitmal Lunia gives details of parallel meetings of Naujawan Bharat Sabha, in which all the fiery leaders of the Congress Party, Subhas Chandra Bose, Jawaharlal Nehru, Ghaffar Khan, and Madan Mohan Malviya had participated. The chapter mentions that Birla contributed Rs 18 lakhs to the Congress and promised another Rs 30 lakhs to the party delegates attending the Round Table Conference in London. To placate left-wingers like Nehru and Bose, Gandhi got a resolution related to 'Fundamental Rights and Economic Change' passed in this session, which gave a slight pro-poor and pro-democratic colour to the social programme of the Congress Party. But how much Gandhi undervalued Bhagat Singh's contribution to the national cause was evident from the letter he wrote to Mehta Anand Kishore on June 26, 1931, in which he refused to be associated with any memorial being built to Bhagat Singh. Rajguru and Sukhdev. (p. 90) Mehta Anand Kishore was a Congress activist of long standing and a close family friend of Kishan Singh, Bhagat Singh's father. In fact, the first Lahore conspiracy case, in 1915, against Ghadar party activists was registered as 'Mehta Anand Kishore vs. the Crown'. Mehta was acquitted in this case, in which young revolutionaries like Kartar Singh Sarabha and Vishnu Ganesh Pingley were executed.

Comrade Ramchandra, President of the Naujawan Bharat Sabha in 1926, has given a lucid account of how the Congress Party sabotaged the Sabha's plan to build a suitable memorial to the three martyrs, in

Lahore. The plan was chalked out during the Karachi Congress itself, but the Congress Party used Bhagat Singh's father, Kishan Singh, to throttle the plan. The party promised to build the memorial on its own, and Mehta Anand Kishore, was made the General Secretary of the All India Bhagat Singh Rajguru Sukhdev Memorial Society. It was on behalf of this society that Mehta wrote to Gandhi, requesting him to issue an appeal for funds for the memorial. Gandhi's response to this letter killed the whole plan. This act of Gandhi's shows how the Congress Party used these young men, when the honour of the country was at stake, and after making some gains through the association, ironically because of the public sympathy for the young revolutionaries, disowned their patriotic acts as 'political violence', thus keeping themselves aloof. But the party reaped the fruits of their sacrifice to get concessions from the British colonial bureaucracy.

In the concluding chapter, Prof. Datta absolves not only Gandhi but even Irwin of any responsibility in matters related to the execution of the revolutionaries. It was beyond Irwin and Gandhi to save these lives he believes, as 'they were not free and independent enough to do whatever they wished as commonly assumed. They had to act within the framework of the British imperial system operating in the country'. (p. 93) One can very well understand Irwin's role as the British imperial system's representative, but, unwittingly, the author has ascribed this uncomplimentary aspect to Gandhi's personality and position as well, though many analysts, including revolutionaries, then and now, have made a similar assessment of Gandhi's role. Prof. Datta has also shown that apart from the issue of Bhagat Singh's death sentence, Gandhi did not even consistently support the abolishing of capital punishment, which almost all democrats the world over have always supported. This makes his moral position even weaker.

There is another error of dates in this chapter: 'Why I Am an Atheist' was published in *The People,* the weekly from Lahore, in the issue of September 27, 1931, and not 31st September, as mentioned. But more significantly, in this chapter, the author again expresses doubts about the authorship of Bhagat Singh's English writings; he believes they were modified by Asaf Ali, though Asaf Ali himself has denied any such editing. For Prof. Datta, it is a 'mystery' how these articles came to be attributed to Bhagat Singh.

Had Prof. Datta matched the proceedings of the Bhagat Singh case, this would not have been a mystery to him. In an exhibition in the Supreme Court Museum, in New Delhi, on 'The Trial of Bhagat Singh', a number of letters are on display, in Bhagat Singh's own handwriting, with no signs of Asaf Ali modifying or 'polishing' them. One may not find even a spelling error in those letters written in the beautiful handwriting of Bhagat Singh.

In his recollections, appearing after the conclusion, the author refers to his meeting with Partap Singh, who tells him that though Irwin had decided to commute the death sentence at Gandhi's request, because of the premature revelation of this decision to the public by Dr. Mohammad Alam, a Congress working committee member, Irwin ordered the execution. These are no more than folk tales created after such a significant incident. Prof. Datta, like Kuldip Nayar, has also taken undue interest in the later life of Hans Raj Vohra, who had turned approver in the case, and who died in Washington as a journalist after a long life. There were seven approvers in the case, out of whom Phaninder Ghosh was murdered in Bihar, and Baikunth Shukal was executed. Jaigopal was shot at in Maharashtra's Jalgaon court by Bhagwan Das Mahour and Sadashiv Malkapurkar. Jaigopal was also hit on the head with sandals by Premdutt, the youngest member of the revolutionary group in the court, since he provoked the revolutionaries by ridiculing them. But none of the other approvers were subjected to any kind of punishment by the revolutionaries, in jail or outside. They understood perfectly that not everyone could stand up to police tortures. Hans Raj Vohra felt guilty and ashamed even during the trial, but since his parents belonged to a high class they sent him out of the country. Had Vohra written his accounts, some truth would have come out about police methods of brutality.

From this image of Bhagat Singh, it would seem as if he achieved nothing and left no legacy or rather left a negative legacy, in Gandhi's terms. But the fact is that Bhagat Singh, exposed the British imperial system as a system of exploitation and oppression to the core. How else would one explain the Jallianwala Bagh episode, the single most brutal incident perpetrated by the British colonial system, in which going by the Congress fact finding team's report, more than one thousand Indians were mowed down by General O'Dwyer's orders?

The names of more than four hundred and fifty of these people have been inscribed now in the memorial itself. Since no punishment was meted out to the brutal killers of all these people, 21 years, after the incidents, Udham Singh, a revolutionary, next to London and shot dead Michael O'Dwyer, who, as Governor of Punjab had defended Dyer. Udham Singh was hanged in London like Madan Lal Dhingra earlier. Would anyone claim that since the Jallianwala Bagh killing was carried out by the imperial system, there was no need to bring the culprits to book? Were Scott or Saunders questioned even once for brutally hitting Lala Lajpat Rai, an old man and respected national leader? Or in neo-colonial times, has any court summoned Bush or Blair for causing more than six lakh murders in Iraq and committing the worst crimes against humanity, as Hitler and Mussolini did earlier?

Whatever Gandhi may have thought, or the historians influenced by him may say, for the common people of the country Bhagat Singh and Udham Singh had defended the dignity of the nation. When political movements succeed, who keeps count of the people killed during the movement? Can anyone dare to book Prachanda today for the political killings his movement carried out; Castro or Che Guevara, for the killings their movements were responsible for? Yes, the colonialists and imperialists have always called Marx, Lenin, Mao, Castro, Che Guevara, etc., all kinds of names; yet their role in the liberation of the people of the world from exploitation and oppression will remain a beacon light for all current and future liberation movements. Bhagat Singh's name also falls in that revolutionary category. That is why, despite all the political tensions between the two countries, Bhagat Singh is as much loved in Pakistan as in India. In fact, one of the major Urdu writers of Pakistan, Zahida Hina has recently described Bhagat Singh as 'the tallest martyr of Pakistan'.

Bhagat Singh and Udham Singh like national heroes did not need reprieve from the colonial system, but they did need proper appreciation from fellow countrymen, politicians, scholars and common people alike. Common people do understand them, and appreciate their noble deeds, but it is the politicians, and sometimes some scholars, who want to defend the colonial system and, in the process, misrepresent history. But as Bhagat Singh is a phoenix, he comes alive as often as he is burnt by the colonialists or their defenders.

In spite of the flaws in his interpretation of history, Prof. Datta must be complimented for bringing out many important documents and facts. The readers of the book will, of course, have a different interpretation.

12

Neither 'Deify' Nor 'Slight' Leaders Nor Martyrs in the Name of 'Democracy'*

Birinder Pal Singh in his piece 'Why Deify Leaders in a Democracy' in the 'open page' of *The Hindu* dated January 25, 2009 has tried to show that Bhagat Singh was made out to be a 'divine' being during his first birth centenary in 2007. He has advised 'the intellectuals' 'to not make mortal beings superhuman. Do his arguments stand the test of objectivity? I am afraid not, because facts do not support the arguments and in absence of facts, arguments become just subjective impressions, which most of the time are reflective of the prejudices of an uncritical mind. Some of the facts in this regard are as followed by:

This is a fact that Bhagat Singh became the icon of youth, patriotism and revolution shortly after his execution along with Sukhdev and Rajguru on March 23, 1931 at Lahore at the hands of British colonialism. The interesting part of his popularity among the Indian masses is that even after 75 years of his execution, he attracted the positive response of Indian masses. This includes *The Hindu* survey which had 64 per cent approval rate along with Dr. Ambedkar and the recent *India Today* survey which gave him the highest approval rate of 37 or 38 per cent, leaving Gandhi, Nehru, etc. way behind. Only Subhas Chandra Bose came a distant second to Bhagat Singh. But one should know the masses covered by these surveys are not fully aware of Bhagat Singh's personality or his ideas. They are more

* Earlier published in *The Hindu.*

impressed by his brave act of avenging the killing of nationalist leader Lala Lajpat Rai at the hands of colonial rulers by killing Saunders and upholding the voice of the freedom struggle by throwing bombs in the Central Assembly 'to make the deaf hear' and *not kill anyone.* This is also a fact that from left to right, all shades of political opinion tried to colour him in their own political interests. RSS like organizations tried to appropriate him as a staunch Hindu nationalist without bothering about his declared ideas. This has recently been done with Subhas Chandra Bose as well, angrily reacted to by Netaji's own established party, Forward Bloc.

The birth centenary of Bhagat Singh was celebrated at two levels, Government of India was rather forced by left pressure to declare it at official level, otherwise it was celebrated mostly at people's level in most parts of the country and abroad–Pakistan, Canada, England, USA, Australia, et cetera. The taste of official functions can be gauged by the spending of nearly four crore rupees by the Punjab Government in sheer wasteful extravagance. Out of these central funds only fifty thousand rupees each was given to Punjabi University, Patiala and Guru Nanak Dev University, Amritsar for holding seminars, which they held in a great hurry without much preparation. Punjab University, Chandigarh held a three-day national seminar sponsored by ICHR and first ever three-day national seminar on Bhagat Singh was held at Mumbai University in March 2007 without any agency or government support. This was by far the best seminar held on Bhagat Singh in the country. At best five-ten more seminars would have been held in Indian academic institutions at official level during the centenary years. In most of these seminars most historians had tried to look at Bhagat Singh from a Gandhian perspective, without bothering to discuss Bhagat Singh's own writings and tried to find fault with his kind of revolutionary transformational approach, which suits the establishment. Very few scholars tried to project Bhagat Singh in his own declared ideological perspective, that is revolutionary socialist perspective. This much limited and objective characterization of Bhagat Singh has pained scholars like Birinder Pal Singh, who see in it Bhagat Singh being lifted to 'divine', 'special status' and 'superhuman'. The fact of the matter is that Bhagat Singh represented one of the three major currents of the national freedom struggle. The most effective was led by the Indian National Congress under the leadership of Mahatma Gandhi, the second was led by RSS and Muslim League like sectarian and communal forces. Bhagat Singh, E.V. Ramasamy Naicker Periyar, Dr. Ambedkar and Netaji Subhas Chandra Bose like leaders represented the third current—to transform Indian society on socialist ideas with some differences on approach. Periyar was the first among those who eulogized Bhagat Singh in his editorial on March 29, 1931 in his journal *Kudai Aarsu*, he also got his essay 'Why I Am an Atheist' translated into Tamil by Com. P. Jivanandam and published it in 1933. This is the first and earliest translation of Bhagat Singh's seminal essay in any Indian language. Bhagat Singh held no special status than Sukhdev and Rajguru or Chandershekhar Azad like revolutionaries. He was given a central figure role as he represented the whole revolutionary current of the freedom struggle, being its ideological and organizational leader, like Gandhi in Congress.

One should also know that the first ever Bhagat Singh chair in any Indian University has been established in JNU, New Delhi only after a protracted campaign. Following this programme, the implementation committee of the Government of India on national anniversaries has sanctioned chairs in the name of Kartar Singh Sarabha, Chandershekhar Azad, Kunwar Singh and Bahadur Shah Zafar like revolutionary figures. In contrast, how many universities and chairs are established in the country in the name of Mahatma Gandhi, Nehru, Sardar Patel, Dr. Ambedkar, Subhas Chandra Bose, Maulana Azad and so many other national figures? Hundreds of books on other national leaders have been published by the Government of India, whereas documents of Bhagat Singh have been published by it for the first time in 2007, a full 76 years after his martyrdom. Ten-twenty seminars attended by 50-60 odd scholars have disturbed Birinder Pal Singh, but he was not bothered by hundreds and hundreds of such seminars on Gandhi, Nehru and other national leaders.

Birinder Pal Singh says that he does not wish to slight Bhagat Singh, but by his narrow and coloured understanding of the freedom struggle, he has done precisely the same.

13

An Emotional Journey Through Lahore and Surroundings*

I was trying to go to Lahore on March 23, 2006, on the seventy-fifth anniversary of Bhagat Singh's martyrdom. I wished that the Indian and Pakistani people could together commemorate this historic event. But the visit did not materialize for various reasons. But I had an unexpected invitation to present a paper on Dr. B.R. Ambedkar, on his birth anniversary, at Lahore, on 13th April. The invitation came from the Ganga Ram Heritage Foundation. The name of Sir Ganga Ram is very familiar in Punjab and Delhi. Delhi, like Lahore, has Ganga Ram Hospital, well known for its service. Sir Ganga Ram, a well known architect, along with Bhai Ram Singh, had designed the most beautiful buildings of Lahore. He had designed some buildings in Patiala and Amritsar too. But it was somewhat perplexing that the Ganga Ram Foundation should be organizing a seminar on Dr. Ambedkar. In any case, I accepted the invitation and prepared my paper. The other participant from India was V.T. Rajshekhar, editor of *Dalit Voice* from Bangalore. There were participants from UK, Nepal and Pakistan as well. On reaching Lahore, I came to know there was a seminar on Dr. Ambedkar at Karachi as well, on 14th April. Indian Dalit scholars participated in the Karachi seminar too.

I was born and brought up in the Indian part of Punjab, after

* Earlier published in *Dalit Voice* (Bangalore) with a different title and in *The Tribune* in an abridged form.

partition. My forefathers were from Mehraj, a village in the Bathinda district; so I had no particular reason to be excited about Lahore or west Punjab. I am an atheist, and so there is no religious reason to go to Pakistan. Yet I was excited. Perhaps, for two reasons. One, I have been involved with the study of Bhagat Singh and his movement. The Ghadar movement and Kartar Singh Sarabha, have also been the focus of my attention. Both these national heroes were executed in the Lahore jail. Bhagat Singh's life and activities were mostly centred round Lahore, and I wanted to visit the places associated with his activities. The other reason was that I had read and heard it said about Lahore that if 'one hasn't seen Lahore, one hasn't been born'. (This folk saying in Punjabi is also the title of a well known Hindi play by Asghar Wajahat, which incidentally, has been staged in Lahore twice.) If going abroad for the first time in life could be considered a reason for excitement that could be counted as the third reason for my excitement. But as it turned out later, not for a moment, did I feel I was in an 'alien' country, where I should move carefully as a 'foreigner', particularly when the relations between the two governments, though at thaw, were not on the best of terms. I was able to move freely in Lahore, at any point of time, day or night, as freely as any 'Lahoria'. This was in spite of the fact that I had some minor trouble at the Lahore airport. I was issued a visa for Sikh pilgrimage, since the *jatha* for Baisakhi coincided with the dates of my visit. In my visa application, I had listed eight different places I wanted to visit, including Taxila, Faislabad (Bhagat Singh's birth place), Islamabad and Peshawar. The Pakistan High Commission office in Delhi did not return to me the two copies of my application that I was supposed to submit at the Lahore airport, one each on arrival and at departure. However, the visa I was issued was one meant for Sikh pilgrimage. I was somewhat apprehensive about this and had twice checked with the official concerned at the Pakistan High Commission, only to be told this was 'no problem'. The young girl on duty at the Lahore airport, who, incidentally, was once sent back from the Delhi airport for a similar reason, was adamant that in the absence of those documents I must be 'sent back' by return flight. Even this situation did not unnerve me. She called her senior officer. I told him that if they wanted to send me back, they could. My tickets were sent by my hosts and they were waiting outside with rose garlands, as is the practice in Lahore while welcoming guests. They were rather more worried than me and sent a message through a security person. I told them not to worry, since I strangely felt confident I would be able to handle this situation. I told the duty girl, addressing her as '*beta*', that I had come for a seminar and was among those who want Punjabis on both sides to meet more frequently and want friendship among people. I showed them my invitation. I talked to them in chaste Punjabi, rather than in Urdu or English. The officer was convinced of my sincerity, and after a while even the girl was no more hostile. I came out of the airport after 45 minutes or so, to the relief of my hosts, who welcomed me warmly.

We stayed at Holiday Inn, which I was told, was the third biggest hotel of Lahore. The seminar was to be held in the conference hall of the same hotel. I reached Lahore on 12th April; and the seminar was on 13th April beginning at 5.00 p.m. On the 13th as is my usual practice in the morning, I came out for a walk, after checking with the hotel staff if I needed to carry my passport with me. They assured me that there was no need for me to do so and I could just mention the hotel name, if someone enquired. As it turned out, not even once, during my eight days' stay, was I checked by any policeman or security person. So I took a walk towards Ferozepur Road, reaching Luxmi Chowk, without, of course, knowing the place. While returning, I passed by the Punjab Assembly, which, too, I did not recognize. The marvellous Allama Iqbal memorial building was in front of the hotel and Al Hamra, the cultural centre of today's Lahore, was just a few steps away; so was Mall Road and Lawrence Garden or Company Bagh, now called Bagh-e-Jinnah. Amritsar and Lahore both had gardens called Lawrence Gardens or Company Bagh, in popular parlance. I wished to go out for a while as the seminar was in the evening, but could not. So what I did was to change my mobile SIM card and use a Pakistani SIM temporarily, to be in touch with acquaintances in Lahore and at some other places. The currency was not a problem. Everyone has told me that the Indian rupee was accepted everywhere. Though I had some American currency with me, I did not spend a single dollar during my stay in Lahore and spent them all at the duty-free shop at Delhi, on my return.

Malwinderjit Singh Waraich had suggested that I meet Wassey Khan, a friend from his ancestral village, Ladhewal Waraich, in Pakistan. Khan became so emotional on receiving my call that he drove for two hours to reach the seminar venue. He wanted me to visit his village, which I could not. The Chief Guest of the seminar was the Governor of Punjab, Khalid Maqbool. The seminar started almost on time, and the Governor arrived when I was speaking. The first speaker of the seminar was Surender Valasai, from Karachi, President of the Scheduled Caste Federation of Pakistan. He spoke in detail about the conditions of the Dalits in Pakistan, who, for some time, had jobs reserved for them, as in India. Reservations were withdrawn subsequently; but the Dalits of Pakistan are demanding the reintroduction of such reservations. Dr. Ambedkar is quite popular among Pakistani Dalits, many of whom are Hindus or Christians, Dr. Rukhsana Siddiqui, a woman scholar from Lahore, was to speak next, followed by Suleman Asif, the UN reprenstative in Islamabad. Asif had during dinner the previous night, bowled me over with his '*shudh* Hindi'. He was so thoroughly exposed to Hindi and Sanskrit literature that I felt ashamed at our ignorance about the people of Pakistan. Dr. Shyam Katuwal, from Tribhuvan University 'Nepal' was the next to speak. Dr. Faqir Mohamad Bhatti, a Pakistani historian from UK, spoke after me, and V.T. Rajshekhar spoke just before the Governor did. Earlier Dr. Yousaf Bukhari, Director Ganga Ram Foundation welcomed the speakers and spoke about the aims of the Foundation. V.T. Rajshekhar and I both spoke about the closeness between the people of both countries. I also spoke, a little emotionally about, Lahore city and Bhagat Singh. Apart from speaking about Dr. Ambedkar's humanist philosophy, I told the audience that the soil of Lahore was as sacred for me as was for them, since it had the blood of martyrs like Bhagat Singh, and Kartar Singh Sarabha in it. I also said that the earth of Jallianwala Bagh was sacred for them as it was for us, as the blood of Hindu, Muslim and Sikh martyrs was part of it. I told my audience that Bhagat Singh belonged to them as much as to us, since he was born in Lahore, did most of his work there and was also martyred there. I almost admonished them for not owning him, while we have made him our national hero. I also spoke about the mad and criminal act of communal frenzy created by vested political interests during 1947, causing untold suffering to lakhs of people of all communities, on both sides of the border. While the past may not be forgotten, lessons can be learnt from it: that was my plea to my Punjabi brothers (and sisters) on the other side of the fence. Governor Khalid Maqbool spoke very rationally and paid tributes to Dr. Ambedkar. After the seminar, many people came and warmly hugged me; they were touched by what I said about our common cultural bonds. At dinner, I met reprenstatives of the Dalit community in Pakistan, most of them of a Christian background, and members of the Punjab Assembly or District Assembly. Pakistan has evolved a system of assemblies from the *tehsil* level to the national assembly. Lt. General (Retd.) Zulifkar Ali Khan, chairman of the Evacuees Property Trust Board, was also present on this occasion. It was interesting to know that the Pakistan Government allowed the formation of the Ganga Ram Foundation, and also the Dayal Singh Research and Cultural Foundation, in the last two or three years. The Ganga Ram Foundation is located in the Aggarwal Dharmshala, in Aggarwal Street. The Dharmshala was in a bad shape and is now being renovated. Many members of the Sikh *jatha* stayed at the Dharmshala. The Pakistan Government, during Baisakhi day celebrations, organized by the Dayal Singh Foundation, at Lahore, announced the setting up of Guru Nanak University, at Nankana Sahib, or Taxila. Both the Governor of Punjab and members of the Sikh *jatha* participated in that programme.

I was in Lahore till the 21st April, and I wanted to use my stay there in the most fruitful way. My purpose was to meet writers/scholars, and other like-minded people, and to visit historical places. I began with the sightseeing. The first stop was the reputed Lahore Museum. The section that attracted me the most was the one that displayed photographs, black and white photographs of the freedom struggle. In Lahore, it was the Pakistan freedom struggle; for me, it was the freedom struggle of both India and Pakistan. I saw the photographs of national leaders like Mahatma Gandhi, Jawaharlal Nehru, Subhas Chandra Bose and Baldev Singh along with those of Jinnah, Liaqat Ali Khan, Khan Abdul Gaffar Khan, etc. There were many photographs of Fatima Jinnah as well. The photographs of Ratti, the Parsi wife of Jinnah, and their daughter, Dina, attracted my attention. Then there was a complete Gandhara Art section, showing Buddhist traditional art of the North-West Frontier Province area. There is now a complete section on Sikh art as well. Old '*deorhies*' (the front door of the house) were too attractive to be missed. The renowned National College of Art is located next to the museum, but I could visit it only later. I saw three books published by the college recently, two of them on Sir Ganga Ram and Bhai Ram Singh. It looks as if slowly but steadily Pakistan, particularly Lahore, is owning up its traditional richness, even that which is not Islamic.

Lahore is a heaven for non-vegetarians. The food streets of Anarkali and Gwalmandi have become such a craze that Lahore remains awake all night. After visiting the food street one night at 1.00 a.m., we moved to Shimla hills of Bagh-e-Jinnah, where a classical music programme was going on at 2.00 a.m. Farida Khanum had just completed her singing. Lahore is such a culturally alive city that it leaves one wonder-struck. I remembered my student days at Jawaharlal Nehru University, Delhi, when we used to go to Mavlankar Hall to listen to classical programmes late at night. Those culturally rich days are over in Delhi, but not in Lahore.

Visiting Shahi Qila (Royal fort) is not so exciting, it is not so well maintained. But the Samadhi of Ranjit Singh, who once ruled from this fort, is almost a part of the fort, which has the gurdwara of the fifth Guru as well. Close by is Minar-e-Pakistan, built after 1947, which on its walls has the resolution of Pakistan, passed on March 23, 1940. This resolution is carved in English, Urdu, Punjabi and Bengali.

Visiting sites associated with Bhagat Singh was another attraction of my Lahore visit. Accompanied by Zubair, a well-known progressive story writer of Punjabi, I first went to Bradlaugh Hall, which few people know now. The hall is in a dilapidated condition and now houses a training school. From the shape of the building, one can well see that it was a grand building once. Fortunately, the foundation plate is still intact. The foundation of this headquarters of the freedom movement was laid by Surender Nath Sen in 1900. It would be desirable for the Government of India to impress upon the Government of Pakistan to have the hall declared a heritage building. The Lajpat Rai Hall of Lahore, which housed the famous Dwarka Das Library, now shifted to Chandigarh, is now occupied by the fingerprint bureau of the Pakistani Police. I could not visit this place; neither could I locate National College, where Bhagat Singh was a student during 1922-26. I could not locate Khwasarian village, near Lahore, which was the abode of Bhagat Singh's family for many years. Even the banks of the river, Ravi, where Lala Lajpat Rai and, later the remains of Bhagat Singh, Rajguru and Sukhdev were cremated, and where Bhagwati Charan Vohra gave his life in an explosion, while he was testing bombs, could not be located. Ravi has perhaps dried up, and people say it has become a *nallah*. They also say that India has stopped releasing water to the river. However I could easily locate the place where Saunders was killed, and the D.A.V. College hostel nearby. There is no great change in that area, except that D.A.V. College and hostel have turned into Government Islamia College and hostel now. But the office of the Senior Superintendent of Police remains the same as it was during Scott's time. I was also able to visit 'Phansighat', the execution spot of Lahore jail, which has now been demolished; Shadman Chowk, or 'Fountain Chowk', has come up in its place. It is a residential colony now, with no trace of the jail or its historicity, where hundreds of freedom fighters were hanged. Democratic Pakistani activists do gather on 23rd March at Shadman Chowk and light candles. They also plan to put a plaque nearby, indicating the historical significance of the place. Bhagat Singh lived in many houses of Lahore during his underground days, and people still talk of those houses. One such house is said to be on Jail Road. Najam Hussain Sayeed, the well known Punjabi writer, lives in the area, but he has no idea of the house Bhagat Singh lived in.

I was able to visit the birthplace of Bhagat Singh with some newly made local friends. Our car took us first to Waris Shah's *mazar* at Jandiala Sheikh. We passed through Sheikhupura town, quite well-known, and from a distance, I was shown 'haran magar', the beautiful place built in memory of a deer, which got killed during a *shikar* by Prince Salim. Visiting Waris Shah *mahar* was a memorable experience. Every year at the *mazhar*, a singing competition, where people sing 'Heer' is held, and it starts with the singing of Amrita Pritam's *Aaj Aakhan Waris Shah nun*.... From Jandiala, we moved to Nankana Sahib. It is a small town, but the access road is broad. Pakistan has paid more attention to its roads and rightly boasts of its motorways from Lahore to Peshawar. But Pakistan lacks railway services. Nankana Sahib has eight gurudwaras in its vicinity, including the main one, where in February 1921, a *morcha* was started against Mahants, who were polluting the pious place. The Mahants, supported by British colonialists, had killed nearly two hundred Sikhs, before vacating the gurdwara. Inside the gurdwara, there is 'Shaheed Jand' (tree), where a protestor, Lachhman Singh, was burnt alive. In Nankana Sahib, most of the gurdwaras relate to Guru Nanak's childhood, where he was born, where he played, where he studied, etc. I had '*langar*' with my Muslim friends of Lahore, who had accompanied me there.

From Nankana Sahib, there was a direct route to Jadanwala, though the road was bad for a few kilometres. Crossing Jadanwala, a *tehsil* town, we reached the road leading to Chak No. 105, where a pleasant surprise awaited us. There was a tin sign on the roadside, with a picture of Bhagat Singh behind bars. A person called Jasbeer Singh, from Faislabad (formerly, Lyallpur) had put up this signboard, with his email address on it. When we were reading the signboard, some people approached us, and seeing our interest in Bhagat Singh, showed us the lane to his village. They suggested that before going to the village, we should meet one Farhan Khan nearby. As it turned out, Farhan Khan is an 82-year-old gentleman, who retired as an excise officer. He now runs a factory called Gulab Farm. The signboard of the factory includes the name, (Bhagat Singh) town. Khan belonged to Chak No. 107, Pathankot, nearby. We reached his place, and he welcomed us warmly. In his drawing room, there was an old framed, black and white photograph, of Bhagat Singh with its glass broken; it was the popular photograph of a hat wearing Bhagat Singh. Farhan Khan was very happy talking about Bhagat Singh family. He was five years old, when Bhagat Singh was martyred. Bhagat Singh's younger brothers, whose names he did not remember (obviously, Kulbir Singh and Kultar Singh), used to meet him. The man was such an admirer of Bhagat Singh that I wanted to present him a copy of his writings, but I had just one copy of the book with me. Farhan Khan got it photocopied, borrowing it for just an hour or so, while we were at Bhagat Singh's house. We went to Chak No. 105, Bhagat Singh's house accompanied by a man sent by Farhan Khan. It was getting dark. The road to the village was not very good. When we reached there, it was not the old house. It was now being shared by the families of three brothers, the Virks–Iqbal, Sadiq and Mushtaq. Pakistan has as many Virks, Randhawas, Sehgals, Bhattis, Cheemas, Waraiches, Gills and Sidhus as in our part of Punjab. The Virk brothers, who were allotted this house after partition, had migrated from Virk village of Amritsar. Of the three, Sadiq Virk is no more. When we arrived there were a few women working at a *chullah*. Later, we met Akhtar Virk, son of Mushtaq Virk, who is an advocate at Faislabad. He told us that apart from the house, the Virks also acquired the 17 acre mango garden of Kishan Singh, father of Bhagat Singh. We were told the current value of the land was six lakhs per acre, which meant that the 17 acres worth more than one crore rupees today. We did not know earlier that, Bhagat Singh's family had a mango garden; yet the information came as no surprise to me. The judge, who wrote the judgment that led to the execution of Kartar Singh Sarabha, had clearly mentioned that Kishan Singh (father of Bhagat Singh) had contributed one thousand rupees (nearly one lakh rupees today) to the Ghadar party, in 1914 or 1915. The legend of Bhagat Singh and family becomes more fascinating, because their commitment to the nation over rode their comforts in life. It is no wonder that Waqar Ahmad, a political science student from Peshawar, became enamoured of Bhagat Singh and contacted me through mail, just to know more about him. Waqar remained in telephonic touch with me during my stay in Lahore, and was hoping to meet me, as the Peshawar University Teachers Association was trying very hard to get visa clearance for me, so that I could visit Peshawar. We had hosted the visit of a Peshawar University teacher's delegation recently at JNU. Also during my stay in Lahore, Raza Naeem, a columnist for the newspapers, *Dawn*, reached me through mail to get a copy of *The Jail Notebook* and other writings of Bhagat Singh, compiled by me and published by Leftword. He wanted to review the book for his paper. I left a copy of the book for him at Lahore. Raza wanted to hold discussions on Bhagat Singh, in Karachi, but there wasn't enough time to organize them.

Lyallpur was built by the British as a planned city. This area has very fertile land, so farmers from other parts of Punjab were encouraged to buy land here, just as many farmers were encouraged to buy land in the Terai region. Interestingly, several people from Doaba went to

Lyallpur. They were allotted plots in villages, demarcated into numbered chaks. The families which shifted to Lyallpur added the name of their village, or area, to these numbered Chaks. Thus Chak no. 65 is Mukundpur, Chak no. 67 is Gidderpindi, Chak no. 104 is Samra, Chak no. 105 is Bange (From Banga of Doaba). Chak no 106 is Khurla, Chak no. 107 is Pathankot, Chak no. 109 is Bajajanwala, and so on. These names continue to be used even now. Only the owners and inhabitants of the houses have changed. We were told that before 1965, there were not many restrictions and many people used to visit these places. After 1965, restrictions increased, though in recent years, there has been some relaxation and people are again coming to visit these places. We were told that a bus full of Punjabis from Canada had come to visit the place last year. After partition, Lyallpur, renamed Faislabad, became the centre of the textile industry of Pakistan. It is now the third biggest city of Pakistan, after Karachi and Lahore. But the city has probably suffered from the same problems as has Ludhiana. The Faislabad cloth is rated high in Asian markets.

From Chak No. 105, we moved to Faislabad; it was night now. From there, we went back to Lahore, and reached the city in about two hours' time. Only a limited number vehicles are allowed on the motorways in Pakistan; so the traffic moves fast, smoothly and safely.

I wanted to go to Taxila and Islamabad as well, but the time was short and I had to meet some more people in Lahore. So I stayed in Lahore for the remaining days. I shifted from the five star hotel to other locations. I spent a night with some young students, one of who, Imran, was teaching Urdu at the Government College at Nankana Sahib. Another night, I spent at the guest house of an NGO, South Asia Participation (SAP), that organized a talk for its researchers and staff. The Deputy Director of SAP, Irfan Mufti, offered to take me to Bulle Shah's *mazhar* at Kasur on one of the evenings. That was a pleasant invitation, which I readily accepted. Though the road to Kasur, which was under reconstruction, was somewhat irritable and the 60 kilometre journey by car took almost three hours, the atmosphere at the *mazhar* made it worth the while. At about eleven at night, the *mazhar* was still full of people, singing and dancing. People were offering flowers, but the women were not allowed inside the sanctorum. They would give the flowers to the caretaker and watch through the windows. That was not a practice Bulle Shah, might have approved of, but everything else was just as he would have liked it to be: people dancing traditional folk dances like *Jhummar* and singing Kafis of Bulle in the most fascinating voices and with the sweetest of musical chords.

After visiting Nankana Sahib, and the *mazhars* of Waris Shah and Bulle Shah and talking to cross sections of people, I felt that the partition had paralyzed the Punjabi body of cultural oneness. On both sides of the border, Punjabis have a strange kind of yearning for each other, and feel incomplete without each other. This overwhelming emotional longing on both sides (perhaps a little more in West Punjab) speaks volumes of the cultural losses which both parts of Punjab have suffered due to this completely irrational division of one complete cultural unit, consisting of three major communities—Muslims, Sikhs and Hindus. I think all Bengalis and Punjabis must be cursing the politicians on both sides of the border, for sacrificing their cultural oneness at the altar of political power. Pakistani Punjab is almost three times bigger than Indian Punjab. The population of Pakistani Punjab is nine crores, which is more than half the total population of Pakistan. It is true that the Punjabi language and literature have developed more in the Indian part of Punjab, but overall Punjabi culture is still more alive in Pakistani Punjab. The ridiculing description of Punjabi culture, that 'it is just agriculture', is the contribution of post-partition Indian Punjab, which has built no strong cultural centre of its own. Lahore was always considered one of the most cultured cities of undivided India, and that tradition is still alive in the city. Lahore has developed tremendously after partition, and its population has grown to nearly one crore. Whereas, before the partition, Amritsar and Lahore were like twin cities, since the partition, Amritsar has shrunk and lost its eminence, except in the religious sense.

I could not move around Androon Lahore (inner city) and see its 12 much known '*darwazas*' (gates). Some of these gates, Yashpal has vividly depicted in his epic Hindi novel, *Jhootha Sach*. Shahlmi gate, the worst centre of communal riots in 1947, Mochi gate, Bhatti gate, Hathi gate, Domoriya gate (like Domoroyia bridge in Jalandhar). The last three nights of my Lahore stay at the guest house of Punjab University, Lahore reminded me a little of my student days at Panjab

University, Chandigarh, in 1971-72. The tiny market on the Lahore campus has a touch of the Chandigarh market, though the Chandigarh market is more developed. The hostels on the Lahore campus, where I had my morning tea and breakfast are similar to the PU hostels in Chandigarh. The name of the University was changed to The University of Punjab, Lahore, after the partition; yet buildings like the library, and the cafeteria carry the old name—Punjab University, Lahore. In Indian Punjab, the spelling of the name of the university was changed to Panjab University, to differentiate it from Punjab University, Lahore. My visit to the Oriental College, on the old campus of the University, which houses the Urdu, Persian, Punjabi and now the revived Hindi Department, was again interesting. To see the names of Dr. Mohan Singh Diwana, Bhai Santokh Singh and Sadhu Ditt Singh in the Punjabi Department was a memorable experience. That the Punjabi Department was set up in 1879 is perhaps not even known on this side of the border. Interestingly, the only teacher working on a temporary basis in the Hindi Department, Shabnam Riaz, turned out to be my student from Punjabi University, Patiala. Shabnam migrated to Lahore from Malerkotla, after marriage and after doing an M.A., in Hindi from Patiala. Incidentally, Lahore is known for its educational institutions. Falling prey to privatization, it has almost 25 universities including one women's university. Even the Government College has been turned into Government College University, an odd name.

Meeting people was an enriching experience for me. I already had some contacts and also many references. I was keen to meet Salima Hashmi, daughter of the legendary poet Faiz Ahmad Faiz, who along with Faqir Aazijudin, both well known artists and art scholars of Pakistan had recently visited the Fine Arts Department of Punjabi University, Patiala, to participate in a seminar. So one evening I spent with the Hashmis at their Model Town house, where once Faiz lived. Prof. Salima Hashmi is now Dean, Visual Arts of Beaconhead University, Lahore, after retiring as Principal of the famous National Art College of Lahore. Her husband, Prof. Shoib Hashmi, retired Economics Professor, is a columnist for some dailies, and a jolly person. Their daughter is named Meera and granddaughter, Anya. Salima told me that Faiz Ahmad Faiz had heard the shots fired on Saunders, as he was somewhere close to D.A.V. College that day. These shots were also heard by the legendary Communist leader of Pakistan, the late Mazhar Ali, this was confirmed by his wife, and mother of the famous writer Tariq Ali, Tahira Mazhar Ali, whom I met at her house. I presented a copy of Bhagat Singh's writings to her, as she is also among those who venerate Bhagat Singh in Pakistan. Tahira Mazhar Ali, at the age of 82 years, and Salima Hashmi, are both active in the democratic movement of Pakistan. Salima took part in a women's rally during my stay. Leftist activists in Pakistan are called 'Surkhe' (Reds) in popular parlance. I met one such 'Surkha' by chance, at Fictionhouse, a progressive publisher and bookseller of Lahore. Fictionhouse has published almost all books of the eminent historian, Mubarak Ali, both in Urdu and English. I had taken some photocards of Bhagat Singh and Dr. Ambedkar to distribute in Lahore, and I handed over one of these cards to the owner of Fictionhouse. An old man present there asked me to give him a card as well. Then he introduced himself as Aslam Raheel Mirza, a member of the Communist Party of Pakistan. He said that they celebrate Bhagat Singh Day every year. There is no ban on the Communist Party in Pakistan these days, but the leftist forces are quite weak. They are splintered into groups like National Workers' Party, Mazdoor Kisan Party and Labour Party, apart from the Communist Party, which has a strong base in Hyderabad Sindh.

About the Communist movement of earlier times, I heard many stories, mostly true, from Prof. Manzoor Ahmad, Prof Aazijudin Ahmad, and Tehseen Ahmad, by whom I was invited to dinner with this group. The 82-year-old Prof. Manzoor Ahmad is considered a Gandhian by his friends. Though no one agrees with his defence of Gandhi, everyone loves this genial man. I heard the fascinating story of Pran Nath Seth, the industrialist of Lahore who refused to leave Lahore in 1947. Pran Nath Seth was the son-in-law of Lala Harikishan Lal, first time minister of Punjab in the Fazal-ul-Hussain ministry. Pran Nath Seth was briefly arrested during the1965 Indo-Pak war. He came to India for some time and fell ill. He declared that he couldn't live outside Lahore. He returned to Lahore and regained his health. During his underground days, Sajjad Zaheer, well-known Urdu writer, who had gone to Pakistan in 1947 to organize the Communist movement, took shelter in Pran Nath's house under an assumed name. When once the police raided the house to arrest Sajjad, who had already escaped, Pran Nath, aristocratic in his habits got angry with the police for raiding his house without informing him, more so when the DIG was his personal friend. Then he was told that the 'professor' he was keeping in his annexe was actually an underground Communist leader. Those were the days when Sahir Ludhianvi also came to work with the Pakistan Communist Party, and stayed with the writer, Ahmad Rahi.

I enjoyed listening to pre-partition and post-partition stories from these grand old men. I also benefited immensely by meeting Mubarak Ali, the historian, who could speak honestly about Jinnah and offend people. One of my most fascinating meetings was with F.E. Chaudhary, the 98-year-old first photo journalist of Pakistan. Chaudhary worked with Faiz Ahmad Faiz, who took over as the Editor of *Pakistan Times*, the newspaper started in the place vacated by *The Tribune*. The earliest photographs of Pakistani leaders were shot by F.E. Chaudhary, a Christian. He was the one who shot the pictures of Central Jail, Lahore, when it was being demolished in the 1960s. He has preserved that file of photographs, which includes the photographs of the *Phansighat*, where Bhagat Singh, Sarabha and so many other freedom fighters were executed. I tried to capture these photos through my ordinary camera, but did not succeed. But I was told that Daljit Ami had shot these on his video camera, few days earlier. Chaudhary, who lives with his son, the Principal of a Christian school in Lahore, wanted to locate his friends of the pre-partition days, most of them photographers who had migrated to Delhi. He mentioned names such as C.L. Soni and Co., and Shankar Dass and Co., Chaudhary remembers so many stories of his early twenties, when all Hindu, Sikh, Muslim and Christian shopkeepers of Lahore lived in complete harmony and in deep friendship. The nostalgia of the past lingers on in Lahore; and it is being passed on to younger generations, who have only heard about the past from their elders. A Pathan family that had migrated from Ludhiana became very friendly with me. A waiter in a hotel, while talking about his ancestors from Ludhiana, became so emotional that he brought me a tubful of fruits and pastry, *Aap hamare mehmaan hain* (You are our guest), is so common a refrain in Lahore that one starts feeling guilty that we never speak of being good hosts and never take care of people coming from the other side of the border as much as Lahoris do.

There are many more things to be recorded here, such as the 'Friday Sangat' at Najam Hussain Sayeed's house on Jail Road. Twenty plus Punjabi writers/scholars, including some women, gather there every Friday evening, and read the Gurbani, and the Najam interprets it. Later they have dinner together before dispersing. Najam is known in East Punjab as well for his enlightened writings. He was the writer, who refused to accept the '*Shiromani Punjabi Sahitkar*' (Videshi) award in 2004, at the World Punjabi Conference held at the Punjabi University, Patiala, and attended, among others by the Pakistani Punjab Chief Minister Parvez Ilahi. The refusal was just on principle and for no other reason. Najam's wife, Sajda, has sung Sufi songs beautifully. One can go on talking about Lahore endlessly, but I shall conclude with the story of an interesting coincidence.

Nawab Mohd. Ahmad Khan was a prosecution witness (*sarkari gawah*) against Bhagat Singh and his comrades in the Lahore conspiracy case. He rose to become an honorary magistrate in Pakistan. He was murdered at the same place, in the 1970s, where Bhagat Singh was executed, that is Shadman Chowk. A further coincidence is that Zulfikar Ali Bhutto was blamed for the murder of this man by Zia-ul-Haq and hanged in Lahore jail in 1977. Now everyone in Pakistan says that Bhutto was framed in this case with US complicity. Also, every Pakistani says that Zia-ul-Haq's eleven-year rule was the blackest period of Pakistan's history, worse than the rule of all other military rulers like Ayub Khan, Yahya Khan and Pervez Musharraf. The Zia regime completely smashed the secular, liberal and democratic character of the Pakistani society and threw it into a prolonged struggle to regain its democratic freedom back. Now the Pakistani society has woken up and is struggling to overcome the most poisonous effects of the Zia regime. Let us wish and hope that they succeed.

14

Bhagat Singh Through the Dalit Perspective from Pakistan*

Returning from the Caribbean after 14 months, I was not able to pay much attention to the 14th Bharat Rang Mahotsav of National School of Drama, however being involved with 1000+ strong 'Indo-Pak-Bangladesh Friendship Forum' on my facebook page and also because of my abiding interest in Bhagat Singh, I could not afford to miss two plays from Pakistan in the festival. So in the last round of the festival, I could manage to see Anwar Jafri directed *Insha ka Intezar* from Karachi Tehrik-e-Niswan group of Sheema Kirmani in Urdu on 18th January, and Shahid Nadeem written Punjabi play *Mera Rang de Basanti Chola* by directed by Madeeha Gauhar from Ajoka theatre group of Lahore on 21st January.

While *Insha ka Intezar* is the Urdu adaptation of Samuel Beckett's world classic 'Waiting for Godot' in specific socio-political Pakistani reality; *Mera Rang de Basanti Chola* as is explicit from the title itself, is based upon the legend of Bhagat Singh, this time coming from Bhagat Singh's political action place Lahore.

Scripted, adapted and directed by Anwar Jafri, *Insha ka Intezar* turns Beckett's absurd and not so progressive play into more realistic and grounded in social reality of Pakistan, devastated by prolonged and frequent military coups and rules. Acted by Sheema Kirmani, the seasoned theatre personality of Pakistan as Zuleikha and her partner

---

* Earlier published in *The Hindu*

Karimuddin (Karmo) by Salim Meraj as a symbol of marginalized people of Pakistan, supported by Naseeban, played by Shama Askari and unnamed girl played by Iman Mirza, these victims of an oppressive system; are sought to be controlled by brutal force represented symbolically by the army officer character of Mansha, played by Hafeez Ali. Zuleikha and Karmo, living a subhuman life are waiting for *Insha*, to free them of the deprivations and made their life liveable with dignity. In Pakistan's political context, Insha symbolizes 'Democratic set up', in opposition to army rule of *Mansha*. While Insha is the shortened version of *Insha Allah*(God willing), which is used in Pakistan in every human situation, *Mansha* literally means 'intention'! While *Insha* is the abstract and always remains elusive, *Mansha* is concrete and functional, oppressing people. He is dragging his maid Naseeban bound with rope, which is in his hand and she serves him more than a slave, except when she is given 'headgear' to wear. Wearing 'headgear', she talks 'philosophy' and becomes a 'free' human being, symbolizing that it is 'thinking', which leads to 'freedom' from all kinds of slavery. At the time of her 'philosophical murmurings', the army officer is spinning his head and is about to 'collapse'. The play concludes with Mansha walking away with roped 'Naseeban'(The fortune) and unending wait for Insha by Zuleikha and Karmo. Anwar Jafri and Sheema Kirmani and their team have given new meaning to 1969 Nobel award winning writer's classic play and turned 'the theatre of the absurd' into the 'theatre of reality'!

Shahid Nadeem written and Madeeha Gauhar directed *Mera Rang de Basanti Chola* presents Bhagat Singh through the Dalit character of Bogha, spelled as Bhoga in the brochure. The legend of Bhagat Singh has many tales, both true and imaginative, linked to his character. Bhagat Singh wrote a seminal essay on the Dalit issue as *Achhut da Sawal* (Issue of Untouchable), giving a stirring call to 'Dalits' to rise up as 'lions' and have their rights. It is mentioned that Bhagat Singh, in response to the query of his 'last wish' before execution, wished to have *roti*, cooked by 'Bebe' (mother), which they used to call Bogha, Dalit prisoner in jail, as mother cleans the shit of her children, so are Dalits performing the task for humanity, so they deserve the respect due to a 'mother'. Bogha was filled with tears at this respect given to him by Bhagat Singh. In the play, Shahid wove the Bhagat Singh legend through Bogha's narration, who stayed behind in Pakistan at the time of partition as 'for low castes', there was no difference in 'Hindustan' or 'Pakistan'. This dialogue is a master stroke by the playwright on the social conditions of both countries even after partition and independence. The legend is further linked to the story of Z.A. Bhutto's hanging, as the Nawab of Kasur-Mohammad Kasuri was the magistrate, who oversaw the hanging of Bhagat Singh, Sukhdev and Rajguru, as many other magistrates at that time declined to perform this 'anti-national' task. And the same Kasuri was murdered at the very place, where Bhagat Singh was hanged, called 'phansighat' of Central Jail Lahore, but which was demolished and turned into Shadman colony after partition. Z.A. Bhutto, ex-Prime Minister of Pakistan was trapped in Kasuri's murder by military ruler Zia-ul-Haq and hanged in 1979. Though Shahid has shown Bhagat Singh to be an atheist and socialist revolutionary, reading Lenin on the verge of execution, turning even Bogha into 'atheist' in honour of his friend Bhagat Singh, yet he links the story to Sufi saint Shah Jamal, who purportedly took the revenge of Bhagat Singh's martyrdom, by getting Kasuri punished for his crimes, as some people in Lahore had the 'vision' of Shah Jamal at the time of execution and pledging revenge! The play is enriched by songs like *Ghori* of Bhagat Singh, sung by Mela Ram Tayar on the streets of Lahore on March 23, 1932, to mark the first anniversary of Bhagat Singh's martyrdom; *Pagri Sambhal Jatta...*, *Mera Rang de Basanti Chola Mayee*...et cetera. It would be music to the ears of some Pakistan haters of India, if they could hear—'Bharat Mata' song in a play from Pakistan. The play got an emotional standing ovation from an overcrowded hall of Kamani Auditorium.

15

Reading Bhagat Singh and Paash

Bhagat Singh and Paash are two illustrious sons of Punjab. Bhagat Singh became the symbol of radical nationalism and socialism in the 1930s. Bhagat Singh's shadow was casting gloom on the Gandhian camp. His martyrdom on March 23, 1931, gave impetus to strong national feelings throughout the country. He became a hero in folk songs from Bihar to Tamil Nadu, from Bengal to Bombay. So many writings depicting him as a national hero were banned during those days.

For Punjabis, Bhagat Singh acquired a very special place and after the Gurus, he became a symbol of Punjabi pride and identity. Mothers would wish their sons to be like Bhagat Singh and in the early 1970s, when Punjabi literature was taking a radical course. The most promising Punjabi poet in his early twenties was impressed most by Bhagat Singh and by a strange coincidence, he achieved martyrdom for the cause of Punjabi identity on the same day, on which Bhagat Singh achieved this pride of place in Indian history. It was on March 23, 1988, 57 years after March 23, 1931, that Paash became a co-symbol of Punjabi pride along with Bhagat Singh. There could not have been a better day for Paash to die and for the same cause, which was so dear to Bhagat Singh, that he chose the gallows.

Bhagat Singh earned his name in history as a political leader of repute. He was a revolutionary leader, just in the short span of five years or so and at the tender age of 18 years to 23 plus, he raised the level of Indian politics and its uncompromising struggle against British colonialism to new heights. There has been a tradition of Indian rebellion against the British since 1857, but it was Bhagat Singh and his comrades, who gave it a true revolutionary shape. For the first time, the Indian revolutionary movement had a clear-cut perspective. They were fighting not just for the ouster of British colonialists from India, but for complete overhauling of Indian society into a socialist society. Their organization of the Hindustan Socialist Republican Association (HSRA) and its military wing Hindustan Socialist Republican Army (HSRA) had a clear programme for the reorganization of Indian society along socialist lines. And in chalking out this new programme, Bhagat Singh had played a leading role as an ideology. For many years, Bhagat Singh was projected only as a brave, militant national hero, who went to the gallows for national freedom. This is a very partial view. He was much more than that. His ideas about Indian society and its reorganization were far more clear than M.K. Gandhi or even Nehru. In fact, revolutionaries like Bhagat Singh had a very clear understanding of the Congress movement and Gandhi's ideas. And Bhagat Singh and other revolutionaries were not leading a complementary movement to Congress for Indian freedom, which most of the history books try to project. Bhagat Singh and his comrades were building a parallel and truly anti-colonial movement against the British and they were exposing the Congress movement as a reformist and collaborationist movement. Bhagat Singh was a real threat to both British colonialism and the Congress movement led by Gandhi. That is why Lord Irwin, the then British Viceroy of India and Gandhi agreed to get rid of Bhagat Singh, which is a historic record now.

But Bhagat Singh could be killed, not the ideas and consciousness created by him and he was absolutely clear in his mind, when he chose the gallows and refused to make any attempt for diluting his sentence. He knew and made it clear in his writings and messages that his and Rajguru, Sukhdev's martyrdom would create a tremendous impact on Indian society and the vibration of that impact can be felt even after 65 years.

In the early 70s, two things happened simultaneously in Indian society. Bhagat Singh's ideas, his writings became known to a large number of Indian people in various Indian languages and it became established that Bhagat Singh was a brilliant intellectual as well, and, he became a pioneer of socialist thought in India. A powerful radical peasant movement arose around the same time, which was popularly known as the Naxalite movement and Bhagat Singh's ideas were inherited in the true sense by sections of this movement. Paash was the product of this movement. Paash was a poet basically, though he had many other facets of his personality. And in two decades he became a cultural symbol of this movement.

In totality, Bhagat Singh and Paash, became political and cultural symbols of the same movement, though there is a gap of four decades between the two. Ideologically, they are part of the same stream, they belong to the tradition of the radical movement for human liberation. The liberation of mankind from all types of exploitation economic, political, social as well as cultural, was the cherished dream of both these proud sons of Punjab. Both of them dreamt of building a society, where both men and women could live a dignified life, where there is no discrimination on the basis of religion, caste or gender, neither on the basis of economic or social status. All men and women realize their fullest potential with their talent and labour, and where no one lives in luxury on the labour of others. Paash depicted this dream in his poetry and other writings.

Unfortunately, Indian society, since the 1980s is sliding downwards. The progressive and liberal stream in Indian society is getting weakened and the reactionary and fascist stream is riding high, whether in the form of communalism or fundamentalism, or in the form of state repression on people and their movements. It is in this context that Bhagat Singh and Paash need to be read and understood to find a way out of this dark tunnel of reaction. Their ideas are like glittering stars, who can shine through any darkness and the lost travellers can try to find the correct path to their destiny.

Till now, more than hundred writings of Bhagat Singh have come to light, which includes letters, articles, translations, court statements, pamphlets, diary and draft political programmes, etc. These writings are in Urdu, Hindi, Punjabi and English. One can well imagine the versatility of the mind of young Bhagat Singh. In this regard, he is comparable only to Dobrolyubov, the early nineteenth century materialist thinker of Russia, who also died almost as young as Bhagat Singh.

On religious fundamentalism and communalism, two articles by Bhagat Singh are well known and well publicized in various languages.

These are 'Religion and Our Freedom Struggle' and 'Communal Riots and Their Resolution'. Apart from these two articles dealing directly with this problem, Bhagat Singh and Bhagwati Charan Vohra discussed the problem of communalism in the manifesto of 'Naujawan Bharat Sabha' in 1928. 'The Question of Untouchability', is another article by Bhagat Singh, which deals with another equally burning, but related problem of Indian society. Again a letter to Lala Lajpat Rai, signed by many comrades of Bhagat Singh in 1929, deals with the problem of Hindu-Muslim tension. And of course, the most important document in this regard is 'Why I Am an Atheist'.

'Communal Riots and Their Resolution' was published in Punjabi in June 1927 in the *Kirti* magazine. This article was written against the backdrop of Kohat's brutal Hindu-Muslim riots in 1924. After the riots, there was a debate going on in the country, on how to tackle the riot situation. At that time it was the key question before the national movement. Congress leaders tried their standard reformist method of getting leaders of the Hindu and Muslim community to reach some compromise, whereas the revolutionary movement of that time dealt with the basic core of these riots. The article begins on a very sharp note, 'India is in a pitiable condition at this moment. The followers of one religion are enemies of the other religion. In these days, to belong to one religion is to be the enemy of the other. If you still do not believe this, see the fresh riots in Lahore. How Muslims have massacred innocent Hindus and Sikhs and how the Hindus and Sikhs have also not proved any lesser than them. Being Hindu or Sikh was enough reason for killing them by Muslims and being Muslim was enough reason for killing them by Hindus or Sikhs. If such is the situation, then only God can save India.'

The article proceeds 'In this situation India's future seems to be very dark. These 'religions' have degenerated India and nobody knows when India will get rid of these religious riots ....'

If the readers are not given a background of the article, one can very well take it as an article on the present situation prevailing in the country and it is a sad comment on the affairs of the country that it is repeating history, in a tragic manner.

What is wrong with our social and political leadership that it is not able to control such riots, which have continued for the last one century or so. It is significant that before the British occupation of India, there are hardly any references to communal riots in the country, though there have been wars for political power between Hindu, Sikh and Muslim rulers. And if British colonialism by its policy of 'divide and rule' has been able to create conditions for communal and caste riots in the country and then trying to project itself as 'the saviour of the country', then the national movement must have addressed itself to these problems in all earnestness. Unfortunately, except for the revolutionary movement, which always remained weak, the other national leadership like the Congress Party, et cetera, never faced these problems squarely. Only Nehru had some perception, but he could never assert himself over Gandhi, whose approach to these problems, was thoroughly reformist.

What are the factors behind these riots? In the same article Bhagat Singh tries to locate the root cause of the communal problem by saying that the root cause of these problems is economic. And he feels that only by economic upliftment of the country can the riots be resolved. 'The economic condition of the common people of the country is so bad that one can get the other one insulted by paying just four *annas* to a man. The suffering of hunger and pain can make any man discard all principles.'

Bhagat Singh is quite clear that economic upliftment in present conditions is rather impossible because of the alien government (even the *desi* is no different). And the best resolve to stop people fight each other is the growth of class consciousness. In Bhagat Singh's own words, 'The class consciousness is needed to stop people fighting each other. The poor workers and peasants should be made to understand clearly that their real enemies are capitalists and they should not fall prey to their trap. The rights of the poor of the world, to whichever caste, race, religion they may belong, are one. Their betterment lies in uniting, forgetting the difference of religion, colour, race, nation and country and attempt to seize the power of the state. By these attempts, they will not lose anything, but some day their fetters will shatter and they will achieve economic freedom.'

This is as much true today? Bhagat Singh exemplifies his argument with Russian conditions during the Czarist regime and after the Bolshevik Revolution. He gives a positive example of the Calcutta riots, where workers belonging to trade unions refused to take part in rioting due to class consciousness.

Bhagat Singh clearly says that religion must be separated from politics, only then can the unity on the political platform be achieved.

In 'Religion and Our Freedom Struggle' published in May 1927, Bhagat Singh deals with the problem from another angle. He differentiates between the religious and communal feelings. He discusses religion from a philosophical viewpoint also by quoting Tolstoy. Tolstoy has differentiated religion in three parts:

(i) Essentials of Religion which includes the moral values like 'speak truth', 'love the others', 'help the poor', et cetera.
(ii) Philosophy of Religion which discusses the questions of birth, rebirth, death, et cetera.
(iii) Rituals of Religion in the form of worship, et cetera.

Bhagat Singh says that the first essential of religion does not harm anyone, but the second and third essential of religion if combined with blind faith, it becomes very explosive and dangerous and in fact that is what turns into 'Religious Fundamentalism'. At the same time, if the second essential is joined to the first essential and is coupled with free thought, it is welcome.

In the manifesto of 'Naujawan Bharat Sabha', Bhagat Singh describes, 'Religious intolerance and prejudices as the big stumbling block in our progress and we should throw these away... The foreign rulers exploit the fundamentalist and reactionary policy of the Hindus, the prejudices of the Muslims and in general the narrowness of all communities.'

In 'Why I Am an Atheist', Bhagat Singh faces the problem at an ideological level. This article, first published in 1930, is quite significant, as it is exemplified by Indian beliefs about religion or God, et cetera. While directly discussing the problem of communalism, Bhagat Singh argues that ultimately 'society has to struggle against the faith in God as it has fought against statue worship and the narrow concept of religion'. Bhagat Singh argues that 'as the man would try to stand on his own feet and become a realist, he would have to throw away the faith in God and to bitterly struggle against every difficulty'.

If one sees the present situation in Punjab and other parts of the country, one cannot help thinking that Indian society, rather than advancing from the time of Bhagat Singh, has been sliding downwards. The controversies like Ram Janmbhoomi-Babri Masjid are symbols of this slide. It is an irony that 'Kar Sevaks' to Ayodhya have been described as Chandershekhar Azad and Bhagat Singh by some communal organizations. It is time that Bhagat Singh's and his comrades' ideas on religion and communalism are propagated to the people.

Nurtured on the thoughts of Bhagat Singh, as part of Marxist-Leninist thought and movement, Paash dealt with the problem of religious fundamentalism and communalism in his writings in a very powerful way. Though his writings are few, but they create a deep impact. His last few poems on the Punjab crisis are a battle cry against all types of fundamentalism, communalism and state oppression. Some of his articles written in USA and *Haak*, a handwritten paper for private circulation also expresses his deep but reasoned hatred for this antihuman thought.

Khuh (The Well) is ideologically a very sound poem against religious fundamentalism. Paash considers the fundamentalist thought as most reactionary, inhuman, fascist thought and its creative expression is found in this powerful poem. He symbolizes the fundamentalism thought as 'the well', 'who are left few in number, but which reward with death to those who want to quench their thirst'. He creates a number of metaphors to exemplify the destructiveness of the fundamentalist thought and movement.

'The wells are nurtured on the songs of the past, they are related to the dead centuries, they are filled with every tenor, they travel with you in buses and makes you beg for life.'

This poem, symbolically very rich, is difficult to render in another language, but the poet conveys that one cannot fight this reactionary thought unarmed and alone.

Begging for Alms of Faith is another powerful indictment of religious fundamentalism. In this poem, a poor mother begs for the life of her only son and yet knows that he would not survive in the storm of religious fundamentalism.

In a very ironic and touching, way the poet describes the situation:

'I have only one son, O Lord of Faith (Dharam Guru)
The poor husband is not there to provide me shelter

—You are omnipotent, O'Lord of faith
Just a frown on your forehead
turns flourishing families into
herds trampling others to dust.

One needs to go through this poem in full to realize the inhuman face of fundamentalism.

In the same vein, Paash has exposed those communal gangsters, who, in the wake of Indira Gandhi's assassination, massacred innocent Sikhs in Delhi and elsewhere and with fullest contempt he expresses his hatred:

Whatever is the name of this Goonda Kingdom
In spite of being its citizen
I am the India
Which hurts the cunning eyes of the pilot
Yes, I am India, which hurts his eyes
If he has any ancestral town
Then strike off my name out of that right now.

How the fascist form of fundamentalism can crush people's spirits, has found expression in another poem in Punjabi, *The Most Menacing*.

Paash has been a rationalist and many of his prose writings are related to the effect of religion and blind beliefs prevalent in our society. In one of his articles 'Back to Ramraj', he argues that we should get rid of the so-called old civilization of India. He explodes the myths of 'India being a golden sparrow', it may be for some, but not for common people. He argues that the slogan of *Ramrajya* is a backward looking reactionary slogan and mankind's liberation lies in the future. He concludes this article by saying, 'Neither Indian culture nor Muslim nor Christian culture can offer comfort by going back. Ahead, more ahead, where all are moving, there will be no Hindu, no Sikh, no Muslim, no Christian. There, only man will survive. The future belongs to man only'.

Bhagat Singh and Paash complement each other. One is a political thinker and the other is a cultural activist of that political thinking. Both give an assurance to mankind and to those who are working for its liberation, that they may die in the cause of liberation, as both these proud sons of Punjab, but the cause would remain dear to millions of toiling people and they are bound to achieve their liberation, despite many odds and many ups and downs.

16

Two Indian Epics on National Heroes

I. THE TRADITION OF INDIAN EPICS

1. Epics in Classical Languages

The tradition of epic poetry writing in India is very old. The ancient literature of India, like in Greece and other ancient cultures, began with the creation of epics and drama.

In the age of classical languages, particularly in Sanskrit and Tamil, many such epics were written, which have become world classics. Monier Williams, in his nineteenth century book, *Indian Epic Poetry*, has discussed the ancient Indian epics in detail.

Two of these Sanskrit epics known worldwide, deserve special mention here—*Ramayana* and *Mahabharata*. The *Ramayana* was written one or two centuries before the *Mahabharata*. The exact time when the *Ramayana* was written has yet not been determined. But it is generally accepted that it was written between the 5th to 1st centuries BC. Two manuscripts of the *Ramayana* were found, the northern and Bengal versions. Of the two, the northern manuscript is considered to be older and purer, whereas the Bengal manuscript is considered to be altered with additions and interpolations.

Not much is known about Valmiki, celebrated author of the *Ramayana*. He is considered to have belonged to the oppressed castes of India, and many modern young Dalit writers, proudly use the surname, Valmiki. The *Ramayana* is the story of Rama, the prince, and later, King of Ayodhya. Rama was exiled for 14 years thanks to the machinations of his stepmother, Kaikayee, who wanted to make her son, Bharat, the king. King Dasratha, Rama's father dies after exiling his son, but Rama refuses to return before the expiry of the 14 years. During the exile, Ravana, the king of Lanka, abducts Rama's wife Sita, who had joined her husband in his exile. There is a war between the armies of Rama and Ravana, and Rama defeats Ravana, brings Sita back from Lanka, and triumphantly returns to Ayodhya, at the end of his exile. Rama is coronated king, but he exiles Sita bothered by the taunt of a commoner that she had stayed at Ravana's place for a year or so. The *Ramayana* consists of 24,000 *shlokas* in seven books. The story continues in Uttarakhand (postchapter), the seventh chapter of the *Ramayana*, which some scholars consider as an interpolation.

Valmiki's *Ramayana* became the source of inspiration for poets in many languages and hundreds of *Ramayanas* have been written in different Indian languages, with different titles and with some difference in storylines. In Tamil *Kamba Ramayanam* is almost as popular as Valmiki's *Ramayana* is in other parts of the country. *Ramcharitmanas*, in Hindi, by Tulsidas written in the 15th century, is a part of many Hindu households in North India, as a religious scripture. Tulsi is considered, and taught, as a major medieval poet of Hindi in academic institutions as well. There have been *Ramayana* stories in almost every Indian language in some form or the other. In some Buddhist *Ramayana* tales, Rama and Sita are depicted as brother and sister. There is a tradition of performing *Ramlila*, a poetic-drama form of the *Ramayana* in large parts of North India. *Ramlila* (story of Rama) is performed by local amateur drama groups in towns and cities for ten days before the 'Dussehra' festival, which falls 20 days prior to 'Diwali' (festival of lights), the day of Rama's return to Ayodhya after completing 14 years of exile. These folk *Ramayana*s and poetical creations are different in art form, but share a common mythical storyline.

After a century or more of the *Ramayana*'s creation, another very popular epic was created in the Sanskrit *Mahabharata. Mahabharata* consists of 220000 lines in 18 chapters, each called a 'parv' in Sanskrit. Its authorship is not as firmly established as that of the *Ramayana*. Its compiler's name is cited as Krishan Dwaipayan, also called Ved Vyas. It is believed that three are more interpolations in the *Mahabharata* than in the *Ramayana*. The *Mahabharata* is much larger in scope and contains stories within stories. It is essentially the story of two mythical dynasties, solar and lunar kings of India. From one of these dynasties descended Dushyanta after whose son Bharat, India is named in Hindi, 'Bharat'. Pandu and Dhritrashtra are two brothers. Pandu has five sons, known as Yudhishtra, Arjuna, Bhima, Nakula and Sahadeva, the five *Pandavas*. Dhritrashtra has a hundred sons, the Kauravas, and a daughter. Dhritrashtra is blind; so his wife Gandhari permanently covers her eyes with a piece of cloth. She will not see with her eyes, as her husband cannot see with his eyes. Kunti, the mother of the *Pandava*s, has another son, Karana, by the Sun God. Karna is taken care of by the *Kaurava*s. Dhritrashtra divides the kingdom between two clans, but Duryodhana, son of Dhritrashtra, and the leader of the *Kaurava*s, through unfair means grabs everything from them. Dhritrashtra, on the advice of Veda Vyasa, the compiler of the *Mahabharata*, returns the kingdom, but Duryodhana again traps the *Pandava*s. This time he turns them into his slaves, and also tries to unrobe Draupadi, the common wife of the five *Pandava*s, but she is saved from this ignominy by the magical power of Krishna, who keeps covering her with clothes. Bhima and Arjuna pledge to take revenge. The *Pandavas* are exiled for 13 years and they stay in disguise at various places, sometimes even acting as servants. Even after the exile, Duryodhana refuses to part with the kingdom. Krishna, who is related to both the *Pandava*s and the *Kaurava*s, and is a close friend of Arjuna's, tries to mediate but to no avail; so a war becomes inevitable. Krishna's army fights for the *Kaurava*s but he himself is chosen by Arjuna to be with him in the Great War. And this bloodiest of wars is fought on the plains of Kurukshetra, near Delhi, the capital of India. The 18 days' war destroys almost everything. The *Pandava*s win but they no longer have the motivation to rule. So they hand over the kingdom to the younger generation and walk towards heaven. All die on the way, except Yudhishtar and his dog. He refuses to enter heaven without his dog. He is allowed in, and is told that Dharma, was accompanying him in the guise of a dog.

There are hundreds of stories within this main story, and they are all immensely interesting. Interestingly, while the *Ramayana* is treated almost as a religious scripture in Hindu homes, and read with devotion, the *Mahabharata* is not brought home. It is said that its presence at home will bring strife. Though Rama and Krishna are both considered gods in the Hindu tradition, and both as incarnations of god Vishnu, Rama is seen as a role model for social conduct, while Krishna is accepted more as a romantic hero, with hundreds of beautiful women as his admirers, even beloveds. Both the *Ramayana* and *Mahabharata* have often been filmed, and in many forms, and are hugely popular with viewers.

The *Ramayana* and *Mahabharata* set certain high standards for epic writing in Sanskrit. Sanskrit produced many significant epics later, including the epics by the greatest Sanskrit poet and dramatist, Kalidas. Kalidas's *Meghdoot* (Cloud Messenger), *Kumarsambhav, Raghuvansh,* etc., are epics that have left an indelible impression on Sanskrit literature and poetics and have made Sanskrit epics treasured world classics. Ashawa Ghosh's *Buddhcharit* (The Story of Buddha) is one of the most famous Sanskrit epics, and it has been translated into English under the title, *Light of Asia*. This Buddhist epic has been translated into many more world and Indian languages.

Classical Tamil also made a significant contribution to the writing of early epics. Thus, in the second century AD, Elango Adigal wrote his *Cilappatikaram,* the story of Princess Kannagi, whose statue is displayed on the famous Marina Beach of Chennai, in India. In the fourth century, a Buddhist epic, *Manimekalahi,* was written in Tamil by Cattanar. It is based on Buddhist tales. The reference to Kamban's *Ramayana* has already been made above. Tamil grew as a very strong language. The first grammar book, *Tolkappiyam,* was written in the first century by Tolkappiyar. This grammar text is considered as significant as *Ashtadhayayi* of Panini, a Sanskrit classic grammar text known the world over.

2. Epics in Modern Indian Languages

The tradition of epic writing continued with modern Indian languages as well. Thus at the beginning of the tenth century, epics appeared in Telugu, Kannada, etc., in South India. Around the same time, epics came to be written in other major Indian languages also, such as in Hindi, Bangla, Oriya, Assamya, Sindhi, Gujarati and Marathi. Two of these modern epics, one each from Hindi and Punjabi, are discussed here, after a brief introduction to the genre of epic poetry in these languages.

Prithviraj Raso by Chand Bardai is considered the first epic in Hindi. It was written in the eleventh century. Most of the epics written in the ancient or medieval period narrate stories of feudal wars or romances or both. Thus Prithviraj Raso tells the story of Prithviraj Raso's bravery in wars and his romance with Samyukta. This is a huge epic consisting of nearly 2500 pages in 69 chapters, though three shorter versions are also found. There are doubts about the authenticity of the author, period and text related to all four versions; the shortest version is considered a little more credible.

Not all epics written in the medieval period need be mentioned here, but some deserve attention. *Padmavat* by Jayasi, a Sufi epic is greatly appreciated for its literary merit. It is a tragic tale of a Sri Lankan princess, Padmavati, who sacrifices her life for love. Around this time Tulsidas's *Ramcharitmanas,* the story of Rama's life appeared. It is by far the most popular book among Hindi-speaking people in India and is treated as both a literary as well as religious text. A century or more later, Keshav's epic, *Ramchandrika,* was published, but it did not catch readers' imagination, though this was also Rama's story. In the eighteenth century, Guru Gobind Singh, the tenth and last Sikh Guru wrote *Chandi Charitar,* the story of goddess Chandi, the war goddess. Guru Gobind Singh wrote mostly in Hindi, as he was born and brought up in Patna, a Hindi-speaking area far away from Punjab.

In the modern period of Hindi literature, epic writing continued, but only with some poets. These poets include Jagannathdas Ratnakar who wrote *Gangavataran* (the story of Ganga), and *Udhav Shatak* in Brajbhasha, Ayodhya Singh Upadhyaya 'Hariaudh' *Priya Pravas* and *Vaidehi, Vanvas* (Exile of Sita), Maithilisharn Gupt's *Saket* (the story of Rama), and *Yashodhra* (the story of Buddha's wife), Gurubhakat Singh's *Noorjehan,* Balkrishan Sharma's *Urmila,* the story of Lakshmana's wife. Rama's younger brother, who accompanied Rama in his exile, while leaving behind his just married wife Urmila, for 14 years and Ramdhari Singh Dinkar, *Urvashi* (the story of the heavenly beauty who was a threat for sages). But the most famous modern Hindi epic is Jaya Shankar Prasad's *Kamayani* (the story of civilization).

It has been translated into many languages including English and is given prime place among modern Indian epics.

There have been hundreds of other Hindi epics; only a few significant ones have been referred to here.

In Punjabi, the epic is not a strong genre. In the ancient period, in place of the epic, there was narrative poetry called *qissa*, somewhat like the *dastaan* of the Persian tradition. *Dastaan* is in prose form, but *qissa* in poetry. The most famous *qissa* of Punjabi are *Heer Ranjha. Sohni Mahiwal, Mirza Sahiban, Sassi Punnu, Shirin Farhad.* All these are earthly romantic tales of young lovers, mostly tragic. Not all these lovers are Punjabi pairs, some are from Sindh, some from Iran, and so forth. One of the tales is, in fact, Arabic in background–the story of Yusuf Zulaikhan–though it is written in Punjabi.

Another form of Punjabi poetry is the ballad of war and strife. *Dulla Bhatti* and *Jaimal* and *Fatta* are two such well known ballads. The ballads are about warriors of medieval times who challenge feudal authority and help the poor after plundering the rich.

Bhai Veer Singh, the first modern Punjabi poet, wrote an epic, *Rana Surat Singh*. Other examples of modern Punjabi poetry include Mohan Singh, *Nankayan* (the story of Guru Nanak), Shiv Kumar's *Luna* (the story of a young bride, married to an old king). *Luna* has been immensely popular in Punjab.

Every language has its own cultural environment, in which its literary creations take place. Punjab has been a land of valour and strife; so Punjabi literature has more ballads and *qissas* than epics.

3. The Freedom Movement and Epic Poetry

India's colonization by the East India Company started in 1757 and culminated in the first war of independence in 1857. In these hundred years there were innumerable revolts in different parts of the country, and the folk literature tales of different Indian languages is full of tales and songs based on these valorous episodes . The 1857 war was lost by the Indians and Britain established its direct rule in India in 1858. The freedom struggle, in various forms, continued till 1947 in all parts of the country, by peaceful means and in some places as revolts, including armed revolts elsewhere. By 1857 modern literature had taken shape in most Indian languages, and one can see hundreds of literary texts in different genres– epic, poetry, drama and novel on the first war of Indian independence, in almost all major Indian languages. Of particular interest to us, in this context, is the PhD thesis of Bhagwan Das Mahour, himself a revolutionary and comrade of Bhagat Singh, on this subject. Mahour wrote his PhD dissertation, in Hindi, on the impact of the first war of independence on Hindi literature. The dissertation, while focusing on Hindi texts also takes a bird's eye view of relevant literature in Sindhi, Bengali, Marathi and Gujarati.

In 1885, the Indian National Congress, later led by Mahatma Gandhi, came into existence. It wanted to achieve independence through constitutional and peaceful means. Congress had a mass following, but the youth were frustrated by its methods, leadership and conservative programmes. Subhas Chandra Bose, like some Congress leaders rebelled against this methodology, and formed the Indian National Army to fight for Indian freedom. This army had bases in East Asian countries as well. Bhagat Singh was the supreme revolutionary youth, who appeared on the political scene during the freedom struggle for a brief period between 1924 and 1931 and became a legend by sacrificing his life for the country. Many revolts, such as the Kakori, Chittagong, and Navy revolts, and the Quit India movement, form the glorious chapters of the Indian freedom movement. A few heroes of the national movement caught the imagination of Indian writers, and they created hundreds of epics, dramas, novels, stories, et cetera, featuring these heroes. The most popular of these heroes were Gandhi, Nehru, Subhas Chandra Bose, Bhagat Singh and Dr. Ambedkar.

Hundreds of these literary texts, particularly books of poetry, were banned by the British colonial regime during the peak of the freedom movement, as they aroused the masses by their emotional appeal. After the execution of Bhagat Singh in 1931, and also during his trial during 1929-31, literary texts appeared in almost all major Indian languages, such as Hindi, Urdu, Punjabi, Sindhi, Gujarati, Marathi, Telugu, Tamil and Bangla and many of them were promptly banned by the regime. Yet the activity of creating literature based on the lives of these heroes never stopped. After independence, in 1947, again there was another flood of literary works on national heroes, and again

Bhagat Singh drew the greatest attention of poets and writers. This trend continues to this day.

II. Epics on Bhagat Singh

1. The Authors

Shree Krishan Saral, the author of the Hindi epic, *Sardar Bhagat Singh*, was born on January 1, 1919, at Guna, in Madhya Pradesh. He was a freedom fighter and after independence, a teacher. He lived a long life and died on September 1, 2000, at Ujjain. He was a prolific writer and wrote more than a hundred books, all in Hindi. These include epics, biographies of freedom fighters and encyclopedias of revolutionaries. One of his epics on the freedom movement, *Kranti Ganga* (the river of Revolution) is considered to be the longest epic. Written in the style of the *Mahabharata*, it has 18 chapters. Each chapter, is a poetic description of a particular phase of the freedom movement. Saral has around 50 books of poetry to his credit and around 60 of prose. His poetry books include 12 epics. His epics are based on the lives of eminent revolutionary freedom fighters like Subhas Chandra Bose, Chandra Shekhar Azad, Ashfaqullah Khan, Bal Gangadhar Tilak, Kartar Singh Sarabha and Bhagat Singh.

Didar Singh, the author of the Punjabi epic on Bhagat Singh, had a shorter life. Born on January 14, 1922, in a Arup, a village in Gujranwala district (now in Pakistan), he became a teacher in 1953 and taught in schools till 1964, before becoming a Professor of English, in a Government College. He retired in 1979 and died on November 30, 1982. Didar Singh has fewer books to his credit. He wrote mainly poetry on historical personalities or movements. He wrote the epics *Mahapandit Carvaka* (on the great scholar Carvaka, who was a materialist thinker of ancient India), *Ajatshatru*, *Baba Punjab Singh*, and *Tripasur*, apart from the epic on Bhagat Singh.

Now let us take a closer look at the epics on Bhagat Singh written by these two authors.

A Brief Introduction to National Hero Bhagat Singh

Bhagat Singh was born on September 28, 1907 in a village called Chak No. 105, Banga in then Lyallpur and now Faislabad district of then India and now Pakistan. Bhagat Singh's grandfather Arjan Singh, his father Kishan Singh and two uncles were all freedom fighters. One of his uncles Swaran Singh died at the young age of 24 years from of tuberculosis that he contracted in jail. Another uncle Ajit Singh was exiled in 1909 and stayed in exile, mostly in Latin America till 1947, a few months before the achievement of independence and he died on the morning of independence, that is August 15, 1947. Bhagat Singh was extremely attached to his exiled uncle Ajit Singh and his wife, who nurtured him like his own child. She herself was childless. Owing to the family environment, Bhagat Singh became aware about his country's condition at a very early age. Though the family was well-off and had fertile lands to till, yet they were prepared to make sacrifices for the country's freedom from British colonial rule. At the age of 12, Bhagat Singh had gone to Jallianwala Bagh in Amritsar, a few miles from Lahore, where he was a school student, in the aftermath of the massacre of Indian people and had brought the bloodstained soil of the place to his home and kept it as a pious symbol. He joined the National College Lahore after his schooling and came under the influence of the underground revolutionary movement. To avoid getting married under pressure from home, he went to Kanpur and further strengthened his bonds with the revolutionary movement. He left his studies and organized student and youth organizations in Lahore and in the whole of Punjab. He was arrested in 1927 and bailed out after five weeks on a huge amount's guarantee. In 1928, Bhagat Singh was instrumental in giving socialist and Marxist direction to his revolutionary organization. The Hindustan Republican Association turned into Hindustan Socialist Republican Association. The organization was planning to organize masses and build mass organizations of youth, students, workers and peasants, when Lala Lajpat Rai, a respected leader of the freedom movement, died following the batons blown upon him by British police officer Saunders in Lahore, when he was leading a mass protest in 1928 against continuation of British rule in India. Another eminent national leader of the freedom movement challenged the youth of the nation to avenge the death of such a respected national leader. So Bhagat Singh and his revolutionary organization decided to kill Saunders, as a symbol of colonial and oppressive power. Exactly a month after the death of

Lala Lajpat Rai, British police officer Saunders, who blew *lathis* (batons) on Lalaji, was murdered in broad daylight in Lahore, when he was coming out of his office. Since Bhagat Singh was part of this action at the age of 21 years, he knew that his fate was now sealed.

The British colonial regime proclaimed two anti-worker ordinances, despite being rejected as bills in the Central Assembly, Delhi forced the revolutionary organization to make a wake up call to Indian workers and other people. Bhagat Singh and B.K. Dutt threw bombs in the Central Assembly on April 8, 1929, when these ordinances were being forced against the wishes of the majority of assembly members. No one was hurt and a few benches were affected by the blast, as the bombs were made to make a noise and not kill. The inspiration to throw harmless bombs 'to make the deaf hear' came from a similar action by French revolutionary Vaillant, who threw a bomb in the French Parliament in 1893 to draw attention towards the hungry masses of France at that time. He was also executed later by the French Government. Bhagat Singh and Dutt could have escaped, but they offered themselves for arrest. Bhagat Singh used British courts for political propaganda during his trial, a thorough miscarriage of justice. He along with his comrades observed the longest hunger strike till then in jail of 115 days. Hunger strikes by revolutionaries and their political statements in courts made them heroes, not only in India, their voice reached the world over. Bhagat Singh was executed along with Sukhdev and Rajguru on March 23, 1931 after a farcical trial in the Saunders' murder. Mass protests by millions of Indians throughout the country made no impact on the colonial government. Bhagat Singh made no appeal against the sentence and all three went to the gallows cheerfully shouting the slogans of *Inqlab Zindabad* (Long Live Revolution). The Communist paper *Daily Worker* published from New York and London published the news of this execution prominently on March 25, 1931 and condemned the British colonial regime for these executions.

Bhagat Singh became a hero of the Indian people during his lifetime and his popularity grew much more after his execution. He became the most respected martyr of the freedom struggle and today his name has become internationally renowned. He is being clubbed with Che Guevara in terms of martyrs for the socialist cause the world over. Books, articles, poetry started getting published on Bhagat Singh during his jail term itself and there were hundreds of publications in all Indian languages after his execution. The Largest number of banned publications in all Indian languages during British rule were focused on Bhagat Singh. Till now more than three hundred publications in all Indian languages, many of these published after independence have come to notice. The maximum number of these publications is in Hindi, more than half of the total publications, followed by Punjabi, English, Urdu, Marathi, Tamil, etc. So these two literary creations of Hindi and Punjabi will be discussed in the above background of Bhagat Singh's life and his popularity in India and elsewhere.

3. The Epics

(i) Hindi Epic: *Sardar Bhagat Singh* by Shree Krishan Saral

This epic by Shree Krishan Saral was first published in 1964, in Ujjain, with the subtitle, 'progressive epic of national consciousness'. It became popular with Hindi readers, and by 1983 went into its fifth edition. It is currently out of print and one has to struggle to locate a copy of the book in libraries or with individuals. The 448 page epic is dedicated to 'that mother from whose womb a son like Bhagat Singh was born'. The epic is divided into 23 chapters, referring to the 23 plus years lived by Bhagat Singh. The preface to the epic is titled, *Visphot*, meaning 'blast'. Saral has narrated a story, or rather a real life experience, in this preface. The poet had gone to Ferozepur, a border town of Punjab, where a memorial to Bhagat Singh and his comrades has been erected by the Punjab Government, on 23rd March, the martyrdom day of Bhagat Singh. There was a huge gathering at the site. The poet was confronted by a person who wanted to know whether he was writing a book on Bhagat Singh. The poet said he was and the unnamed person tried to dissuade him from doing so, as 'whatever had been written on Bhagat Singh earlier was all trash and he did not want that trash to further increase.' The poet assured the person that he would write correctly and accurately about Bhagat Singh, but the stranger warned him that he would shoot him if he wrote anything wrong. This threat shocked the poet, but also made him realize that he could not write such a significant book casually or for pleasure. He had to be strong on facts about historical events. So he contacted the family members and living comrades of Bhagat Singh and collected facts. He started writing the epic on March 23, 1963 at the memorial of the martyr and completed it in seven months and 23 days, on November 14, 1963. Incidentally, 14th November is the birthday of the first Prime Minister of independent India, and freedom fighter himself, Jawaharlal Nehru. The poet wanted to complete the epic during the lifetime of the martyr's mother, and he was able to do so. The poet explains the process by which he wrote this epic. He says he made sure that:

(a) the epic was based only on true events, and had no fictional elements;
(b) he used only information gathered from Bhagat Singh's family and comrades; his focus being on Bhagat Singh's personality, he did not pack the book with events from his hero's life;
(c) he projected Bhagat Singh's ideas accurately by trying to read all the books Bhagat Singh himself had read during his lifetime.

While the poet introduces all the male members of Bhagat Singh's family, including his grandfather, father, uncles, and five brothers, he strangely skips the grandmother, the mother, the aunts and three sisters, one of who is still alive. He then moves on to describe Bhagat Singh's personality and his contribution to the armed revolutionary movement of India. After this long introduction, the poet starts his first chapter, titled *The Lion's Mother*.

The first five chapters of the epic deal with the childhood of Bhagat Singh, when he was exposed to the national movement at home. Bhagat Singh is depicted here as a mischievous child, who used to amuse even the neighbours with his mischief. In one playful incident, the child throws away some jewellery, but is attracted by a gun. The child was the centre of affection for all his aunts. In the second chapter, the mother hands over the child to his aunt, the wife of his exiled uncle, Ajit Singh, with whom the child was even otherwise attached. In his third year, described in the third chapter of the epic, the child is shown as sowing guns on the family farm and declaring to his father's friend that he was going to 'organize his own army and with the pistols growing on the farm, he would arm his soldiers suitably, and throw the British out.' The father of the child is worried at such talk, but his friend explains that it is natural in his case as the child is always listening to anti-British discourses at home. In the fourth chapter, we see the child comforting his aunt and pledging to take revenge on the British for exiling his uncle.

From his sixth year, as depicted from the sixth chapter onwards, the critical mind of Bhagat Singh develops and he starts questioning his father on the role of the Congress Party in the freedom struggle. His father was a Congress Party activist. The growing child also questions the landlord's exploitation of poor peasants and asks why he does not himself labour in the farms? He also asks why the *Goras* (Whites), who are so few in number, do not leave our country? Bhagat Singh is shown as building a tough body as well. At the age of nine, Bhagat Singh has a dream, in which he sees the British forces killing Indians; they are firing on them, having horses crush them, and so forth. The child says that an old man saves him from this torture, while narrating the dream to his aunt. His father goes to the school and discusses the dream with Bhagat Singh's teacher, who tells him not to worry as the child has listened to a story of the freedom struggle during the day at school, and that led to the dream at night. At the age of 11, Bhagat Singh is sent to a city school in Lahore, where he is admitted into the sixth class. Here his personality develops further. When he is 12 years old, the massacre of Jallianwala Bagh takes place in the nearby city of Amritsar, and Bhagat Singh goes to Amritsar, straight from his school, without informing the family. He brings a bottle full of blood soaked soil from the site of the massacre and pays respect to what he calls 'the blood of martyrs' every day, along with his sister. In the thirteenth and fourteenth year of his life, the adolescent Bhagat Singh sees the oppression of Indians by the British. In 1921, Mahatma Gandhi begins his mass movement against British rule. Under the impact of this even school students replace the 'Union Jack', the British flag, with the tricolour Indian flag and get baton charged by the British police. Bhagat Singh also takes part in these activities. But when Gandhi withdraws his mass movement, following the burning of police personnel in Chauri Chaura village of Gorakhpur district in north India, Bhagat Singh is shocked and starts thinking about the futility of a peaceful struggle. In this section, the poet also mentions Bhagat Singh's association with the Sikh movement to free gurdwaras from the hands of corrupt preachers appointed with British collaboration.

In 1923, at the age of 16, Bhagat Singh joins National College, Lahore, set up an alternative education system to counter the British colonial education system. In national schools and colleges established in various cities of India, lessons in patriotism are part of the curriculum and education system. National College, Lahore is being looked after by an ex-revolutionary of the Ghadar Party, who escapes the gallows by a whisker. Here Bhagat Singh grows into a full-fledged revolutionary, drawing inspiration from his teachers as well. Poet Saral devotes a whole chapter to National College, Lahore and depicts the youthful behaviour of his hero. The poet describes the friendship among five friends in the college, who grew up to be part of the revolutionary movement. These friends are Jaidev Gupta, Sukhdev, Bhagwati Charan Vohra, Yashpal and Bhagat Singh. Of these five, Sukhdev is executed with Bhagat Singh, and Bhagwati Charan Vohra dies while testing a bomb, a year before the execution of Bhagat Singh. Yashpal turns into a major Hindi writer at a later stage and writes many memorable novels in Hindi, apart from memoirs of the revolutionary movement. Jaidev Gupta takes care of Bhagat Singh during his lifetime and sends books to his friend in jail. His memoirs are most valuable in helping us understand the personality of Bhagat Singh. The friends spend whole nights on the banks of the river in Lahore, in serious discussion. Bhagat Singh wins a prize in an essay competition in Hindi during this period. The poet narrates the bravery of the 'Babbar Akali' movement of this period. Bhagat Singh writes an article on the movement after six 'Babbar' revolutionaries are hanged in 1926. During his Lahore college days, Bhagat Singh is a member of the drama group of the college, and this group stages many plays, in which Bhagat Singh plays the hero's role many times.

The family starts looking for a bride for Bhagat Singh, and this alarms him, as he considers his life committed to the nation. With an introduction from his teachers, he goes to Kanpur and meets national leaders as well as revolutionaries there. The poet refers here to Yogesh Chatterji and Ganesh Shankar Vidyarthi as 'two great teachers' of revolution. Bhagat Singh works for the daily *Partap* here, under a fictitious name and writes many articles in it. He takes part in flood relief work and also teaches at a national school, near Aligarh. His friend Jaidev Gupta arrives in Kanpur, to take him home as his grandmother has fallen sick missing him. He returns home, and the talk of his marriage is abandoned altogether by the family. In 1926, during the Dussehra festival in Lahore, there is a bomb blast. Bhagat Singh is arrested in that case in May 1927, and is released after a five week detention. The real reason for the arrest is the organization of Naujawan Bharat Sabha (National Youth Organization), on the pattern of 'Young Italy', inspired by Garibaldi and Mazzini, national heroes of Italy. The epic is now in its twenty-first chapter, and describes how the young revolutionaries try to by showing the slide show of martyrs for the national cause. This show is organized in Bradlaugh Hall of Lahore. The hall was built in the memory of pro Indian freedom British MP Charles Bradlaugh by the Indian National Congress. During the bail period Bhagat Singh is confined to the milk farm of his father, but he has no interest in farming. He invites his comrades to the farm and serves milk in abundance. His father does not like this and chastises him. This time he bids a final goodbye to the family. The poet described the Delhi meeting of the revolutionaries, in September, 1928, where the organization is given a socialist direction and a decision taken to create mass organizations. But following the death of national leader, Lala Lajpat Rai, in a baton charge by the British officer, Saunders, the youth avenge Lalaji's death by shooting down Saunders in broad daylight, in Lahore, in front of the police headquarters. While Bhagat Singh and his comrades escape from Lahore after this action, they plan another act of throwing bombs in the Central Assembly, to protest against anti-people laws. The poet while describing these historic events has not forgotten to depict the most sensitive and friendly feelings among the revolutionary youth, and their cheerfulness. Thus the poet writes about the physical strength contest between Bhagat Singh and Chandershekhar Azad, who was more strongly built. But Bhagat Singh defeats him in this contest. The poet also mentions the young revolutionaries' liking for good food and their habit of eating from each others' plates. These are very human pictures of the self-sacrificing youth. When Bhagat Singh and Dutt are going to the Central Assembly in Delhi, they are bade goodbye by very close comrades in a park, where Durga Bhabhi, widow of Bhagwati Charan Vohra brings sweets and oranges for them. Bhagat Singh, had very affectionate relations with Durga Bhabhi.

Following the bomb-throwing incident, it is a two-year political struggle in the jail and courts for Bhagat Singh and comrades. This is the period when through his acts of going on hunger strikes, making revolutionary statements in court, and writing articles to inspire his countrymen Bhagat Singh evolves into the most popular hero of the nation. He almost becomes a folk hero in his lifetime. The poet has depicted the last two years of Bhagat Singh in Chapters 22 and 23, with great sensitivity. Jatin Das, a close friend and comrade of Bhagat Singh, dies on the 63rd day of his hunger strike. In this context, the poet refers to Bhagat Singh's record 16-week hunger strike, which ultimately gets them the status of political prisoners. Before the execution of Bhagat Singh and his fellow accused, their most precious comrades and leaders, Bhagwati Charan Vohra and Chandershekhar Azad lost their lives in May 1930, and February 1931, respectively. This makes Bhagat Singh extremely sad in jail, but he faces the gallows in a most heroic manner. Embracing each other, Bhagat Singh, Sukhdev, and Rajguru raise the sky shattering slogans of 'Long Live Revolution' and 'Death to Imperialism'. The poet concludes his epic with this comment: 'It seems you live in every particle of this world. It seems you live in every patriot's pledge. It seems that you are alive in the revolutionary spirit of the age. You live in our hearts, on the touchstone of sacrifice.'

In conclusion, one can say that Saral's epic would have been more effective, had it been slightly shorter and more compact. However, throughout the long epic the poet has maintained the rhythm and the metre. Generally Indian epics focus on feudal heroes, but Shri Krishan Saral has broken this tradition and made rebels and revolutionaries his heroes. The poet has used the form of the epic quite effectively to convey both his emotions and ideas. Though the poet had made a promise to the stranger he met at Ferozepur that he would remain faithful to the facts about, and ideas of, the hero, he has not been able to do justice to the socialist and atheist ideas that Bhagat Singh propounded most assertively. Here one can also see the weakness of the epic. The ideology and perspective of the poet seem to override those of Bhagat Singh himself. The non-socialist and non-atheist perspective of the poet hinder the true depiction of his hero's declared ideas. Yet, in totality, one has a positive assessment of this epic, as it was the first full-fledged biographical poetic creation on Bhagat Singh's life, which is quite fascinating to creative artists.

(ii) Punjabi Epic: *Shaheed Bhagat Singh* by Prof. Didar Singh

This epic by Prof. Didar Singh is available in two forms. It was first published in 1968 in an abridged form. It was published by Yuvak Kendra, Jalandhar, Punjab, without mentioning the name of the author. It has since been reprinted as a *qissa* by another publisher, with an introduction by Malwinderjit Singh Waraich.

The second form of this ballad was published in 1984, by the Shaheed Bhagat Singh Research Committee, Ludhiana, Punjab. This is a larger and fuller edition of the epic. The edition came out after the death of the author, and its introduction was written by the eminent Punjabi critic Prof. Kesar Singh. While the earlier version has 14 chapters, this enlarged edition contains 30 chapters and this is more than double in size compared to the earlier version.

Prof. Kesar Singh, in his introduction, has described Didar Singh's work as an epic, and underlined the fact that its contents are based on research and recorded history. According to critics, this epic authentically presents three main aspects— (a) Bhagat Singh's ancestral background and the political events of his life, (b) the aims, programme and struggle of the Hindustan Socialist Republican Army (HSRA), the ideologically strong organization that was part of the Indian freedom struggle, and (c) the national-international politics of a decade (1921-31), its background and future. Prof. Kesar Singh appreciates the language, folk metre, rhythm and simplicity of the epic, but he believes its real literary strength is the choice of the subject and hero, and its mature ideological truthfulness. Kesar Singh also notes that the poet has created a character conforming to the norms of the realism theory of literature, particularly propounded by Hungarian Marxist critics George Lukacs. Kesar Singh concludes with the observation that so long as the system of economic exploitation of workers and peasants continues, the relevance and literary value of this epic will remain intact.

Except for a few pages, both the versions of this epic share the content. The poet follows the typical formula of epic writing. The first chapter is a 'Prayer' (of the poet), where he expresses his resolve to create a truthful account of the hero. The second chapter begins with the description of the birth of the hero. The poet says that fortune-tellers had predicted that 'the child will either get political power or go to the gallows'. The poet also describes Bhagat Singh's birth as signalling 'good fortune for the Sandhu clan of Jats' (Punjabi dominant caste). In the third chapter the poet describes the mythical story of the phoenix, and narrates the history of the clan, whose ancient members even fought the Greek aggressors of India, during Alexander's time. The poet mentions Charmak as the king of the Sandhu clan, based in Narli village of the erstwhile Lahore district of undivided India. At a later stage, the family shifted to Khatkar Kalan, a village where an ancestor of the clan was married to the only daughter of the local lord. As Bhagat Singh's grandfather takes the nine-year-old child to the ancestral village and narrates the story of the clan, the attempt of the poet is to show the readers the ruling class background of the would be martyr. The poet refers to the mythical image of the phoenix here to show that the brave ones continue to be reborn in one form or another. The poet also shows the child taking a pledge to turn into a phoenix. In family accounts, Bhagat Singh was born in Faislabad district, and lived mostly at Lahore, and perhaps rarely visited his ancestral place. In the next chapter, the poet refers to the Bolshevik Revolution in Russia, in 1917, led by Lenin, and he describes this event as the 'making up of the sons of the soil'. Further, the poet refers to the growth of Bhagat Singh into a young man, and then describes 'the night of the alien rule.' In this chapter the poet refers to the organization of young men by Bhagat Singh. In the next chapter, the poet poetically describes 'the manifesto of the youth organization'. He focuses on the youth's sacrificing spirit. The manifesto declares the aim of the revolution as 'bringing power to proletarian hands'. In the next chapter, the poet jumps to the Saunders' murder in Lahore and poetically presents the poster put up on Lahore walls that night. The chapter that follows narrates the escape of Bhagat Singh from Lahore to Calcutta, with Durga Bhabhi, the wife of his comrade, Bhagwati Charan Vohra, shielding Bhagat Singh, in a British officer's dress, as her husband.

The revolutionaries decide to throw bombs in the Central

Assembly 'to make the deaf hear' and not to harm anyone. After throwing the bombs, Bhagat Singh and his comrade, B.K. Dutt, both loudly raise the slogans of *Inqlab Zindabad* (Long Live Revolution) and *Samrjyavad murdabad* (Death to Imperialism). Incidentally, one of these slogans, *Inqlab Zindabad* became a clarion call of Indians afterwards, and it is as much popular in present-day Pakistan, Bangladesh and Nepal as in India. The poet then moves on to the Bhagat Singh trial in British courts, and poetically presents the historic statement made by Bhagat Singh and Dutt in the session's courts, on June 6, 1929. Even after they proclaim that their only purpose in throwing the bombs is to draw the attention of the law makers towards the people's plight and that they stand for a revolutionary transformation of the whole society, to free it from all kinds of exploitation, they are sentenced to 'transportation for life'.

The poet then focuses on the ideological development of Bhagat Singh and moves to the message he sent to the students' conference of Punjab, held in Lahore, on October 19, 1929, in which he declares that 'it is not advisable for students to take the path of bombs and pistols. It is advisable for them to move to workers and peasants and other poor to organize them in mass organizations'. Continuing with this theme, the poet mentions the letter addressed by Bhagat Singh to the editor of *Modern Review*, who had ridiculed the concept of 'revolution' by attacking the slogan, 'Long Live Revolution' in his journal. Published in *The Tribune*, the most respected daily of Lahore on December 22, 1929, the letter clarifies the concept of 'revolution', which is not just 'sanguinary strife'; it is a total transformation of the society on socialist principles. Moving further, the poet now recreates 'the manifesto HSRA', at that time titled 'The Philosophy of the Bomb'. It is a rejoinder to Mahatma Gandhi's editorial in his paper, titled 'The Cult of the Bomb'. By this time, it is clear that there are two perceptions about the Indian freedom struggle, one propounded by Mahatma Gandhi, the non-violent movement, and the other propounded by revolutionaries like Bhagat Singh, which emphasized the revolutionary transformation of society by all means, including armed struggle.

Though close friends Bhagat Singh and Sukhdev, the two intellectual stars of the group have occasional differences as well. On two issues, they exchange strong notes. One is on the sensitive issue of 'Love', which Bhagat Singh appreciates as an inspiring feeling, and Sukhdev's somewhat puritan approach frowns on. When the revolutionaries are on a hunger strike, Sukhdev becomes a votary of the idea of committing 'suicide', though, earlier, he used to condemn it in very harsh terms. Here Bhagat Singh snubs his friend by saying that revolutionaries have to remain prepared for suffering of the worst kinds and suicide can only be seen as an easy escape from those troubles. Bhagat Singh has a more compassionate view of suicide in normal circumstances. Both Bhagat Singh and Sukhdev are so well read that the notes they exchange make frequent references to Russian literature and other aesthetic aspects of life.

The poet then narrates the courtroom scenes and refers to the boycott of the courts by the revolutionaries, who believed they were a sham. In this context, the poet presents, in verse, one of the most important essays of Bhagat Singh, titled—'Why I Am an Atheist'. Written on October 4, 1930, a few months before his execution, this essay is Bhagat Singh's swan song. Around the same time, Bhagat Singh also writes a very strong letter to his father censuring him for interfering in his political life, in order to save his life. He declares that for him, his 'principles are far more important than his life'. He instructs his father to get the letter published in the media and strictly forbids him to interfere in his political life. The father follows the instructions of his son and has the letter published before the day of pronouncement of the death sentence.

A significant aspect of Prof. Didar Singh's epic on Bhagat Singh is his poetical transcreation of the major documents associated with Bhagat Singh. Two of these are Bhagat Singh's letter on 'how to fight revolutionaries' court cases' and the very important political document of February 2, 1931, titled 'Letter to Young Political Workers'. Bhagat Singh is in his best philosophical and political form in this second letter and declares that except for a very brief period of his early revolutionary life, he was never 'a terrorist', as the British colonial government tried to project him. He declares himself to be 'a professional revolutionary' in the Leninist sense.

In one sensitive chapter, the poet recreates the emotional exchanges between Bhagat Singh and members of his family: his grandfather, mother and father, two aunts, sister, and two younger brothers. This meeting, held on March 3, 1931, three weeks before his execution, is his last meeting with his family. Bhagat Singh inspires his brothers and the rest of the family to work for the nation. After this chapter, the poet moves to Bhagat Singh's historic letter addressed to the Punjab Governor, exhorting him to send an armed squad to shoot him and his comrades as they are 'at war with British colonialism' and therefore they should be treated as 'war prisoners' and should be 'shot dead' by a firing squad. A day before his execution, Bhagat Singh writes his final goodbye to his comrades, telling them to live and continue the struggle for freedom. He underscores the fact that living in adverse conditions is much more difficult than dying, and as true revolutionaries they 'must live in the most adverse conditions' to continue their struggle for the revolution. The poet gives free flow to his imagination in the chapter, 'The Last Night of the Martyr'. He recreates Bhagat Singh's last moments very well. He shows Bhagat Singh as reading a book of Lenin's, when suddenly, in the evening, he is asked to be ready to go to the gallows, though the practice the world over is to conduct executions in the early morning. Bhagat Singh is not surprised, as he understands the British colonial rulers only too well. He tells the jail warder to wait for a few minutes, and completes the page he was reading. He then closes the book and announces that he is ready to go. As Bhagat Singh, Rajguru and Sukhdev are taken to the gallows, they hug each other warmly and shout slogans, which resonate in the whole jail *Inqlab Zindabad* and 'Death to Imperialism'. The poet creates two more emotional scenes, in one of which Bhagat Singh's grandfather sees him in a dream, before to his death, in 1932; in the other scene, the poet presents a message written by Vidyawati, Bhagat Singh's mother, in the 1970s when she was 86 years old. The poet concludes his epic at this juncture.

Prof. Didar Singh's Punjabi epic tries to depict the ideas of Bhagat Singh in a more objective manner than the Hindi epic by Saral. However, Didar Singh also falters when he eulogizes the ruling class background of his hero and him being part of a higher caste than the Sandhu Jats.

We need not pay too much critical attention to the literary merits or demerits of these two epics here as their theme outweighs such considerations. One can say that both poets have tried their best to remain close to the principles of realism in their literary creation. But one may have to add that in the present age, the novel is a more effective genre to depict such characters and movements.

REFERENCES

1. Shree Krishan Saral, *Sardar Bhagat Singh*, Rashtriya Prakashan, Ujjain, 5th edition 1983 (Ist ed. ,1964).
2. Didar Singh, *Qissa Shaheed Bhagat Singh*, Tarakbharti Prakashan, Barnala, ed. 2006.
3. Didar Singh, *Shaheed Bhagat Singh*, Shaheed Bhagat Singh Research Committee, Ludhiana, ed. 1984.
4. W. J. Wilkins, *Hindu Mythology*, D.K. Printword Delhi, ed. 2006 (1st ed. 1882).
5. John Dowson, *A Classical Dictionary of Hindu Mythology and Religion*, D.K. Printworld, New Delhi, ed. 2005.
6. John Garrett, *A Classical Dictionary of India*, Low Price Publications, Delhi, ed. 1996 (1st 1871).
7. Monier Williams, *Indian Epic Poetry*.
8. William Jones, *Discourses and Essays*, PPH, New Delhi, 1984.
9. Sant Singh Sekhon/Kartar Singh Duggal, *A History of Punjabi Literature*, Sahitya Akademi, New Delhi, 1992.
10. Ramchander Shukla, *Hindi Sahitya Ka Itihas* (History of Hindi Literature), Nagri Pracharini Sabha, Benaras.

* Paper presented at an international workshop on the 'Vietnam Epic', in Buon Ma Thout, Vietnam, (October 24-26, 2008) .

17

Inqlab Zindabad: In Lieu of Post Script

It is 23rd March now on the clock, the most significant day for revolutionary movement of not only India, but for the whole of South Asia, at least as important for Pakistan as for India. The greatest martyr of both India and Pakistan held the head of dignity of the Indian nation of 1931 and revolutionary movement of the whole world, high, with the resounding sounds of *Inqlab Zindabad* and 'Down with Imperialism'. The event made the British colonialism hang its head in shame before the brave three—Bhagat Singh, Rajguru and Sukhdev!

I am trying to imagine the three days of March 1931. On 20th March, Bhagat Singh wrote to the Governor of Punjab, daring him to send a firing squad in order to shoot them, as they were 'war prisoners', since the war was on between the Indian nation and British colonialism. On 22nd March, Bhagat Singh wrote a letter to his comrades, exhorting them to continue the struggle, though they would face immense hardships, more than dying; living and struggling will be more difficult... And on the 23rd itself, I presume they all three slept well at night, after singing revolutionary songs. They knew only about 24th March, as the day of execution. At the time of meetings, Pran Nath Mehta their friend and advocate brought the book on or by Lenin as sought by Bhagat Singh , a day earlier. In all likelihood Pran Nath Mehta must have informed Bhagat Singh, Rajguru and Sukhdev that their families refused to avail themselves of the last meeting with them, though all three families were present in Lahore that day for the last meeting. Rajguru's poor mother travelled all the way from Maharashtra to be with her son. Sukhdev's mother was there with Sukhdev's uncle Lala Achint Ram Thapar, who was like a father to Sukhdev after the death of his father earlier. Jail authorities refused permission to Lala Achint Ram to accompany them for the last meeting, because of 'not being a blood relation'. To protest against this, the all three families refused to attend the meeting. I was trying to gauge the pain of three mothers, particularly of Rajguru's poor mother, who came all the way from a village near Pune in Maharashtra, who had not got many chances to meet her son during the trial, being far away. At least Bhagat Singh and Sukhdev families had many chances to meet them, being in Punjab. Bhagat Singh was worried that at the last meeting his mother might not cry, so he advised her not to come, she did come, but now showing exemplary courage bearing pain, refused to see their sons for the last time, exposing the British colonial regime's cruelty in its worst form.

Bhagat Singh could understood everything, when Bogha, Dalit jail worker came, Bhagat Singh asked him to cook lunch for them. In 1931, Bogha cried, he could not commit this 'sin' to cook for a 'high caste', but Bhagat Singh told him that before going to the gallows, he had to eat from the hands of 'Bebe', they used to call Bogha, bebe(mother), since like mother he cleansed their toilet. Bhagat Singh had his way and got his last food from 'Bebe'. Then he started reading Lenin and around four the jail warder Chatar Singh requested them to have a bath, could not explain anything except crying. Bhagat Singh understood that the 'time was up', they got ready for the 'last and final journey'. Bhagat Singh again continued reading Lenin's book, when around six, the jail staff came to fetch them. Bhagat Singh smiled and said, 'wait for a while', 'let me finish this page, a revolutionary is meeting another revolutionary, don't spoil the beauty of their meeting', they waited.

All three arm in arm, singing started moving towards the gallows. Bhagat Singh's weight increased by ten pounds, with the expectation of execution, mind 'expectation and not apprehension', as he was so happy and excited to sacrifice his life for the country and people, in order to awaken them. I sometimes wonder whether we shall celebrate 23rd March, with happiness or express sorrow as many people do. Bhagat Singh would have said, 'Celebrate your struggles on this day, don't spread gloom, be cheerful and strong'.

At 7 p.m. or around, they were at the gallows, Bhagat Singh refused to wear the black cloth on his face and told the British officer, 'you are lucky to see how happily Indians go to the gallows for the nation'. Saddam Hussein was not the first to go to the gallows with uncovered face; Bhagat Singh was the first one.

And what did the British do after the executions were over? Scared of people's anger, gathered at the jail gate, the news spread fast. They mutilated the bodies by cutting them into pieces, put into sacks and took from the back gate towards Hussainiwala, had burnt the bodies with kerosene oil with some Pandit/Granthi around from Kasur. A large number of people walking by foot collected the half burnt body pieces, brought to Lahore and a lakh of people joined the funeral march to Ravi bank in Lahore on 24th March evening. Thus ended the saga of one of the bravest men and patriots of history at the age of 23 years and five months plus, whose slogan *Inqlab Zindabad* became the war cry of the freedom struggle after their martyrdom.

Inqlab Zindabad II—Long Live Revolution

Writing *Inqlab Zindabad* on 23rd March, I wrote that I would write part two of it, so now trying to jot it down, I wish to share here that what brought me closer to Bhagat Singh in my life. After passing matriculation in my home town Rampura Phul with rather low marks, I was almost lost in the wilderness. There was no college in those days in town and father was not in a position to support my college education in nearby towns, Bathinda or Barnala at an equal distance of 30 kilometres on opposite sides, where the colleges were located. My father, a petty trader, always under some debt, did not join as a school teacher, being middle pass in his days, due to 'little pay', had no such sensitivity to educate his children by all means. Under the circumstances, Public Library Rampura Phul took me out of the morose by opening a whole new world of literary creativity before me. Started with Munshi Prem Chand's *Godan,* I could never settle for a lower level of literary creation, that's why Punjabi novels did not bind me as much, as Hindi ones and translations of Indian and world classics in Hindi. After a while, I became a member of Hind Pocket Books, Delhi's scheme of 'Readers Club', getting nine rupees worth books for eight rupees, with postage free. And one book for one rupee by Manmath Nath Gupta, *Bharat Ke Krantikari* having 16 sketches, including of Bhagat Singh brought my first encounter with revolutionary freedom fighters. Manmath Nath Gupta, who was himself part of the Kakori conspiracy case and got life conviction, though being just 15 years or so at that time. I was so impressed that I started translating the book into my mother tongue Punjabi. By that time I had done JBT, teachers training course and passed Prabhakar (Hons. in Hindi) examination as a private candidate, securing first position in Punjab. This got me a job as a Hindi teacher in a Government High School in Poohla village of Bathinda district. These sketches were serialized in *Desh Bhagat Yaadan*, fortnightly brought out by legendary Ghadarite Baba Gurmukh Singh Lalton from Desh Bhagat Yàdgar Hall, Jalandhar. Some of the pieces were published in *Preetlari* and *Aarsee* like respected literary journals also. Till that time I could read and understood books in Hindi and Punjabi only, English was a distant dream yet. So I read many books in these languages on revolutionary heroes and got particularly enchanted with Bhagat Singh. Perhaps the first meeting on Bhagat Singh, I attended on March 23, 1969 in the Public Library, Bathinda on his martyrdom day, which was addressed by well-known Punjabi short story writer and joint editor of *Preetlari,* Navtej Singh, with his father Gurbux Singh Preetlari at that time.

But I had to struggle a lot, while doing a job, passed graduation privately and even M.A. part-I, too privately. I joined Panjab University, Chandigarh to complete M.A. part-II in Hindi. This opened new paths of life for me. Though continued with my school job, even after completing my M.A., my teacher's union activity and doing M.A., Punjabi again privately, kept me close to study about revolutionaries as well as studying a lot of creative Indian and world literature. Though registered for PhD in Hindi with Prof. Romesh Kuntal Megh, I could not proceed much. In this period, I became quite active in the Punjabi cultural movement and with some writings and translations to credit, became known as Chaman Lal 'Prabhakar' in literary circles. Kumar Vikal, Mohan Bhandari and Bhushan known as Dhianpuri at that time, became part of a circle and by organizing Punjabi Sahitya Sabha at Rampura Phul; came into contact with stalwarts of Punjabi literature as well, Prof. Mohan Singh, Sant Singh Sekhon, Gurdial Singh, and Paash, Waryam Sandhu, Surinder Hemjyoti, Ajmer Aulakh, Amarjit Chandan, Harbhajan Halwarvi, Attarjeet, Sant Ram Udasi, Lal Singh Dil, et cetera, were all part of same stream at that time. We worked together in *Panjabi Sahitya Sabhiachar Manch*, with guidance from Nagi Reddy group of ML movement in Punjab at that time. In the 1975 Emergency, I spent seven months in Bathinda and Patiala jails.

In 1977, I joined JNU for research and left the school job. Five years in JNU, as a student, had been the best period of my life so far. After doing a Hindi officer's job for sometime in Bombay, I had a short stint in *Jansatta*, Hindi daily from *Indian Express* group as sub-editor, before getting a long-term job at Punjabi University, Patiala as an academician. Before leaving for Patiala, I completed editing *Bhagat Singh aur Unke Sathiyon Ke Dastavez* with Jagmohan Singh for Rajkamal Prakashan, Delhi, which got published in 1986, to become an all time bestseller till now. From 1985 to 2002, I remained confined to literature and have many publications in Hindi, Punjabi and English, books as well as articles in journals/newspapers.

Again after 2002, my interest returned to Bhagat Singh and this time I collected documents of Bhagat Singh alone with the title, *Bhagat Singh ke Sampuran Dastavez* (Complete Documents of Bhagat Singh). The Preface of the book was written by Kultar Singh, younger brother of Bhagat Singh and the book was released during the World Book Fair in Delhi in February 2004. This also became as much a hit as was the early collection. In the meantime, National Book Trust Chairman, Prof. Bipan Chandra, assigned me to write a monograph on Kartar Singh Sarabha, which I completed only after joining JNU as Professor in Hindi Translation in 2005. By this time, I got the Central Hindi Directorate award for translating Surjit Patar's poetry in Hindi, Sahitya Akademi Translation Prize for translating Paash's poetry in Hindi in 2002 and Punjab Government's Shiromani Hindi Sahityakar award in 2003.

By the time I joined JNU, I had enough publications on Hindi and Punjabi literature, including that of criticism and translation, which were getting published every year. However, from 2006, my whole interest seemed to be concentrated on Bhagat Singh and other revolutionary heroes during the 75th martyrdom centenary (2006) and in 2007 the birth centenary of Bhagat Singh. I became an active campaigner and writer on Bhagat Singh in this period, more at non-official level, but some at official level also. By impressing upon left parliamentary parties, which were supporting the UPA government in those days, I got Bhagat Singh centenaries included in official functions also, which resulted in publication of Bhagat Singh's documents from the Publications Division for the first time in 60 years. This was edited by me as *Shaheed Bhagat Singh:Dastavezon ke Aaine Mein*, which is coming in Urdu also shortly. Also got *Jail Notebook and Other Writings* with my introduction, published from Leftword Books, Delhi, which has got many reprints in paperback till now. NBT also got *Bhagat Singh ke Rajnitik Dastavez* edited from me. On my own I prepared a book in Punjabi, my mother tongue, *Bhagat Singh: Vicharvan Inqlabi*, published by Navyug Press, Delhi, best in Punjabi language publications. My own writings in Hindi on Bhagat Singh were published in 2009 under the title, *Bhagat Singh* by Medha Books, Delhi. Another collection of my writings on Bhagat Singh, including some in *EPW* and *Monthly Review* is now being published as *Understanding Bhagat Singh* from Aakar Books, Delhi and Foreign Languages University Hyderabad. Hindi literary monthly *Gyanoudey* also got a column on Indian revolutionaries from me during 2007, which is now ready to be published in book form any time. In Punjabi my book appeared as *Inqlabi Itihas De Sunehare Panne,* in 2006, by Tarak Bharti Publishers, Barnala. During 2006-10, I delivered fifty plus lectures on Bhagat Singh in different parts of the country and abroad. My NBT collection of Bhagat Singh documents has recently come out in Urdu translation also, which I hope reaches Pakistan.

Why did I get so involved with this theme? As part of the left and democratic movement, I realized that one needs to have heroes from one's own tradition to have emotional appeal among the masses. Bhagat Singh is one such hero, who has mass appeal, and who has the best enlightened leftist ideas during the freedom movement. Bhagat Singh like Che Guevara is an ideal hero for not only India, but for South Asia as a whole, as Che Guevara is for the whole of Latin America and both together for the whole world. The other reason was, to place

Bhagat Singh in proper ideological perspective, he was just projected as a brave, fearless patriot, but despite his writings being available, he was not projected as a clear socialist revolutionary thinker, to some extent deliberately. Prof. Bipan Chandra brought his ideological position clearly in the 1970s, I took the task further by bringing into light his writings in focus, so that people could know him directly from his writings. I have more material to focus on him, like official documents from the National Archives including intelligence reports, which I want to use in a book, *Bhagat Singh: Through Colonial and Nationalist Perspectives*. I have a desire to get a complete set of articles published in *Mainstream* journal, in a book form, which could prove to be the best collection of articles on Bhagat Singh. I am working now on the *Bhagat Singh Reader*, assigned to me by Penguin India for the international edition, may be completed in this year. This will bring Bhagat Singh's complete documents in English at an international level. This will provide me with the greatest satisfaction of my life, as and when it comes out. Amen! *Inqlab Zindabad* (Long Live Revolution).

PART II
ANNEXURES

Annexure 1

Why I am an Atheist

By Bhagat Singh

[By special arrangement *The People* is permitted to print some of Bhagat Singh's writings in jail. The things placed at our disposal are mostly non-political. Copyright vests in S. Kishan Singh.—Editor.]

A new question has cropped up. Is it due to vanity that I do not believe in the existence of an omnipotent, omnipresent and omniscient God ? I had never imagined that I would ever have to confront such a question. But conversation with some friends has given me a hint that certain of my friends—if I am not claiming too much in thinking them to be so—are inclined to conclude from the brief contact they have had with me, that it was too much on my part to deny the existence of God and that there was a certain amount of vanity that actuated my disbelief. Well, the problem is a serious one. I do not boast to be quite above these human traits. I am a man and nothing more. None can claim to be more. I also have this weakness in me. Vanity does form a part of my nature. Amongst my comrades I was called an autocrat. Even my friend Mr. B. K. Dutt sometimes called me so. On certain occasions I was decried as a despot. Some friends do complain and very seriously too that I involuntarily thrust my opinions upon others and get my proposals accepted. That this is true up to a certain extent, I do not deny. This may amount to egotism. There is vanity in me inasmuch as our cult as opposed to other popular creeds is concerned. But that is not personal. It may be, it is only legitimate pride in our cult and does not amount to vanity. Vanity or to be more precise "Akankar" is the excess of undue pride in one's self. Whether it is such an undue pride that has led me to atheism or whether it is after very careful study of the subject and after much consideration that I have come to disbelieve in God, is a question that I intend to discuss here. Let me first make it clear that egotism and vanity are two different things.

In the first place, I have altogether failed to comprehened as to how undue pride or vaingloriousness could ever stand in the way of a man in believing in God. I can refuse to recognize the greatness of a really great man provided I have also achieved a certain amount of popularity without deserving it or without having possessed the qualities really essential or indispensible for the same purpose. That much is conceivable. But in what way can a man believing in God cease believing due to his personal vanity ? There are only two ways. The man should either begin to think himself a rival of God or he may begin to believe himself to be God. In neither case can he become a genuine athiest. In the first case he does not even deny the existence of his rival. In the second case as well he admits the existence of a conscious being behind the screen guiding all the movements of nature. It is of no importance to us whether he thinks himself to be that supreme being or whether he thinks the supreme conscious being to be somebody apart from himself. The fundamental is there. His belief is there. He is by no means an athiest. Well, here I am. I neither belong to the first category nor to the second. I deny the very existence of that Almighty Supreme being. Why I deny it shall be dealt with later on. Here I want to clear one thing, that it is not vanity that has actuated me to adopt the doctrines of athiesm. I am neither a rival nor an incarnation nor the Supreme Being Himself. One point is decided, that it is not vanity that has led me to this mode of thinking. Let me examine the facts to disprove this allegation. According to these friends of mine I have grown vainglorious perhaps due to the undue popularity gained during the trials—both Delhi Bomb and Lahore conspiracy cases Well, let us see if their premises are correct. My atheism is not of so recent origin. I had stopped believing in God when I was an obscure young man, of whose existence my above mentioned friends were not even aware. At least a college student cannot cherish any sort of undue pride which may lead him to atheism. Though a favourite with some professors and disliked by certain others, I was never an industrious or a studious boy. I could not get any chance of indulging to such feelings as vanity. I was rather a boy with a very shy nature, who had certain pessimistic dispositions about the future career. And in those days, I was not a perfect atheist. My grand-father under whose influence I was brought up is an orthodox Arya Samajist An Arya Samajist is anything but an atheist. After finishing my primary education I joined the D. A. V. School of Lahore and stayed in its Boarding House for full one year. There does not lead towards progress. It is rather too obviously reactionary.

Because our forefathers had set up a faith in some supreme being—the Almighty God—therefore any man who dares to challenge the validity of that faith, or the very exitence of that supreme being, he shall have to be called an apostate, a renegade. If his arguments are too sound to be refuted by counter-arguments and spirit too strong to be cowed down by the threat of misfortunes that may befall him by the wrath of the Almighty—he shall be decried as vainglorious, his spirit to be denominated as vanity. Then why to waste time in this vain discussion? Why try to argue out the whole thing? This question is coming before the public for the first time, and is being handled in this matter of fact way for the first time, hence this lengthy discussion.

As for the first question, I think I have cleared that it is not vanity that has led me to atheism. My way of argument has proved to be convincing or-not, that is to be judged by my readers, not me. I know in the present circumstances my faith in God would have made my life easier, my burden lighter and my disbelief in Him has turned all the circumstances too dry and the situation may assume too harsh a shape. A little bit of mysticism can make it poetical. But I do not want the help of any intoxication to meet my fate. I am a realist. I have been trying to overpower the instinct in me by the help of reason. I have not always been successful in achieving this end. But man's duty is to try and endeavour, success depends upon chance and environments

As for the second question that if it was not vanity, then there ought to be some reason to disbelieve the old and still prevailing faith of the existence of God. Yes; I come to that now. Reason there is. According to me, any man who has got some reasoning power at his command always tries to reason out his environments. Where direct proofs are laking, philosophy occupies the important place. As I have already stated, a certain revolutionary friend used to say that Philosophy is the outcome of human weakness. When our ancestors had leisure enough to try to solve out the mystery of this world, its past, present and the future, its whys and wherefores, they having been terribly short of direct proofs, everybody tried to solve the problem in his own way. Hence we find the wide differences in the fundamentals of various religious creeds, which sometimes assume very antagonistic and conflicting shapes. Not only the Oriental and Occidental philosophies differ, there are differences even amongst various shools of thoughts in each hemisphere. Amongst Oriental religions, the Moslem faith is not at all compatible with Hindu faith. In India alone Buddhism and Jainism are sometimes quite separate from Brahmanism, in which there are again conflicting faiths as Arya Samaj and Sanatan Dharma. Charwak is still another independent thinker of the past ages. He challenged the authority of God in the old times. All these creeds differ from each other on the fundamental question; and everybody considers himself to be on the right. There lies the misfortune. Instead of using the experiments and expressions of the ancient Savants and thinkers as a basis for our future struggle against ignorance and to try to find out a solution to this mysterious problem, we lethargical as we have proved to be raise the hue and cry of faith, unflinching and unwavering faith in their versions and thus are guilty of stagnation in human progress.

Any man who stands for progress has to criticise, disbelieve and challenge every item of the old faith. Item by item he has to reason out every nook and corner of the prevailing faith. If after considerable reasoning one is led to believe in any theory or philosophy, his faith is welcomed. His reasoning can be mistaken, wrong, misled and sometimes fallacious. But he is liable to correction because reason is the guiding star of his life. But mere faith and blind faith is dangerous: it dulls the brain, and makes a man reactionary. A man who claims to be a realist has to challenge the whole of the ancient faith. If it does not stand the onslaught of reason it crumbles down. Then the first thing for him is to shatter the whole down and clear a space for the erection of a new philosophy. This is the negative side. After it begins the positive work in which sometimes some material of the old faith may be used for the purpose of reconstruction. As far as I am concerned, let me admit at the very outset that I have not been able to study much on this point. I had a great desire to study the Oriental Philosophy but I could not get any chance or opportunity to do the same. But so far as the negative study is under discussion, I think I am convinced to the extent of questioning the soundness of the old faith. I have been convinced as to non-existence of a conscious supreme being who is guiding and directing the movements of nature. We believe in nature and the whole progressive movement aims at the domination of man over nature for his service. There is on consious power behind it to direct. This is what our philosophy is.

As for the negative side, we ask a few questions from the 'believers.'

(1) If, as you believe, there is an almighty, omnipresent, omniscient and omnipotent God—who created the earth or world, please let me know why did he create it? This world of woes and miseries, a veritable, eternal combination of num-

berless ttagedies! Not a single soul being perfectly satisfied.

Pray, don't say that it is His Law! If he is bound by any law, he is not omnipotent. He is another slave like ourselves. Please don't say that it is his enjoyment. Nero burnt one Rome. He killed a very limited number of people. He created very few tragedies, all to his perfect enjoyment. And what is his place in History? By what names do the historians mention him? All the venomous epithets are showered upon him. Pages are blackened with invective diatribes condemning Nero, the tyrant, the heartless, the wicked. One Changezkhan sacrificed a few thousand lives to seek pleasure in it and we hate the very name. Then how are you going to justify your almighty, eternal Nero, who has been, and is still causing numberless tragedies every day, every hour and every minute? How do you think to support his misdoings which surpass those of Changez every single moment? I say why did he create this world—a veritable hell, a place of constant and bitter unrest? Why did the Almighty create man when he had the power not to do it? What is the justification for all this? Do you say to award the innocent sufferers hereafter and to punish the wrong-doers as well? Well, well! How far shall you justify a man who may dare to inflict wounds upon your body to apply a very soft and soothing liniment upon it afterwards? How far the supporters and organisers of the Gladiator Institution were justified in throwing man before the half-starved furious lions to be cared for and well looked after if they could survive and could manage to escape death by the wild beasts? That is why I ask, 'Why did the consious supreme-being created this world and man in it? To seek pleasure? Where then is the differerce between him and Nero?

You Mohammadens and Christians! Hindu Philosophy shall still linger on to offer another argument. I ask you what is your answer to the above-mentioned question? You don't believe in previous birth. Like Hindus you cannot advance the argument of previous misdoings of the apparently quite innocent sufferers? I ask you why did the omnipotent labour for six days to create the world through word and each day to say—that all was well. Call him to-day. Show him the past history. Make him study the present situation. Let us see if he dares to say, "All is well."

From the 'dungeons of prisons, from the stores of starvation consuming millions upon millions of human beings in slums and huts, from the exploited labourers, patiently or say apathetically watching the procedure of their blood being sucked by the Capitalist vampires, and the wastage of human energy that will make a man with the least common sense shiver with horror, and from the preference of throwing the surplus of production in oceans rather than to distribute amongst the needy producers—to the palaces of kings built upon the foundation laid with human bones......let him see all this and let him say "All is well." Why and wherefore? That is my question. You are sileut. Alright then, I proceed.

Well, you Hindus, you say all the present sufferers belong to the class of sinners of the previous births. Good. You say the present oppressors were saintly people in their previous births, hence they enjoy power. Let me admit that your ancesstors were very shrewed people, they tried to find out theories strong enough to hammer down all the efforts of reason and disbelief. But let us analyse how far this argument can really stand.

From the point of view of the most famous jurists punishment can be justified only from three or four ends to meet which it is inflicted upon the wrongdoer. They are retributive, reformative and deterrent. The retributive theory is now being condemned by all the advanced thinkers. Deterrent theory is a so following the same fate. Reformative theory is the only one which is essential, and indispensable for human progress. It aims at returning the offender as a most competent and a peace-loving citizen to the society. But what is the nature of punishment inflicted by God upon men even if we suppose them to be offenders. You say he sends them to be born as a cow, a cat, a tree, a herb or a beast. You enumerate these punishments to be 84 lakhs. I ask you what is its reformative effect upon man? How many men have met you who say that they were born as a donkey in previous birth for having committed any sin? None. Don't quote your Puranas. I have no scope to touch your mythologies. Moreover do you know that the greatest sin in this world is to be poor. Poverty is a sin, it is a punishment. I ask you how far would you appreciate a criminologist, a jurist or a legislator who proposes such measures of punishment which shall inevitably force man to commit more offences? Had not your God thought of this or he also had to learn these things by experience, but at the cost of untold sufferings to be borne by humanity? What do you think shall be the fate of a man who has been born in a poor and illiterate family of say a chamar or a sweeper. He is poor, hence he cannot study. He is hated and shunned by his fellow human beings who think themselves to be his superiors apart from morning and evening prayers, I used to recite "Gayatri Mantra" for hours and hours. I was a perfect devotee in those days. Later on I began to live with my father. He is a liberal inasmuch as the orthodoxy of religions is concerned It was through his teachings that I aspired to devote my life to the cause of freedom. But he is not an atheist. He is a firm believer. He used to encourage me for offering prayers daily. So this is how I was brought up. In the Non-Co-operation days I joined the National College. It was there that I began to think liberally and discuss and criticise all the religious problems, even about God. But still I was a devout believer. By that time I had begun to preserve the unshorn and unclipped long hair but I could never believe in the mythology and doctrines of Sikhism or any other religion. But I had a firm faith in God's existence.

Later on I joined the revolutionary party. The first leader with whom I came in contact, though not convinced, could not dare to deny the existence of God. On my persistent inquiries about God, he used to say, "Pray whenever you want to." Now this is atheism less courage required for the adoption of that creed. The second leader with whom I came in contact was a firm believer. Let me mention his name—respected comrade Sachindra Nath Sanyal, now undergoing life transportation in connexion with the Karachi conspiracy case. From the very first page of his famous and only book, "Bandi Jivan" (or Incarcerated Life) the Glory of God is sung vehemently. In the last page of the second part of that beautiful book his mystic—because of vedantism—praises showered upon God form a very conspicuous part of his thoughts. "The Revolutionary leaflet" distributed throughout India on January 28th 1925, was according to the pro secution story the result of his intellectual labour. Now, as is inevitable in the secret work the prominent leader expresses his own views—which are very dear to his person and the rest of the workers have to acquiesce in them—in spite of differences which they might have. In that leaflet one full paragraph was devoted to praise the Almighty and His rejoicings and doing. That is all mysticism. What I wanted to point out was that the idea of disbelief had not even germinated in the revolutionary party. The famous Kakori martyrs—all four of them—passed their last day in prayers. Ram Prasad Bismil was an orthodox Arya Samajist. Despite his wide studies in the field of Socialism and Communism, Rajen Lahiri could not suppress his desire of reciting hymns of the Upanishads and the Gita. I saw only one man amongst them, who never prayed and used to say, "Philosophy is the outcome of human weakness or limitations of knowledge." He is also undergoing a sentence of transportation for life. But he also never dared to deny the existence of God.

Up to that period I was only a romantic idealist revolutionary. Uptil then we were to follow. Now came the time to shoulder the whole responsibility. Due to the inevitable reaction for some time the very existence of the Party seemed impossible. Enthusiastic comrades—nay leaders—began to jeer at us. For some time I was afraid that some day I also might not be convinced of the futility of our own programme. That was a turning point in my revolutionary career. "Study" was the cry that reverberated in the corridors of my mind. Study to enable yourself to face the arguments advanced by opposition. Study to arm yourself with arguments in favour of your cult. I began to study. My previous faith and convictions underwent a remarkable modification. The Romance of the violent methods alone which was so prominent amongst our predecessors, was replaced by serious ideas. No more mysticism, no more blind faith. Realism became our cult. Use of force justifiable when resorted to as a matter of terrible necessity; non-violence as policy indispensible for all mass movements. So much about methods. The most important thing was the clear conception of the ideal for which we were to fight. As there were no important activities in the field of action, I got ample opportunity to study various ideals of the world revolution. I studied Bakunin, the Anarchist leader, something of Marx the father of Communism and much of Lenin, Trotsky and others, the men who had successfully carried out a revolution in their country. They were all atheists. Bakunin's "God 'and State', though only fragmentary, is an interesting study of the subject. Later still I came across a book entitled 'Common Sense' by Nirlamba Swami. It was only a sort of mystic atheism. This subject became of utmost interest to me. By the end of 1926 I had been convinced as to the baselessness of the theory of existence of an almighty supreme being who created, guided and controlled the universe. I had given out this disbelief of mine. I began discussion on the subjects with my friends. I had become a pronounced athiest. But what it meant, will presently be discussed.

In May 1927 I was arrested at Lahore. The arrest was a surprise. I was quite unaware of the fact that the police wanted me. All of a sudden while passing through a garden I found myself surrounded by police. To my own surprise, I was very calm at that time. I did not feel any sensation, neither did I experience any excitement. I was taken into police custody. Next day I was taken to the Railway Police lock-up where I was to pass full one month. After many days' conversation with the Police officials I guessed that they had some information regarding my connexion with the Kakori Party and my other activities in connexion with the revolutionary movement. They told me that I had been to Lucknow while the trial was going on there, that I had negotiated a certain scheme about their rescue, that after obtaining their approval, we had procured some bombs, that by way of test one of the bombs was thrown in the crowd on the occasion of Dussehra 1926. They further informed me, in my interest, that if I could give any statement throwing some light on the activities of the revolutionary party, I was not to be imprisoned but on the contrary set free and rewarded even without being produced as an approver in the Court. I laughed at the proposal. It was all humbug. People holding ideas like ours do not throw bombs on their own innocent people. One fine morning Mr. Newman, the then Senior Superintendent of C. I. D., came to me. And after much sympathetic talk with me imparted—to him—the extremely sad news that if I did not give any statement as demanded by them, they would be forced to send me up for trial for conspiracy to wage war in connexion with Kakori Case and for brutal murders in connexion with Dussehra Bomb outrage. And he further informed me that they had evidence enough to get me convicted and hanged. In those days I believed—though I was quite innocent —the police could do it if if they desired. That very day certain police officials began to persuade me to offer my prayers te God regularly both the times. Now I was an atheist. I wanted to settle for myself whether it was in the days of peace and enjoyment alone that I could boast of being an atheist or whether during such hard times as well I could stick to those principles of mine. After great consideration I decided that I could not lead myself to believe in and pray to God. No, I never did. That was the real test and I came out successful. Never for a moment did I desire to save my neck at the cost of certain other things. So I was a staunch disbeliever; and have ever since been. It was not an easy job to stand that test. 'Belief' softens the hardships, even can make them pleasant. In God man can find very strong consolation and support. Without Him man has to depend upon himself. To stand upon one's own legs amid storms and hurricanes is not a child's play. At such testing moments, vanity—if any—evaporates, and man cannot dare to defy the general beliefs. If he does, then we must conclude that he has got certain other strength than mere vanity. This is exactly the situation now. Judgment is already too well known. Within a week it is to be pronounced. What is the consolation with the exception of the idea that I am going to sacrifice my life for a cause? A God-believing Hindu might be expecting to be reborn as a king, a Muslim or a Christian might dream of the luxuries to be enjoyed in paradise and the reward he is to get for his sufferings and sacrifices. But what am I to expect? I know the moment the rope is fitted round my neck and rafters removed, from under my feet, that will be the final moment —that will be the last moment. I, or to be more precise, my soul, as interpreted in the metaphysical terminology, shall all be finished there. Nothing further. A short life of struggle with no such magnificent end, shall in itself be the reward if I have the courage to take it in that light. That is all. With no selfish motive, or desire to be awarded here or hereafter, quite disinterestedly have I devoted my life to the cause of independence, because I could not do otherwise. The day we find a great number of men and women with this psychology who cannot devote themselves to anything else than the service of mankind and emancipation of the suffering humanity; that day shall inaugurate the era of liberty. Not to become a king, nor to gain any other rewards here, or in the next birth or after death in paradise, shall they be inspired to challenge the oppressors, exploiters, and tyrants, but to cast off the yoke of serdom from the neck of humanity and to establish liberty and peace shall they tread this—to their individual selves perilous and to their noble selves the only glorious imaginable—path. Is the pride in their noble cause to be misinterpreted as vanity? Who dares to utter such an abominable epithet? To him I say either he is a fool or a knave. Let us forgive him for he can not realize the depth, the emotion, the sentiment and the noble feelings that surge in that heart. His heart is dead as a mere lump of flesh, his eyes are weak, the evils of other interests having been cast over them. Self reliance is always liable to be interpreted as vanity. It is sad and miserable but there is no help.

You go and oppose the prevailing faith, you go and criticise a hero, a great man, who is generally believed to be above criticism because he is thought to be infallible, the strength of your argument shall force the multitude to decry you as vainglorious. This is due to the mental stagnation. Criticism and independent thinking are the two indispensable qualities of a revolutionary. Because Mahatmaji is great, therefore none should criticise him. Because he has risen above, therefore everything he says—may be in the field of Politics or Religion, Economics or Ethics—is right. Whether you are convinced or not you must say, "Yes; that's true". This mentality having been born in say a higher caste. His ignorance, his poverty and the treatment meted out to him shall harden his heart towards society. Suppose he commits a sin, who shall bear the consequences? God, he or the learned ones of the society? What about the punishment of those people who were deliberately kept ignorant by the haughty and egotist Brahmans and who had to pay the penalty by bearing the stream of being led in their ears for having heard a few sentences of your Sacred Books of learning—the Vedas? If they commited any offence—who was to be responsible for them and who was to bear the brunt? My dear friends! These theories are the inventions of the privileged ones! They justify their usurped power, riches and superiority by the help of these theories. Yes! It was perhaps Upton Sinclair, that wrote at some place, that just make a man a believer in immortality and then rob him of all his riches and possessions. He shall help you even in that ungrudgingly. The coalition amongst the religions preachers and possessors of power brought forth jails, gallows, knouts and these theories.

I ask why your omnipotent God, does not stop every man when he is committing any sin or offence? He can do it quite easily. Why did he not kill the war lords or kill the fury of war in them and thus avoid the catastrophe hurled down on the head of humanity by the Great War? Why does he not just produce a certain sentiment in the mind of the British people to liberate India? Why does he not infuse the altruistic enthusiasm in the hearts of all capitalists to forgo their rights of personal possessions of means of production and thus redeem the whole labouring community—nay the whole human society from the bondage of Capitalism. You want to reason out the practicability of socialist theory, I leave it for your almighty to enforce it. People recognize the merits of socialism inasmuch as the general welfare is concerned. They oppose it under the pretext of its being impracticable. Let the Almighty step in and arrange everything in an orderly fashion. Now don't try to advance round-about arguments, they are out of order. Let me tell you, British rule here not because God wills it but because they possesses power and we do not dare to oppose them. Not that it is with the help of God that they are keeping us under their subjection but it is with the help of guns, and rifles, bomb and bullets, police and militia and our apathy that they are successfully committing the most deplorable sin against society—the outrageous exploitation of one nation by an other. Where is God? What is he doing? Is he enjoying all these woes of human race? A Nero; A change!! Down with him!

Do you ask me how I explain the origin of this world and origin of man? Alright I tell you, Charles Darwin has tried to throw some light on the subject. Study him. Read Soham Swami's "Commonsense." It shall answer your question to some extent. This is a phenomenon of nature. The accidental mixture of different substances in the shape of nebulæ produced this earth. When? Consult history. The same process produced animals and in the long run man. Read Darwin's 'Origin of Species'. And all the later progress is due to man's constant conflict with nature and his efforts to override it This is the briefest possible explanation of this phenomenon.

Your other argument may be just to ask why a child is born blind or lame if not due to his deeds committed in the previous birth? This problem has been explained away by biologists as a mere biological phenomenon. According to them the whole burden rests upon the shoulders of the parents who may be conscious or ignorant of their own deeds that led to mutilation of the child previous to its birth.

Naturally you may ask another question—though it is quite childish in essence. If no God existed, how did the people come to believe in him? My answer is clear and brief. As they came to believe in ghosts, and evil spirits; the only difference is that belief in God is almost universal and the philosophy well developed. Unlike certain of the radicals I would not attribute its orgion to the ingenuity of the exploiters who wanted to keep the people under their subjection by preaching the existence of a supreme being and then claiming an authority and sanction from him for their privileged positions. Though I do not differ with them on the essential point that all faiths, religions, creeds and such other institutions became in turn the mere supporters of the tyrannical and exploiting institutions, men and classes. Rebellion against king is always a sin according to every religion.

As regards the origin of God my own idea is that having realized the limitations of man, his weaknesses and shortcoming having been taken into consideration, God was brought into imaginary existence to encourage man to face boldly all the trying circumstances, to meet all dangers manfully and to check and restrain his outbursts in prosperity and affluence. God both with his private laws and parental generosity was imagined and painted in greater details. He was to serve as a deterren factors when his fury and private laws were discussed so that man may not become a danger to society. He was to serve a father, mother, sister and brother, friend and helpers when his parental qualifications were to be explained. So that when man be in great distress having been betrayed and deserted by all friends he may find consolation in the idea that an ever true friend was still there to help him, to support him and that He was almighty and could do anything. Really that was useful to the society in the primitive age. The idea of God is helpful to man in distress.

Society has to fight out this belief as well as was fought the idol worship and the narrow conception of religion. Similarly when man tries to stand on his own legs, and become a realist he shall have to throw the faith aside, and to face manfully all the distress, trouble, in which the circumstances may throw him. That is exactly my state of affairs. It is not my vanity, my friends. It is my mode of thinking that has made me an athiest. I don't know whether in my case belief in God and offering of daily prayers which I consider to be most selfish and degraded act on the part of man whether these prayers can prove to be helpful or they shall make my case worse still. I have read of athiests facing all troubles quite boldly, so am I trying to stand like a man with an erect head to the last; even on the gallows.

Let us see how I carry on; one friend asked me to pray. When informed of my atheism, he said, "During your last days you will begin to believe"! I said, No, dear sir, it shall not be. I will think that to be an act of degradation and demoralization on my part. For selfish motives I am not going to pray. Readers and friends, "Is this vanity?" If it is, I stand for it.

Annexure 2

Scanned Copies of Bhagat Singh Letters Published in *The Hindu*

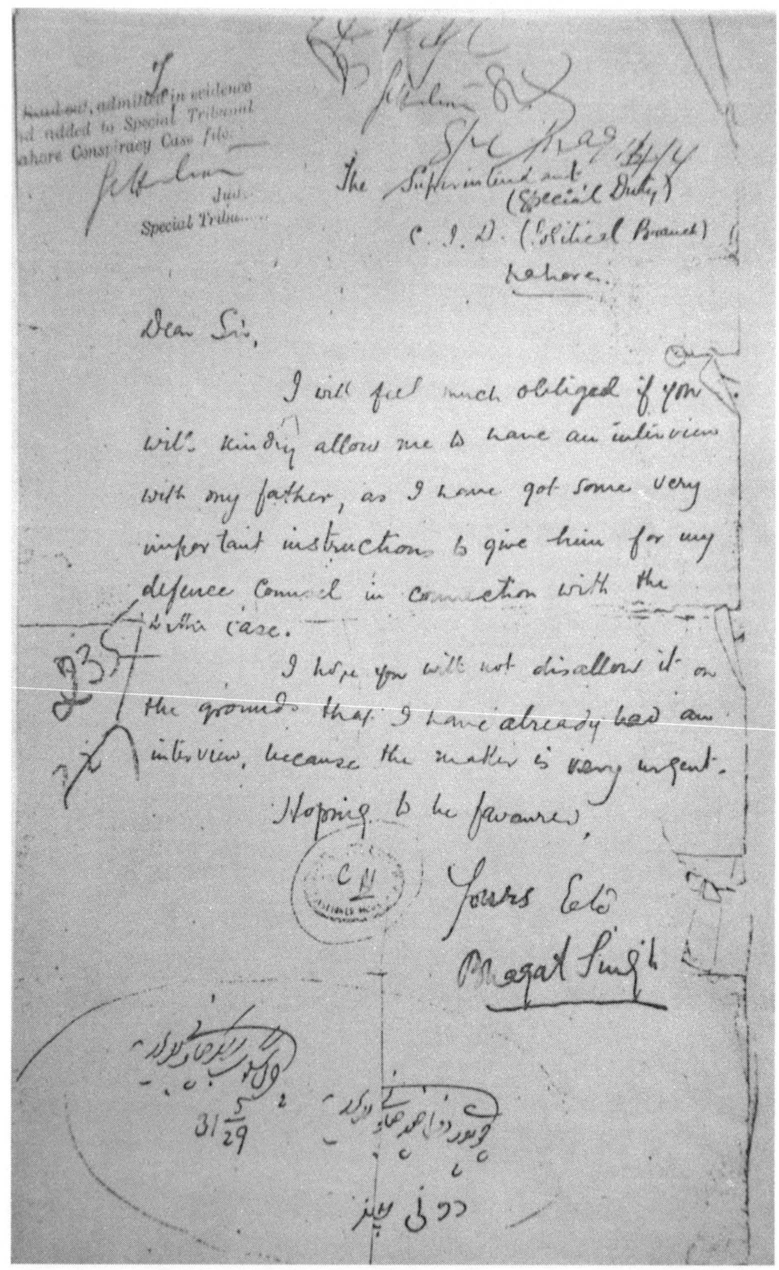

The Superintendent
(Special Duty)
C.I.D. (Political Branch)
Lahore.

Dear Sir,

I will feel much obliged if you will kindly allow me to have an interview with my father, as I have got some very important instructions to give him for my defence Counsel in connection with the Lahore case.

I hope you will not disallow it on the grounds that I have already had an interview, because the matter is very urgent.

Hoping to be favoured,

Yours Etc

Bhagat Singh

31/5/29

In the Court of the special magistrate,
Lahore

Crown VS. Sukhdeo & others.

Charged under Section 121 A 302+120B.

This humble petition of the accused Bhagat Singh most humbly Sheweth:—

1. That the petitioner is going unrepresented in this case,

2. That evidence has been produced in this court ~~of~~ entangling the petitioner in the murders of Mr. Saunders and Sardar Chanan Singh,

3. That the petitioner may be able to effectively cross-examine the witnesses, ~~that~~ it is necessary that the petitioner may be given an opportunity to visit the spot and see the roads and other surroundings in connection with the alleged incident.

4. That the petitioner therefore ~~requests~~ prays that proper facilities to be afforded him for the said purpose and that the production of further witnesses regarding the particular incident may be postponed till the petitioner has been able to examine the locality.

D/ 4th Nov. 29

Bhagat Singh
Petitioner

47

To,

The Registrar,
The Special Tribunal,
Lahore Conspiracy Case,
Lahore

Sir,

Kindly supply me with an attested copy of the order of the Special Magistrate dated 3rd May 1930, according to which the inquiry proceedings in that court were stayed.

Thanking you in anticipation,
Yours Etc.

Dt 19th June 1930.

Bhagat Singh
Undertrial,
Lahore Conspiracy Case
Lahore

To,

The Registrar,
Special Tribunal, Poonch House,
Lahore

Through
The Superintendent,
Central Jail, Lahore.

No 76y Dt 20th June 1930 Special Tribunal, Poonch House

Forwarded to the Registrar, ~~High Court Punjab~~ Lahore, for favour of necessary action as he deems fit.

[illegible] Major IMS
Superintendent Central Jail
Lahore

Let a copy be given
[illegible] [illegible]-6-30

61

In the Court of the Special Tribunal, Lahore Conspiracy Case Lahore
constituted under the Lahore C.C. Special Ordinance

Crown vs Bhagat Singh & others
Charged under Sections 121, 121A, 302, 120B etc.

Most respectfully Sheweth:—

1. That the petitioner is an accused in the above case.

2. That he is not attending the Court, due to the reasons given in a previous letter, submitted by him before this court.

3. That he went on hunger strike in protest against certain Rules and Regulations of jail department and that the hungerstrike had nothing to do with the trial whatsoever.

4. That according to the provisions of the special ordinance, accused still have the right to be represented by a Counsel if so desired.

5. That the case is entering a new stage i.e. the prosecution evidence is going to be closed and the accused shall be called upon to produce defence or to make statements if desired.

6. That at this delicate moment the petitioner wants the help of his relatives and legal advisers.

7. That all the interviews with relatives and legal advisors have been stopped by the jail authorities due to the so-called breach of jail discipline caused by his hungerstrike.

8. That this purely executive affair is hampering the course of justice.

9. That it is prayed in the interests of justice and fairplay that the court be pleased to issue orders to the jail authorities to allow him all these interviews which are very essential for defence purposes.

Bhagat Singh
convict, undertrial
Central Jail
Lahore

11/8/30

No. 483-P.D/11.8.30

Registrar

Forwarded to the Hon'ble Special Tribunal Lahore Conspiracy Case, Lahore for favour of disposal.

Lahore
11.8.30

M. [illegible]
Major
Supdt. Central Jail
Lahore

173

In the Hon'ble High Court of Judicature (Punjab) Lahore

Crown Vs Bhagat Singh & others
[Lahore Conspiracy Case, Lahore]

Charged under Section 302, 121, 121A Etc of I.P.C.

Most respectfully Sheweth:—

1. That the petitioner ~~[illegible]~~ is an accused in the Lahore Conspiracy Case, being tried by the Special Tribunal constituted under the Lahore Conspiracy Ordinance.

2. That the petitioner and his coaccused refused to attend the court in protest of a certain order passed and treatment meted out to the accused.

3. That the petitioner went on hunger strike on July 28th '30 in protest against certain regulations of the jail department.

4. That the trial is entering a new stage i.e. the Prosecution evidence is about to be closed and the petitioner is to be called upon to make his statement and to offer any defence if desired.

5. That the jail authorities have altogether stopped all the interviews of the petitioner with his relatives and legal advisers.

6. That this purely executive affair is hampering the cause of justice and these orders of the executive are highly illegal.

7. That the petitioner wants the help of his relatives and legal advisers in deciding the most delicate question of defence.

8. That there is a special provision in the Lahore Conspiracy Case Ordinance to the effect that if any accused voluntarily disables himself by hunger striking or otherwise or resists his production before the Court, he shall still have the right to be represented by a counsel in his absence.

9. That in the present circumstances the accused feels quite handicapped due to the above mentioned orders of the jail authorities.

10. That it is prayed that in the interest of justice and fair-play, the court be pleased to intervene in this affair and to issue such instructions to the authorities concerned, as would be necessary to give full and proper facilities for arranging defence adequately in a case where the petitioner is being tried for such serious offences ~~which~~ as may bring the extreme penalty of Law.

11. That it is prayed that the court be pleased to issue urgent orders for allowing interviews etc at the earliest convenience.

[illegible] 11/8/30

Bhagat Singh
convict-undertrial
Lahore Conspiracy Case,
Lahore
Central Jail Lahore

Through
The Supdt.
Central Jail
Lahore

No. 127-[illegible] 11/8/30

Forwarded to the Registrar to the High Court of Judicature for favour of disposal.

Lahore [illegible]

181

In the Hon'ble High Court of Judicature (Punjab) Lahore

Crown Vs Bhagat Singh & others
[Lahore conspiracy case]

Charged under Sections 302, 121, 121 A, etc of the I.P.C.

Most respectfully sheweth:—

1. That the petitioner submitted a petition on 11th August 1930 to this learned court through the Supdt. Central Jail, Lahore, praying the court to intervene in the ~~affairs~~ matter of interviews essential for defence purposes, with coaccused, relatives, and legal advisers; which have been stopped due to his resorting to hunger-strike as a protest against certain jail-rules.

2. That a full week has elapsed since and no orders have been received by the petitioner.

3. That his defence is being unnecessarily handicapped and he is suffering simply due to high handedness of the executive authorities.

4. That it is prayed that immediate orders be passed to this effect and the petitioner be informed of that.

Bhagat Singh
Petitioner
Convict - undertrial
Central Jail,
Lahore

D/16/8/30

159

To,

The Special Commissioners,
Lahore Conspiracy Case Tribunal,
Lahore

Through.

The Supdt.,
Central Jail,
Lahore

Sirs,

I have just been informed by the jail-authorities that the learned Court was pleased to pass order on my application dated 11th Aug. '30, to the effect that interviews with legal adviser alone may be allowed. I was at a loss to understand the reason of such an order. Why should I not be allowed to see my relatives, when the said interviews are very essential for defence purposes? If the order is meant simply to make a show that the accused are given proper facilities regarding their defence, though in reality nothing of the sort is done, on the contrary the defence is hampered at every step, then all my petitions and representations are useless.

My legal adviser, L. Duni Chand Bar-at-Law is in jail. I want to engage a new one, which I can not without the help and advice of my father. Therefore the interview is very essential. I have to consult my father about offering the defence. I want to ascertain how far he can help me in this respect. If interviews will not be allowed, the Court and jail authorities shall stand responsible for the serious consequences that I might have to bear for this high-handedness.

With no stretch of imagination can I understand as to why should the court of law join hands with the executive in such matters as are immediately concerned with the administration of justice and be a party to the unnecessary harassment of the accused.

I most earnestly request the court to reconsider their orders passed on my said application and to issue instructions to the jail authorities to allow all my interviews so long as the trial is going on. They shall have time enough to treat us as they like after conviction.

Hoping to be favoured with an early decision,

Yours etc.
Bhagat Singh
Convict-undertrial

D/ 15th Aug 30

In the Court of the Special Tribunal, 163
Lahore Conspiracy Case, Lahore

Crown Vs Sukhdev & others.

Charged under Sections 121, 121A, 302 & 120B etc.

Most respectfully Sheweth :—

1. That the petitioner has today on 22nd Aug. '30 been supplied with the copies of the orders of the learned court bearing the dates 11th August and ~~22nd August~~ 22nd August '30.

2. That inspite of the order of 11th August, no interview has so far been allowed to him.

3. That it is impossible for the petitioner to represent his case personally before the Court on 25th August due to the weakness caused by hunger-strike.

4. That unless and until he is allowed to see his relatives he is not in a position to engage any counsel.

5. That unless and until he is allowed to consult his coaccused he can not decide about other matters concerning the defence.

6. That it is for the Court to see that their orders are carried into effect properly.

7. That it is prayed that the court be pleased to issue immediate orders to the jail-authorities to allow these interviews without any further delay.

D/22nd Aug '30

Bhagat Singh
Central Jail,
Lahore

B.S.
Str...

This application was handed over to me by Bhagat Singh at the Central Jail on the 22nd of August 1930.

Fatehkhan
Regr.

207

In the Court of the Special Tribunal,
Lahore Conspiracy Case, Lahore.

Crown VS Sukhdev & others.

Charged under Sections 302, 120B,
121, 121A Etc of I.P.C.

Most respectfully Sheweth:—

1. That the petitioner has just been furnished with a copy of the order of the learned Court regarding the close of the prosecution evidence.

2. That, since the accused – petitioner – has not been given any opportunity to interview his relatives and particularly his father, who is the only person interested in his defence, he is not in a position to engage any counsel or legal adviser, and without whose help he can not decide any thing regarding such a delicate matter as the defence.

3. That it is prayed that the court be pleased to see if it is proper in these circumstances to deprive a man of all facilities of defence; and to do what ever is thought proper to meet the ends of justice.

Bhagat Singh
Petitioner
Central Jail
Lahore

D/ 26/8/30

Seen by all the members of Tribunal
Placed on the record

[signature]
27/8/30

In the Court of the Special Tribunal,
Lahore Conspiracy Case, Lahore

Crown Vs Sukhdev & others. 219

Charged under Sections 121, 121 A, 302 & 120 B. Etc.

Most respectfully Sheweth:—

1. That yesterday on 29th August '30 the petitioner was informed by the jail authorities that orders have been received from the local govt. to allow him interviews with his legal advisers, relatives and concerned for discussing and deciding finally about our defence in this case on 29th, 30th and 31st August '30.

2. That father of the petitioner who is at Ludhiana standing his own trial, has been sent for and is expected today.

3. That the petitioner shall have an interview with his concerned tomorrow viz 31st August '30.

4. That in the present circumstances, the petitioner shall be able to decide about his defence, and will inform the court about the same on Monday i.e. 1st September 1930.

5. That it is therefore prayed that the learned court be pleased to postpone the passing of any final orders on the question of defence till Monday when the petitioner shall be in a position to inform the Court of his final decision regarding the same.

D/ 30th Aug: 30

Bhagat Singh
Petitioner

No. 182-C D/ 30.8.30

Forwarded to the Registrar of the Court of [illegible]cial Tribunal Lahore Conspiracy Case Lahore [illegible] favour of disposal.

Lahore Central Jail
30.8.30

M. [illegible]
Major
[illegible] Supdt.
Central Jail

In the Court of the Special Magistrate, Lahore

Crown ....Versus Sukhdev Etc.

It is submitted as follows:-

That on 21st (October, 1929-Ed.) instant an unhappy incident occurred in the court. While an approver named Jai Gopal was giving his evidence standing in the dock, he adopted such a provocative posture that apart from twisting his moustaches, he addressed the accused, Janab ye Sab ap ke kartut Hai Sachchi Sachi Baten keh raha hun.(Sirs, these are all your misdeeds, telling the true incidents!-Ed.) In these most provocative circumstances the youngest of all the accused, Prem Dutt(who was just 18 years at that time, born in 1911-Ed.) , got excited and threw a sleeper at the approver. All the accused disapproved of his act and disassociated themselves from it. They wanted to make a statement in connection with that affair. But their statement was not recorded. They then submitted a joint statement. In spite of their statement to that effect, orders were passed against all the accused and all were subjected to undergo humiliation and brutal statement for the fault of one person, which was against the principle of Justice.

Comrade Bijoy Kumar Sinha has already submitted a statement about what happened in the Borstal Jail on 22nd instant. On the 23rd Bhagat Singh and B.K.Dutt were brought to the gate of the court by the Jail authorities. But the notice wanted to handcuff them on both hands which they refused. Then a large number of policemen and a few sub-inspectors and inspector pounced upon them. A few sat on their bodies and others xxxxx(word cancelled after writing) continued violently kicking and beating. These blows were dealt with mercilessly on their heads and chests. Then both of them were dragged to court-room. They asked if the police officials were acting under his orders and if he would ask for explanation from their officials for such brutal and illegal conduct. But no attention was paid to these.........

Ed.- Second page of this statement is not found in Supreme Court digital records. Many of the accused including Bijoy Kumar Sinha and Kanwalnath Tiwari, had submitted written statements on police brutalities after this incident to the court, some of which were not recorded faithfully and distorted by court officials. This statement also seems to be part of the same records, which probably was submitted on behalf of Bhagat Singh and B.K.Dutt. Most of the jail statements were drafted by Bhagat Singh.

Available in the Supreme Court records in typed form only

In the court of the Special Magistrate, Lahore

Crown VS. Sukhdev &Others

Charged under sections 120B+302, 121A

The petitioners respectfully submit the following:—

1. That majority of the petitioners have been in confinement for the last nine months in the above case and the rest have been so confined for terms varying from two to six months, and the case will yet take a very long time.
2. That the charges against the petitioners are of a very serious nature.
3. That the petitioners are being deprived of the fundamental right of being defended by a counsel as they are not permitted to see their attorneys and friends, a matter which the learned court has delegated to the jail authorities who have refused to allow their interview with their attorneys and friends.
4. That although the police and other officials are permitted to come freely into the court room, the petitioners friends are not even permitted to enter the court room.
5. That the dock in which the petitioners are kept in the course of the inquiry is always surrounded by police and jail officials and even those petitioners who are represented by counsel feel handicapped in communicating with and giving full instructions to them.
6. That an unprecedented practice of keeping an assistant jailor and some jail officials present always around the dock is being daily pursued.
7. That the petitioners have been deprived of the right of having access to newspapers which they need very badly in connection with the defence.
8. That they are being persecuted and punished by the jail authorities for matters which have occurred in the court.
9. That the petitioners are unable to take legal steps in respect of the illegal punishment inflicted on them and the illegal treatment meted out to them by the jail authorities.
10. That definite complaints filed by some of the petitioners in respect of the ill treatment and assault by the police officials have not been attended to by the authorities and while in custody the petitioners are unable to prosecute them...........

Here ends the first page of the petition and second and likely final page is not in digital records of the Supreme Court. It seems the second page may be having just one or two more submissions and comments of jail authorities, if at all, if they had forwarded the petition. The petition could be of Jan.-Feb., 1930, when trial was in progress at such stage, where lot many unpleasant incidents taken place in the course of the trial by Special Magistrate Rai Saheb Pandit Sri Kishan. (Chaman Lal)

Available in the Supreme Court records in typed form only

Annexure 3

Periyar on Bhagat Singh

"The aim of life is no more to control the mind, but to develop it harmoniously: not to achieve salvation here after, but to make the best use of life here below; and not to realise truth, beauty and good only in contemplation, but also in the actual experience of daily life; social progress depends not upon the ennoblement of the few but on the enrichment of democracy; universal brotherhood can be achieved only when there is an equality of opportunity of opportuniyt in the social, political and individual life."

The following is the editorial Periyar E.V. Ramasamy wrote in his Tamil weekly *Kudi Arasu* dated 29th March, 1931. Translation by Aasaan.

The editorial highlights the point that Bhagat Singh's outspoken progressive views and supreme sacrifice have disabused the minds of the people and made them realise the retrograde nature of the ideals and methods of Mahatma Gandhi.

Periyar's Editorial dated 29th March, 1931

There is no one who has not condoled the death of Mr. Bhagat Singh by hanging. There is none who has not condemned the government for hanging him. Besides, we now see serval people known as patriots and national heroes scolding Mr. Gandhi for the happening of this event.

While this happens in one place, let us see what the same group of people do in another place. They congratulate Lord Irwin, the Viceroy. They praise Mr. Gandhi for coming to an agreement with him. They are not only satisfied that the agreement has been reached without laying down the condition of not to hang Bhagat Singh, but also consider the signing of such an agreement as a great victory and celebrate the same. In addition, Mr. Gandhi says that Lord Irwin is a Mahatma (great soul), and has ordered the common people of the country to address the Viceroy the same way. Lord Irwin publicises Mr. Gandhi among the white people as a great man endowed with divinity.

The same people who have been hailing Mr. Gandhi as a great leader are now shouting 'Down with Gandhi' and 'Down with Congress'. They show black flags wherever he goes, and disturb the meetings he addresses. These things have become common.

When we witness these things we are at a loss to find out either the opinion of the public or the principle they entertain regarding political affiars. We also doubt if they really adhere to any principle.

Whatever be the position of the public, even when Gandhi started the agitation of Salt Satyagraha, we explained elaborately that it would not only be of no use to the people, but also hostile to the progress of the country and to the liberation of the suffering class.

Even Gandhi has said clearly and openly admitting that the reason for starting the agitation had been to spoil and undo the work done by persons like Bhagat Singh.

To supplement (these things), the real socialists among the neighbours have been proclaiming loudly: 'Mr. Gandhi has betrayed the poor. He does these things to eradicate the socialist principles. Down with Gandhi, down with Congress.' But our known national heroes and patriots never cared for these reactions. They did not realize the pros and cons of anything. Like those who fall into the well holding the lamp, like those who dash against the rock accepting the challenge, they were blindly and wildly enthusiastic (about the Salt Agitation). They went to prison and returned 'triumphantly'. They accepted the honour connected with it. And now after finding Bhagat Singh hanged, they also shoult, 'Down with Gandhi', 'Down with Congress'. We do not understand what benefit will ensue due to such behaviour.

As far as we are concerned, let us tell the truth. There are idiots and fools in this land. They do not think of the pros and cons of a course of action, but selfishly seek their own honour. Had Bagat Singh lived long, he would have to suffer every second the agony of witnessing the activities of such people. Instead, it is good that Bhagat Singh is dead and has found 'peace'. I am sad that I cannot get such a great rare chance (*paeru*).

The issue is whether a man has done his duty or not. The issue is not whether the action has borne fruit. Yet we agree that we should do our duty taking into account the time and place. We are sure that time, place and the general trend are not hostile to the principle upheld by Bhagat Singh. Though it occurs to our mind that he has erred a little in choosing the means to translate his principle into practice, we will never at any time he emboldened to say that his principle is a flawed one. It alone will make peace prevail in this world.

It Bhagat Singh had come to the firm and sincere conclusion that all his principles were correct, and that the method he had used were the just ones, then he should have definitely condacted himself, we could not say he was an honest person. So we now say that he is a true man. It is our strong view that only Bhagat Singh's principle is needed to India.

As far as we know Bhagat Singh's principle represented socialism and communlism. As an evidence to this view, we find the following lines in the letter the wrote to the governor of the province of the Punjab.

'Till Communist Party comes to power and people live without unequal status, our struggle will continue, it cannot be brought to an end by killing us; it will continue openly and secretly.'

Further, we think that Bhagat Singh had no faith in god and in divine dispensation, but was a man of self-confidence. Holding such views is not a crime under any law. Even if it is considered to be against any law, no one need to be afraid of it because, we are sure, that following those principles (that Bhagat Singh upheld) will not do any harm or cause any loss to the public. If by chance any harm or loss takes place, it will be unintentional. We endeavour to put the principle into practice whole cheartedly, without entertaining personal hatred towards individuals or towards communities or towards the people of any other land. We do our work without causing injury to any person, but we are ready to undergo extreme suffering forth cause we espouse. So we need not worry about or afraid of anything.

The same philosophy that underlies our endeavour to eradicate untouchability also forms the basis of the efforts to remove poverty. To abolish untouchability we have to abolish the principle of upper and lower castes. In the same manner, to remove poverty we have to do away with the principle of capitalists and wage earners. So socialism and communism are nothing but getting rid of these concepts and systems. These are the principles Bhagat Singh stood for. It is not wonder that those who consider them just and necessary call for the downfall of Gandhi and Congress. What is very strange is that those who advocate these priciples or hail Gandhi and Congress.

The day when Gandhi said that god alone guides him, the *Varnasharma Dharma* is a superior system fit to govern the affairs of the world, and that everything happens according to god's will, we came to the conclusion that there is no difference between Gandhism and Brahminism. We also concluded that unless the Congress party that subscribes to such philosophy and principle is abolished, it will not be good to the country. But now this fact has been found out at least by some of the people. They have gained the wisdom and courage to call for the downfall of Gandhism. This is a great victory to our cause. If Bhagat Singh had not died by being hanged, there would not have been any chance for this victory to take place in such a popular manner. We even venture to say that Gandhism would have gained more ground if Bhagat Singh had not been hanged.

Bhagat Singh had not fallen sick, suffered and died as it normally happens with people. He gave his life for the noble cause of showing to India, nay to the world, the path of real equality and peace. He has reached a great height, a feat never achieved normally by any one else. We applaud and sing of his matrydom from the depth of our heart. At the same time, we request those in our government to find out and hang four true persons like Bhagat Singh in each of the provinces.

Annexure 4

Jinnah's Speech on Bhagat Singh in the Central Legislative Assembly on September 12 and 14, 1929*

Sir, one is placed somewhat in a difficult position when one has got to deal with a speaker like the last one. It was his maiden speech, and it is the tradition of this House, that when a Member makes his maiden speech, he is in a privileged position and is not to be attacked. Whatever reasons or grounds, therefore, he may have given me for criticizing him, I will not wish to depart from that tradition which, I think, ought to be maintained in the House. But I would say this, that in his concluding portions he remarked that the Hon'ble Members may have admiration and sympathy for the accused in the Lahore case. I think I am speaking on behalf of a very large body of people when I say that, if there is sympathy and admiration for the accused, it is only to this extent, that they are the victim of the system of government. It is not that we approve or applaud their actions if they are guilty, which still remains to be proved. If they are guilty of the offences of which they are charged, then I am sure it is not that we admire them or approve of their actions, but, on the contrary, I am sure a large body of thinking people feel that these young men, whatever be the provocations, are misguided in resorting to actions for which they now stand charged.

Now, Sir, the Hon'ble Home Member asked the House that we must approach this question without prejudice, and impartially. Sir, I am sure the Hon'ble Home Member himself tried his best to follow the same principle, but has he been able to apply the same principle

* Courtsey: A.G. Norrani's book, *The Trial of Bhagat Singh.*

when he brings this before the House ? Do the facts justify that ? The last speaker, whom I am not going to attack, almost gave away the case in his concluding remarks when he said that the only way to break the hunger-strike is to pass this Bill.

Well, I am not concerned at present so much with the account that was given by the Hon'ble Member with regard to the treatment in jails of various classes of prisoners, but one thing is clear, and it is this. From the statement that issued by Bhagat Singh and Dutt, what is an admitted fact now, even from the speech of the Hon'ble Member who spoke last, is that they were not given the treatment–not on racial grounds–but according to the standard and the scale which is laid down for Europeans in the matter of diet and bare necessities of life. It is not a mere question that they want to be treated as Europeans. As a matter of fact, according to the admission and the definition given by the Hon'ble Member who spoke last on behalf of the Treasury Benches, so far as I know, Bhagat Singh and Dutt wear topees, and their figures appeared in shorts. Therefore, they ought to have been treated as Europeans. The Hon'ble Member in reply to a question said that whether the man is a European or an Indian–and he accepted the definition of my honourable friend Mr. Neogy–if one wears a topee, then one is a European for the purpose of jail rules. Then why should you not treat Bhagat Singh and Dutt, who wear topees and European clothes, as such for the purpose of treatment in jails? Why do not the Punjab Government give them the treatment that they are entitled to, at once, and be done with ? They wear topees and they are entitled to that treatment.

What do they say in their statement which was read out ? This is what they say:

> "We, Bhagat Singh and Dutt, were sentenced to life transportation in the Assembly bomb case, Delhi, on 19th May, 1929. As long as we were undertrial prisoners in Delhi jail we were accorded very good treatment and we were given good diet. But since our transfer from the Delhi Jail to Mianwali Jail and Lahore Central Jail,–

Which is represented by the Hon'ble Member, who spoke last–the Punjab seems to be a terrible place . . .

Mian Muhammad Shah Nawaz (West Central Punjab): Don't go there.

M.A. Jinnah: I won't. To continue what they say:

'We are being treated as ordinary criminals'.

So, in Delhi they received very good treatment and in the Punjab they are treated as ordinary criminals. Surely, Sir, if the Government of the Punjab was not wanting in statesmanship, if the Government of the Punjab had any brains, they would have found a solution to this question very easily and long ago. But, Sir, it is a question–the more I examine it and the more I analyse it, I find–it is a question of declaration of war. As far as the Punjab Government are concerned, the Government do not merely wish to bring these men to trial and get them convicted by a judicial tribunal, but Government go to war against these men. They seem to me in this frame of mind: 'We will pursue every possible course, every possible method, but we will see that you are sent either to the gallows or transported for life, and in the meantime we will not treat you as decent men.'

Sir, the whole spirit behind this is that and nothing else. I do not for a moment wish to say that the Government are not bound–in fact, it is their bounden duty–to prosecute those people that commit offences. I do not wish to say that the Government should not do every thing in their power to see that their convictions are secured. But may I ask, with whom are you at war ? What are the resources of these few young men who, according to you, have committed certain offences ? You want to prosecute them, and after due trial, you want to secure their convictions. But before they are convicted, surely this is not a matter on which there should be this struggle, that you should not at once yield to their demands for bare necessities of life. After all, so far as the Lahore case prisoners are concerned, surely they are political prisoners and undertrial. You ask me, what is a political prisoner ? It is very difficult to define a political prisoner. It is very difficult to lay down any particular definition. But if you use your common sense, if you use your intelligence, surely you can come to the conclusion with regard to the particular case and say, here are these men who are political prisoners, and we do not wish to give them proper treatment. We want to give them treatment as undertrial prisoners. If you has said that, the question would have been solved long ago. Do you wish to prosecute them or persecute them ?

Sir, I do not wish to base my opposition to this Bill on this issue of bad treatment, because this is only one aspect of the issue, or rather one aspect of the Bill before us. This Bill has got to the looked at, as far as I can see, from three points of view. The *first,* from the point of view of criminal jurisprudence; *second,* political point of view or the policy of the Bill; and *third,* treatment to the accused when they are under trial. I think it will be admitted, I think even the Hon'ble Home Member conceded, that be the Bill which he has brought before the House, he is introducing a principle, in the criminal jurisprudence, of a very unprecedented character. I do not think, Sir, there is any system of jurisprudence in any civilized country where you will find such a principle existence as is involved in this Bill. Some of the Hon'ble Members who are not lawyers might not have appreciated fully the implications of this Bill. This Bill not only dispenses with the presence of the accused at the trial, but I will give you a picture as to what will happen under this Bill. Under this Bill the Government will apply to the Magistrate before whom the inquiry is going on and say, 'Here is a law which we have secured from the Legislature. Now the accused have voluntarily made themselves incapable of attending the courts and, therefore, you have to dispense with their presence'. The inquiry will then proceed *ex parte* before the Magistrate. Evidence will be led, oral and documentary, which will go without being tested by cross-examination. The documentary evidence will go without being even seen by the accused, against whom it is produced, and how will you identify the accused in their absence ? Then we know, and particularly those who are lawyers would know, that when the Magistrate has concluded the recording of the evidence for the prosecution, under Section 209 of the Criminal Procedure Code, he must ask the accused whether he has any explanation to offer with regard to the evidence which is recorded by him against the accused. It is after that statement is made that the Magistrate has got the power either to commit or discharge the accused. That statement of the accused under Section 209 is absolutely obligatory. It is not the choice of the Magistrate. The Privy Council has laid down that an omission in that regard would vitiate the whole trial. Under this Bill the accused will not be there to give any explanation to the Magistrate with regard to the evidence that has been already recorded *ex parte.*

Then, Sir, we come to important Sections. Under Section 287 that statement again will have to be made before the Sessions Court. There also, the accused will not be present. The evidence before the Sessions Court will be recorded *ex parte* and if it is a jury, the jury will be asked to return their verdict. If it is a case of assessors, they will be asked to express their opinion, and the Judge will pass his judgement or sentence, as the case may be. I ask the Hon'ble Home Member, and I ask the Hon'ble Law Member of the Government of India whether that will be a trial or a farce ?

Sir Brojendra Mitter (Law Member): Not a farce. The accused can always go before the Court if he chooses to.

Gaya Prasasd Singh: But what about the evidence that has already been recorded in his absence ?

M. A. Jinnah: I am very glad that the Hon'ble Law Member has given me a reply. Then you want by this Bill really to break the hunger-strikers. You want this House to give you a Statute laying down a principle generally in the criminal jurisprudence for this particular case, so that you have no other case that you can cite. One swallow does not make a summer. It is the Lahore case. Well, you know perfectly well that these men are determined to die. It is not a joke. I ask the Hon'ble Law Member to realize that it is not everybody who can go on starving himself to death. Try it for a little while and you will see. Sir, have you heard anywhere in the world, except the American case, which may honourable friend Mr. Jamnadas Mehta pointed out, of an accused person going on hungerstrike ? The man who goes on hungerstrike has a soul. He is moved by the soul and he believes in the justice of his cause; he is not and ordinary criminal who is guilty of cold-blooded, sordid, wicked crime.

Mind you, Sir, I do not approve of the action of Bhagat Singh, and I say this on the floor of this House. I regret that, rightly or wrongly, youth today in India is stirred up, and you cannot, when you have three hundred and odd millions of people, you cannot prevent such crimes being committed, however much you may deplore them and however much you may say that they are misguided. It is the system, this damnable system of Government, which is resented by the people. You may be a cold-blooded logician; I am a patient cool-headed man and can calmly go on making speeches here, persuading and influencing the Treasury Bench. But, remember, there are thousands of young men outside. This is not only country where these actions are resorted to. It has happened in other countries, not youths, but greybearded men have committed serious offences, moved by patriotic impulses. What happened to Mr. Congrave, the Prime Minister of Ireland ? He was under sentence of death a fortnight before he got an invitation from His Majesty's Government to go and settle terms ? Was he a youth ? Was he a young man ? What about Collins? So what is the good of your putting forward this arrgument? You have got a situation which you have got to meet, not by introducing and enacting measures which go to the root of the fundamental principles of criminal jurisprudence, and lightly, saying, 'Oh! but it is common sense!' Law is common sense; it is not common sense of one individual

Mr. President: I hope the Hon'ble Member is not inconvenienced when I ask him to resume his speech at the next meeting.

Pandit Madan Mohan Malaviya: Sir, cannot we go on for another 15 minutes?

Mr. President: What is the idea of going on for another 15 minutes? I can understand the House asking me to sit till 6 o'clock, but there is no idea in sitting for another 15 minutes only.

> The House was then adjourned. Mr. Jinnah concluded his speech at the next sitting, after the adjournment motion had been admitted for discussion.

Sir, when the House last adjourned I was dealing with this Bill from the point of view of criminal jurisprudence–and I brought to the notice of the House what would be the position if this Bill was passed, so far as the trial and proceedings of this particular case, or any other case under it, were concerned. It is quite clear, as I said, that the trial will be a travesty of justice. Let us consider the point further. The trial would proceed in the absence of the accused. I ask the Home Member, is there a Judge or jury who would feel that they were administering law or justice in that case? The moment this Bill is passed, the prosecution can go before the court and say, 'Here is a voluntary act of the accused persons; he has or they have incapacitated himself or themselves, and we ask you now to proceed *ex parte*'. Remember, Sir, that in a particular case that procedure may be adopted from the very start. Even the plea of the accused may not be empanel a jury and the jury will be empanelled. You will have a Judge on the Bench and the jury by his side. What will they do? They hear the *ex parte* evidence, oral and documentary. I ask the Home Member, I ask this House, what would you consider of that Judge, what would you think of that Judge or jury, sitting there solemnly, seriously, proceeding with a charge of murder, going through this farce as His Majesty's Court–what conclusion do you think any jury can come to under those circumstances? That prisoner stands already condemned. What is the good of this face? I say that no Judge who has got an iota of a judicial mind or a sense of justice can ever be a party to a trial of that character and pass sentence of death without a shudder and a pang of conscience. This is the farce which you propose to enact under this procedure! I say this, that if ever there was a conscientious Judge and he was strong enough, if he had a judicial mind, and if he had any independence, let me tell you, that, in spite of this provision of yours, he would say, 'True, the law has to be administered; I am obliged to make the order that the trial shall proceed *ex parte;* but I realize and I feel that it will be a travesty of justice and I cannot be a party to it; and I shall, therefore, adjourn this case until further orders'. Have you considered that? I suppose you have not. It seems to me, Sir, that the great and fundamental doctrine of British jurisprudence, which is incorporated and codified in the Penal Code and the Criminal Procedure Code, has very wisely not made such and absurd provision in the criminal law of his country and I am not satisfied that there is a lacuna in our system of criminal law.

The Home Member said that it is a well known doctrine and a fundamental doctrine of criminal jurisprudence that the man is taken to the innocent until he is proved to be guilty. May I remind him of another doctrine which goes to the very root of the criminal jurisprudence, or for the matter of that of even civil law, that no man is to be condemned until he is given a hearing? Sir, I think there cannot be the slightest doubt that we are now engaged in considering a cardinal principle, a principle of very vital and paramount character, to be introduced into the criminal jurisprudence of this country. It must be admitted that this is a most revolutionary, unheard of, unprecedented change that is proposed in our criminal jurisprudence. I know the Home Member will tell me, 'Yes, the doctrine is that no man shall be condemned unless he is heard and until he is given a hearing; but here it is the voluntary act of the accused, and if he chooses not to go there and insist upon his being heard, it is his fault.' Sir, this is not a new question; it has been considered in England and there is a long history about it and behind it and you will find that in old days there was the strictest formality observed as to the recording of the plea of the prisoner. And if the prisoner was mute of malice, that is to say, if he refused deliberately to open his mouth when he was arraigned in a court of law and when the question was put to him as to whether he pleaded guilty or not–he had to make his plea, and there are cases where he refused to speak, and the old law was–even England has advanced–in that case he was condemned and executed or must be committed to imprisonment . . .

E. L. Price (Bombay: European): Torture.

M. A. Jinnah: I am glad that you are up to date. I know that. I am only dealing with this one point, that he used to be executed or committed to prison. Further, when it was thought that it was rather a serious thing that, because a man was mute of malice, he should be condemned to death or imprisonment–then comes the point of my learned friend over there, who I understand is a member of the Bar–that they resorted to torture. Torture for what? That he should make his plea, not that an *ex parte* trial should proceed. That is what you want to do here by this Bill, that *ex parte* trial should proceed. The old law was then altered, because the result the torture was that some of them died and the form of torture was the most cruel form of torture, and I will read to you a passage from Stephen's *History of the Criminal Law:*

'If he was accused of felony, he was condemned, after much exhortation to the peine fore et dure, that is to be stretched, naked on his back, and to have 'iron laid upon him as much as he could bear and more', and so to continue, fed upon bad bread and stagnant water on alternate days, till he either pleaded or died.'

But they did not proceed *ex parte.* Then the old form of trial was trial by ordeal. That was done away with because the plea that a prisoner had to put forward was in a particular form. When he was asked he had to say

> that he wanted to be tried 'By God and by my country'. That was the trial by ordeal. That was done away with and in 1827 by a Statute it was enacted that in such cases a plea of not guilty should be entered. Now, Sir, before that statute was passed there is one case which I will bring to the notice of this House and which will illustrate how much importance was attached to the form and the procedure even in olden days. Of course, my honourable friend Sir Darcy Lindsay will say that matters of this kind can be decided by the common sense of a single individual such as himself. Sir, I must remind him–for he is a man of peace, and especially when we get old we love peace, and common sense is sometimes regulated by that state of mind–, I will remind him, and I think the House will agree with me, that law is nothing but the essence of common sense, that law is the concentrated essence of experience, of knowledge, of practice of centuries and generations, and even Sir James Stephen will point out to you that, when these rules, when these forms have been laid down as the essence of common sense and experience of generations, they are not lightly to be departed from.

What to we find in this House now? Have we not got forms and are we not slavishly following them? Some of them would appear to the strangers in the gallery or any outsider to be most absurd and against common sense, at first sight. If any one passes across between you and the speaker he will be guilty of a gross breach of the forms of this House and you would call him to order at once. Why is that? Without meaning? Without reason ? Without experience? What common sense is there? Why should the man not pass across? It is, therefore, What common sense is there? Why should the man not pass across? It is, therefore, no use treating these matters lightly and saying that we have got to decide everything by the common sense of an individual. The instance that I was going to refer to is this. In one case:

> Mr. Pike produces some evidence to show that in the early part of Edward I's reign, people who refused to put themselves on their trial were executed . . .

Better, people who refuse to put themselves to trial, execute them, rather than go through the farce of an *ex parte* trial; much better.

> " . . . but this practice was opposed to the statute which provided that 'notorious felons' and which openly be of evil name and will not put themselves in inquests of felonies that men shall charge them with before

> the justices at the King's suit, shall have strong and hard imprisonment, as they which refuse to stand to the common law of the land."

Then he cites a case which I think will interest the House. He says this:

> 'But this is not to be understood of such prisoners as be taken of light suspicion. According to Barrington this meant that the prisoner who refused to plead was to be starved till he died, but not tortured–(so they improved later on)–and he quotes in proof of it a pardon granted in the reign of Edward III to a woman who *pro eo quod se tenuit mutam* was put in *areta prisona* and there lived without eating or drinking for forty days, which was regarded as a miracle.'

Well, Sir, I know that there is a passage which is likely to be quoted in this House in Stephen's *Digest of Criminal Procedure.* It is a curious thing that the Government of India, who have hardly given this House even seven days' notice and call upon this House to endorse a vital, cardinal principle of a novel or unheard of character, do not possess in their library even an edition of the *Law of Criminal Procedure* by Stephen of a later date than 1883. And they seriously ask this House, 'The Government case is that they find that a deadlock is created. The law is paralysed, and in fact, even the Government of India might tumble down altogether, and we, therefore, call upon the Legislature to come to our rescue–we admit it is unprecedented, we admit it is unheard of, we admit it is unknown to any system of jurisprudence; but you as a responsible body–would you not endorse this Bill straightaway within these few day's notice ?' You do not possess in your library an edition of a textbook which is the standard book except of the year 1883! And it is a tall order to ask the House to pass the Bill now and here. I will read the passage now, which is likely to be quoted, and I want the House not to be misled by it. But before I do so, I will request the Law Member, to consider what I am going to submit. That is a branch of the law which comes under the category of contempt of court, and we know that the King's Bench in England and superior courts in India, who have inherited the jurisdiction under the Charter, have got unfettered power to deal with cases of contempt. That is the one branch of the law which is neither codified nor restricted by and law. It is entirely left to the Supreme Court or the

High Courts in India to deal with cases of contempt as they think proper. That is a branch which comes under that doctrine of law of contempt of court and even there, while the courts have asserted that they have the power to refuse to hear the party who is guilty of contempt of court, the footnote says that it has never been done in a criminal case. I will read to you what it says:

> 'The prisoner has a right to be present at the trial so long as he conducts himself properly, but the Court may, in its discretion, permit his absence in cases of misdemeanour, and may proceed with the trial in his absence in cases in which he has pleaded to an indictment or information in the High Court (Queen's Bench Division).
>
> 'If a prisoner so misconducts himself as to make it impossible to try him with decency, the Court, it seems, may order him to be removed and proceed in his absence.'

The footnote says this:

> 'I have never known or heard of this being done, but Lord Cranworth (then Rolfe, B.) threatened to have Rush removed from Court, at his trial for murder at Norwich in 1849, if he persisted in a singularly indecent and outrageous course of cross-examination. I have heard from eye-witness an account of a trial before Shee, J. (then acting as Commissioner) at Dorchester, where the prisoner (a convict at Portland, tried for the murder of a warder) behaved with such desperate violence that it was necessary to fasten him down with chains and straps. He was not, however, removed from the Court. and it is obvious that in capital cases, or indeed in any trial involving severe punishment, almost any measures, short of removing the prisoner, should be resorted to.'

The *raison d'etre* of this principle is very different and requires no more words to understand it. Now, Sir, I shall not weary the House with any further legal quotations. I am driven to think the object of Government in bringing in this Bill is political, but if their real object is to supply a lacuna, not for the purpose of this particular case, but in the general interest of the country and the administration of justice, if that is their object, let them remove this case from their mind, for Heaven's sake. Come to us dispassionately and without prejudice. Let them tell us that they find a lacuna, and that it is necessary to make some provision. If that is their object, then their honest and straightforward course is to come before the House and place all the facts before us. Now, I do not admit for a moment that there is a lacuna, and I do not admit that such a principle should be introduced in the criminal jurisprudence of our country, especially and admittedly when it does not exist anywhere else. I am prepared to assume that you honestly and sincerely believe that it is necessary, in the interest of the people and the administration of justice, that some such measure of the kind should be introduced. Then your honest course is to go slowly. Pause and consider. Let those outside this House who are competent to speak, express their opinion. What are you going to lose? What is the harm that will be done? Remove from your mind this Lahore conspiracy case. But if you say that this course will cause you inconvenience and that you want this instrument now and at once, then I say that I am not satisfied with your plea and I can't support it, nor am I satisfied with the version that you have placed before the House about you difficulties. I am not going to give you this power standing on the floor of this House, today, now and here.

Sir, can you imagine a more horrible form of torture than hungerstrike? If, rightly or wrongly, these men are inflicting this punishment upon themselves and thereby you are inconvenienced, is that any reason why you should ask us to abandon one of the cardinal principles of criminal jurisprudence? If these young men pursue this course, and I am sorry to hear that one of them has died, what will happen? Is this a matter which can continue indefinitely? Certainly not. As I say, I am not satisfied with the version that you have placed before this House. I understand that some of the prisoners are not on strike. If you are solicitous and anxious that their trial should proceed and should not be delayed, then split up the trial. Proceed against them and bring home the guilt to them if you can. I am told that it means expense. I am told that 400 witnesses are going to be produced and 200 more maybe added. Now, I appeal to the common sense of the House and not only of Sir Darcy Lindsay. Can you imagine that 600 witnesses are necessary to prove the case against each one of the accused? And, Sir, I ask, is it not an amazing fact that, in order to prove this case, 600 persons should have been cited as witnesses? Well, Sir, it may seem a joke and it may seem that I am making fun of the statement made to this effect, but the first impression that one gets is that, when a case cannot be proved without the testimony of 600 witnesses, that case is a very bad case. Therefore, I say that it is open to Government to split up the case. You think of expense? But are we here to abandon this cardinal principle because it is going to cost some money to Government? Is that the reason? Is that a plea which can be accepted by any responsible Legislature?

Well, Sir, I was told that some of them go on a hungerstrike for a short time and then they get better for a little while and again and again they start, and so it goes on. Sir, I cannot understand the anxiety of the Government to proceed with this trial when these men are inflicting the greatest possible punishment upon themselves by prolonged fasting? Is it your fault? Does it mean that you are not treating them properly and, therefore you are compelling them to resort to these extreme methods? Well, then I appeal to you with all the emphasis I can command do not be vindictive. Show that you are fair, generous, that you are willing to treat these men decently. At any rate, before they are released or sentenced, give them proper treatment. What treatment do they want? What is it that bothers them? Do they want spring mattresses? Do they want dressing tables? Do they want a set of toilet requisites? No, Sir, they ask for noting but bare necessities and a little better treatment. I ask you in all decency, why cannot you concede this small thing? Well, Sir, if this Bill is passed, perhaps I might ask the Hon'ble Member when he goes to Court how would he base his application? Will he base his application on the point that the period of a hungerstrike which has already taken place for a short period is not to be counted? Or is it to be counted? Or is it to be counted? Supposing I tried to put myself in the position of a Judge when the application is made that the presence of the accused in this case should be dispensed with, because by their own voluntary act they have rendered themselves incapable. Now, from what period shall I take the disability? From the period after this statute is passed? Shall I disregard the disability which has already taken place before the passing of the Act? Supposing something else happens to these men on hunger-strike and they do not get well for two or three months. Will the trial not be delayed? Do you think you can avoid considerable delay even if the Bill is passed? Further, can you give a guarantee that all the prisoners will be well enough in the course of these two or three months from now to stand their trial. Even if they abandon hungerstrike? When you say that this Bill will not have retrospective effect, how is it going to work? Then will you give them notice that in view of the fact that this measure is passed, if you do not cease your hungerstrike from today and if you are not better within two or three months, as you ought to be, then we shall apply to the court that your presence will be dispensed with and we shall proceed *ex parte*? Does it not come to this, that you want to carry this Bill, you want to have this Bill placed on the Statute-book, and then you want to give notice to the prisoners that, unless they cease their hungerstrike within a certain period, you are going to proceed *ex parte*? Under that threat you think these prisoners will cease their hungerstrike? Can you give the House that assurance, and if they do not cease their hungerstrike, what will you do? You will proceed *ex parte*? Just imagine the absurdity of the whole position.

Sir, now I have finished from the point of view of the jurisprudence. I do not wish to go into details so far as their treatment is concerned. I have, in the course of my speech, already indicated their grievances and how they can be met. But there is a political aspect of this Bill and the policy underlying this measure. I think the Hon'ble Home Member must admit that this is not a measure which is only brought here for the purpose of putting the law in order. Sir, it reminds me of a story, an old Persian story. A man got stomachache because he had eaten some very rotten bread. So he went to the doctor and told him that he had stomachache. The doctor said, yes, and he promptly started treating his eyes. Then he said, 'What have my eyes got to do with my complaint ?' Then the doctor said, 'Well, if you had eyes, you would never have got stomachache because you would not have eaten rotten bread'.

Similarly I would say to the Hon'ble Home Member, 'Have you got eyes? Well, if you had, you would never gave got this stomachache'. Now, will you open your eyes? Will you have a little more imagination? Have you got any statesmanship left? Have you got any political wisdom? This is not the way you are going to solve the root cause of the trouble. You may temporarily, provisionally, get over this particular trial. But now let us see what is the real cause of the trouble.

I ask this House to consider this. Is there today in any part of the globe a civilized government that is engaged, day in and day out, week in and week out, month in and month out, in prosecuting their people? You have read the daily papers for the last six, eight months. You will find prosecutions in Bengal, prosecutions in Madras, prosecutions in the Punjab, prosecutions all over the country. In fact I am afraid you will soon have to open a new department and to have an additional member to manage these prosecutions if you go on at this rate and in this way. Do you think that any man wants to go to jail ? Is it an easy thing ? Do you think any man wants to exceed the bounds of law for the purpose of making a speech which your law characterizes as a seditious speech, knowing full well the consequences, that he may have to go to jail for six months or a year? Do you think that this springs out of a mere joke or fun or amusement? Do you not realise yourself, if you open your eyes, that there is resentment, universal resentment, against your policy, against your programme?

Then, Sir, what has happened so far as this House is concerned? What have you done since 1924 with regard to the protests that we have made session after session? Have you accepted the proposal or suggestion of any reasonable section of this House? I do not wish to go into the details, Sir, but what has been the attitude of the Government towards this House and the country outside over the constitutional reforms since 1924, leave alone the past prior history ? The reply is, 'We have appointed the Simon Commission and we must must await its Report.' Well, the Simon Commission was not accepted by this House–but that does not matter. What is the answer in regard to the Indianization of the Army? You appointed a Committee to go into that very important question; I attach more importance to it than to any other question. What have you done with the unanimous report of the Skeen Committee which was endorsed by this House, without a division, the responsible House as you call it today and to which you appeal today in the name of 'responsibility'? This House endorsed that report without a division. What have you done with it? The attitude of Government has been amazing one. The Army Secretary stood there on the floor of this House last session and said, 'We cannot get even 20 suitable candidates'. Sir, the apparent untruth of that statement is enough to condemn the Government. You cannot get 20 young men out of 300 odd millions of people, who are suitable candidates for the King's Commission?

Then, there are many other matters. What has been your attitude always?

Don't you think that, instead of trying to proceed with an iron hand and pursuing a policy of repression against your own subjects, it would be better if you realized the root causes of the resentment and of the struggle that the people are carrying on? Don't you think that it is high time that you made you position more clear? I understand that there is something in the atmosphere– I hope it is true–that some satisfactory announcement is going to be made in Parliament very soon, when it meets next, which I trust will satisfy this House and the people. Do you want to prepare an atmosphere for it, or you do not ? Do you want reconciliation between the Government and the people or you do not? Don't you think that these difficulties and troubles of yours are of a temporary character? They are an obstruction in the trial of this particular case which can be managed by other methods, but that is a very small matter when you compare it with the bigger issues which are awaiting the decision of the Government, this House and the country.

Sir, the Hon'ble Member asked, what are the Government to do? I think I understood the Hon'ble Member aright when he said that the Government have no other course. What are the Government to do? They are, therefore, compelled to bring this Bill. Now, let me tell you that your course is to open your eyes, have more imagination, do not be guilty of bankruptcy of statesmanship, do not merely sit there as if the wheels of the Secretariat must not be clogged at any cost, but try and understand the root cause and deal with the situation as politicians, as statesmen and not as bureaucrats, who can see no other way but to come forward before this House and ask for more statutory powers the moment any difficulty arises. You have got several courses open to you. The first and the foremost course open to you is this. Give these men decent treatment, and I think you will get over your difficulty. At least I hope so. If you do not, you will, at any rate, be exonerated in the eyes of the public and at the Bar of public opinion. Behave as a humane and decent Government, and that is enough for you. I am not going to urge upon the Government to withdraw prosecution cases against men if they have evidence enough to bring home to them their guilt. So try that better treatment first. Secondly, if you do not succeed, split up the trials. Try those with whose trial you can proceed, and leave the rest. After you have made it clear to them that you stand for a decent treatment being given to them and they still wish to torture themselves and follow that course, then you cannot help it; and I venture to say that it will not last very long or indefinitely. And the last words I wish to address the Government are, try and concentrate your mind on the root cause and the more you concentrate on the root cause the less difficulties and inconveniences there will be for you to face, and thank Heaven that the money of the taxpayer will not be wasted in prosecuting men, nay citizens, who are fighting and struggling for the freedom of their country.

Legislative Assembly Debates, Vol. IV, Part I,
pp. 752-55 and 757-65.

Annexure 5

Daily Workers (New York) Report March 25 and 27, 1931

LABOR GOV'T EXECUTES 3 INDIA REBELS

Frame-up Revolutionists For British Imperialism

(Cable By Inprecorr.)

LONDON, March 24.—The three Lahore prisoners; Bhagat Singh, Raj Guru and Sukh Dev, fighters for the independence of India, have been executed by the British labor government in the interest of British imperialism. This is one of the bloodiest deeds ever undertaken by the British labor government, under the leadership of MacDonald.

The Indian National Congress opens at Karachi on Thursday. Indignation against the executions is causing mass opposition to the Gandhi-Irwin agreement. The Punjab members of the legislature propose an adjournment and censure of the government for the execution. The London press declares the Karachi congress is the supreme test of Gandhi's authority and doubts Gandhi's success.

* * *

The execution of the three Indian revolutionists, on a deliberate political frame-up, at the orders of the labor government, shows the lengths to which the MacDonald regime will go to save British imperialism in India. The MacDonald government, which weeps bitter tears over the trial of the counter-revolutionary Mensheviks in the Soviet Union who received splendid treatment although they plotted for war against the workers and peasants of the Soviet Union, deliberately fosters the most brutal tortures against Indian revolutionaries.

The three executed Indian revolutionists were arrested on the charge of setting off a bomb last April, as well as for the murder of Lieutenant Saunders, a police official, who had beaten thousands and killed many Indian workers.

Against the suspects arrested, the labor government vented its wrath and hate. All of the prisoners were beaten and tortured through special methods invented by the British imperialists and the "labor" administrators.

* * * * * * * * *

Jatin Das, one of the accused, who died before he could be executed, was tortured for 63 days. He was paralyzed and blinded by the torture. His blood circulation had stopped except around his heart. His body was reduced to 19 pounds at his death. His funeral was attended by 50,000 bearing slogans and banners saying: "Long Live the Revolution," and "Down With Imperialism."

The other prisoners were all tortured and beaten repeatedly. They were handcuffed and flogged by the "civilizers" of the British labor government. One Indian paper describes the tortures as follows:

"Each prisoner was assaulted by at least 20 to 25 policemen, the methods of assault being most inhuman." (The actual details are unprintable.) "One method employed was the penetration of the fingers into the rectum and kicking the private parts. The assault continued for more than one hour, after which five prisoners got fever; all others had acute pains in different parts of the body. Mahabi Singh and Raj Gure fell down senseless on the spot. Canes were frequently used, and marks can be actually seen on these prisoners."

Now they are executed. The "socialist" leaders of the British imperialist government go to all lengths to stop the rising tide of revolution. Neither they nor their bourgeois tool, Gandhi, nor all their tortures and killings will be able to stop the growing struggles of the great masses of Indian workers and peasants.

Extract from the *Daily Worker* (New York) No. 75

dated 27th, the March 1931.

75 KILLED; 500 HURT BY LABOR GOV'T SOLDIERS

Fighting Spreading in India; Gandhi for Real Betrayal

(Cable by Inprecorr)

BERLIN, March 26.—A rigid censorship has been clamped down in Cawnpore, India, by the British labor government to prevent the truth of the widespread fighting from being known.

Seventy-five are already dead and at least 500 have been wounded. An exodus of 30,000 people took place from the city last night, due to the fighting. Large British military forces are enforcing martial law. All railroad bookings to Cawnpore have been stopped, unless a special permit is issued.

New fighting has started in the Tharawaddy forest where two British platoons were reported to have killed 22 rebels . The outbreak is spreading. Reinforcements, including armored trains are being rushed by the British to the affected district.

The fighting in Cawnpore followed the lynching by the British imperialist labor government of three Indian revolutionists, after they had been frightfully tortured.

Latest reports from Karachi, India, by the Associated Press and the United Press tell of the growing opposition to Gandhi. Gandhi is trying to put over his sell-out with Lord Irwin, British viceroy of India, by all means, threatening to retire for life if the betrayal is not accepted.

The United Press staff correspondent in Karchi where the Indian National Congress is meeting writes:

"The independence leader, who was the object of hostile demonstrations by 'red shirts' throughout last night, told newspapermen that the execution of Nationalist extremists at Lahore had not affected his position toward the peace settlement." That is to say, Gandhi's object is to do the dirty work for British imperialism, despite everything. He said that the British or with his lieutenantDWILNNUPNI government had "committed a first-class blunder," making it harder for Gandhi to put over the sell-out.

Refused an interview with Gandhi or with his lieutenant, Jawarhalal Nehru, who is parading as a "left," the "red shirt" representatives departed shouting: "Who killed Bhagat Singh?" and answering, "Gandhi! Gandhi"!

More "red shirts" are arriving at Karachi. The "red shirts" are a militant youth organization who do not approve of Gandhi's program of uniting with the British imperialists.

Not only are there reports of fighting in Cawnpore and the Tharwaddy forest as well as the Insein regions, but mass demonstrations against the British are taking place in Bombay and Calcutta.

E. F. S. (Breach of Anglo Russian Agreement file) to P.A.

Sd/- F. F. P. Gill
4. 5. 31.

Annexure 6

Bhagat Singh Ki Moorat (Statue of Bhagat Singh)

—Fahmida Riyaz

There is news from Delhi
alas! Alas!!
What a mess they have made
Of Bhagat Singh
In the Parliament Complex!

For 60 years they petitioned
The British rejected him
But YOU! Our own government.
Erect his statue
in the Parliament Complex
At last the government thumped its chest
and said why not!
and erected the statue in the Parliament Complex.
But when the veil was lifted
You discover it is not Bhagat Singh
That 24 year old beautiful lad
Nor his young limbs that they could not properly burn
On the fateful night when they hanged him

It is some 60 years old guy
Flabby and tired looking

With upturned mustaches
Oh what the hell is this.
This is not our Bhagat Singh
In the Parliament Square
Who the hell is he ?

Ha ha ha ! Dear friends
Wipe your tears look closely
At all the other statues in the Parliament
Is it the same Jawahar Lal as he was? Is it the same Gandhi?
The same Abul Kalam Azad?

The in-coming and out-going respected parliamentarians
Have made an omelete of their reality
And gobbled them up long long ago.
In this grand square
Only cissored and edited versions
Can find a lasting place.

Bhagat Singh was the child of his time
And times have changed. He loved Urdu poetry and Ghalib
And Ghalib, getting rid of his robe
Is Galib now, winking and singing some trashy "*gajal*"
Aishwarya Rai is dancing on it
So kind of her.

And in his city Lahore
Bhagat Singh is a Sikh
Who perhaps migrated to India in '47
Such names make people nervous
Is the god-damn man coming back?
to claim his property??
We shall never let that happen
After all we left fields and barns
shops and houses
in Ludhyana.

Bhagat Singh was a pure Indian
His times are swept away with the wind
He was a purely Indian earth-song
Light in the water
Rustling in the wind
He was a purely Indian passion of his time
And times have changed.

Let his statue remain where it has remained for 60 years
Across both sides of the border
In a heart or two.
There every morning
Longings as innocent and ignorant as little children
Cover his young body with fresh garlands of marigold
Bathe his limbs with tears of love and adoration
He belongs there
He is happy there.

"The aim of life is no more to control the mind, but to develop it

(Urdu original—English translation by the poet)

Bibliography

Hindi Readings

1. 'भविष्य', भगत सिंह विशेषांक, संपादक रामरख सिंह सहगल, इलाहाबाद (जब्त) 16 अप्रैल, 1931
2. 'अभ्युदय' भगत सिंह विशेषांक, संपादक पद्मकांत मालवीय इलाहाबाद (जब्त), 8 मई, 1931
3. 'चाँद' (फाँसी अंक), संपादक चतुर सेन शास्त्री नवंबर, 1928 इलाहाबाद (जब्त)
4. भगत सिंह की जेल डायरी, वेदस्वरूप नीरज एवं ज्ञान कौर कपूर, राज पब्लिशिंग, जयपुर
5. पल प्रतिपल, (पंचकूला) भगत सिंह विशेषांक, सं. देश निर्मोही, 2006
6. उद्भावना, भगत सिंह विशेषांक, सं. अजय कुमार, दिल्ली, 2007
7. उत्तरार्द्ध, सं. सव्यसाची, भगत सिंह विशेषांक, मथुरा, अक्टूबर 1988
8. वे इन्कलाबी दिन, वीरेंद्र, राजपाल एंड संज, संस्करण, 1986
9. सरदार भगत सिंह (महाकाव्य), श्रीकृष्ण सरल, राष्ट्रीय प्रकाशन, उज्जैन, प्रथम संस्करण, 1964
10. स्मारिका: शहीद भगत सिंह विशेषांक, ज्ञान-विज्ञान समिति, वाराणसी, 2007
11. भगत सिंह: दुर्गा भाभी स्मारिका, शहीद स्मारक, लखनऊ, 2007
12. भगत सिंह: तब और अब, संपादक राम कविंद्र, सुभाष गुप्त, जमशेदपुर, 2001
13. पांचजन्य, सं. तरुण विजय, दिल्ली, मार्च 2007
14. विचारों की सान पर (भगत सिंह स्मारिका) सं. सुधीर सुमन, आरा, 2007
15. युवा संवाद, सं. ए. के. अरूण, भगत सिंह का भारत, दिल्ली, नवंबर 2007
16. भगत सिंह स्मारिका, श्रमिक संघ, मुंबई, 1981
17. उज्ज्वल ध्रुवतारा, सं. जी.पी. मिश्र, इलाहाबाद, जुलाई-सितंबर 2007

18. फिलहाल, सं. प्रीति सिन्हा, शहीद भगत सिंह स्मृति अंक, पटना, अप्रैल 2007
19. अमर शहीद भगत सिंह, सरस्वती पुस्तक एजेंसी, कलकत्ता, (जब्त) 1931
20. आज़ादी के चिराग, रामचंद्र चंद्रदेव, गया, (जब्त) 1932
21. आज़ादी के दीवाने, पंडित शिव संपति उपाध्याय, बनारस, (जब्त)
22. आज़ादी की आग (काव्य), चिरंजी लाल शर्मा, बनारस (जब्त)
23. आज़ादी की तान (काव्य), रामनंदन शाह, छपरा, (जब्त) 1932
24. आज़ादी की तरंग (काव्य), काले सिंह, सोनीपत, (जब्त) 1931
25. बलिवेदी पर (काव्य) युवक हृदय, (जब्त) 1931
26. भगत सिंह (काव्य), हर्षदत्त पांडेय 'श्याम', कानपुर (जब्त)
27. भगत सिंह की वीरता (काव्य), सरस्वती पुस्तक एजेंसी, कलकत्ता, (जब्त) 1931
28. भारतीय वीर, दिल्ली, (जब्त) 1931
29. दुनिया का चाँद उर्फगम का ढोला, फगर साओ हलवाई, कोलकाता, (जब्त) 1932
30. फाँसी के शहीद (काव्य), राजाराम नायर, प्रयाग, (जब्त) 1931
31. जिगर के टुकडे, शिव शभू मिश्र, हावडा, (जब्त) 1931
32. कराची कांग्रेस, हिंदी साहित्य मंदिर, अजमेर, (जब्त) 1931
33. कौमी परवाना, पन्नालाल गुजराती, कोलकाता, (जब्त) 1931
34. खून के आँसू, सरस्वती पुस्तक एजेंसी, कोलकाता, (जब्त) 1931
35. क्रांति की चिंगारी (काव्य), रामचंद्र सर्राफ, बनारस, (जब्त) 1931
36. क्रांति का पुजारी, मोहन लाल 'अरमान', कानपुर, (जब्त) 1931
37. क्रांति पुष्पांजलि (काव्य), सुमेंद्र मुकर्जी, देहरादून, (जब्त) 1931
38. लाहौर की सूली अर्थात सरदार भगत सिंह मस्ताना, शभूनारायण मिश्र, गया, (जब्त) 1931
39. लाहौर के शहीद, स्वामी, आजाद ग्रंथ माला, जबलपुर, (जब्त) 1931
40. लाहौर की फाँसी अर्थात भगत सिंह का तराना, एन. एल. ए. बामलट, बनारस (जब्त) 1931
41. मर्दाना भगत सिंह (काव्य), श्रीयुत प्रताप सुतंतर, अलीगढ़, (जब्त) 1931
42. मतवाला गायन, माता प्रसाद शुक्ल, बनारस, (जब्त) 1931
43. नई कजली सावन बम केस उर्फ भगत सिंह की फाँसी और बनारस के दंगे की नई कजली (हिंदी गीत), मार्कण्डेय, बनारस, (जब्त) 1931
44. प्रभात फेरी (गीत), संपादक पीण्बी पाठक, मुंबई, (जब्त) 1931
45. राष्ट्रीय आल्हा यानि भगत सिंह की लडाई (काव्य), सूर्यप्रसाद मिश्र, कानपुर, (जब्त) 1931
46. शहीदों की आहें, मिर्जापुर, (जब्त) 1931

47. सरदार भगत सिंह, के. एल. गुप्ता, आगरा, (जब्त) 1931
48. सरदार भगत सिंह की नई कजरी: सावन के सिंह (गीत), गोपाल गुप्ता, बनारस, (जब्त) 1931
49. सरदार भगत सिंह के गाने (गीत), पं. रामविलास अवस्थी, लखनऊ, (जब्त) 1931
50. शहीद भगत सिंह, शभू प्रसाद मिश्र, कलकत्ता, (जब्त) 1931
51. शहीदे नवरत्न (गीत), शर्मा शिवकलश् कानपुर, (जब्त) 1931-52. शहीदे वतन, प्रभाकर जी, कलकत्ता, (जब्त) 1931
53. शहीदों का संदेश, गांधी की जंग (काव्य), मनोहर चंद्र, दिल्ली, (जब्त) 1931
54. शहीदों का तराना, शंभू प्रसाद मिश्र, कलकत्ता, (जब्त) 1931
55. शहीदों के गाने, शिवदत्त अवस्थी, लखनऊ, (जब्त) 1931
56. शहीदों की यादगार (काव्य), सत्यनारायण धौरिया, अभ्युदय प्रेस, इलाहाबाद, (जब्त) 1931
57. सुलह और राष्ट्रीय पुकार (काव्य), रामविलास अवस्थी, लखनऊ, (जब्त) 1931
58. स्वतंत्रता भगत सिंह और जेलों की खुशबस्ती, फकीरा शर्मा, मुजफ्फरपुर, (जब्त) 1931
59. तराने सरदार भगत सिंह, धर्म सिंह आर्य, दिल्ली, (जब्त) 1931
60. वीरों के गानेरू फाँसी के पुजारी, धर्म सिंह आर्य, दिल्ली, (जब्त) 1931
61. वीरों का झूला (काव्य), लक्ष्मण लाल, झाँसी, (जब्त) 1931
62. युवक गर्जना (काव्य), काशीराम तिवारी, इलाहाबाद, (जब्त) 1931
63. क्रांतिकारी भगत सिंह, सुरेश, हिंद पॉकेट बुक्स, दिल्ली
64. अमर शहीद भगत सिंह, सं. वीरेंद्र संधू, प्रकाशन विभाग भारत सरकार, 1974
65. मेरे क्रांतिकारी साथी—भगत सिंह, सं. वीरेंद्र संधू, राजपाल एंड संज, दिल्ली, 1977
66. पत्र और दस्तावेज, सं. वीरेंद्र संधू, राजपाल एंड संज, दिल्ली, 1977
67. युगद्रष्टा भगत सिंह और उनके मृत्युंजय पुरखे, वीरेंद्र संधू, ज्ञानपीठ प्रकाशन, 1968
68. शहीद भगत सिंह, रामदुलारे त्रिवेदी, कानपुर, 1938
69. क्रांतिकारी भगत सिंह, शकर सुलतानपुरी, हिंद पॉकेट बुक्स, दिल्ली, 1969
70. आज़ादी के परवाने, आरण्सहगल
71. भगत सिंह, रमेश विद्रोही, भावना प्रकाशन, दिल्ली, 1982
72. जब ज्योति जगी, सुखदेव राज, क्रांतिकारी प्रकाशन, मिर्जापुर, 1971, विश्वभारती प्रकाशन, नागपुर, 2007
73. विप्लव यज्ञ की आहुतियाँ, बटुकनाथ अग्रवाल, क्रांतिकारी प्रकाशन, मिर्जापुर, 1971

74. यादों की परछाइयाँ, चतुरसेन शास्त्री, राजपाल एंड संज, दिल्ली
75. शहीदे आजम भगत सिंह, सत्यशकुन, सन्मार्ग प्रकाशन, दिल्ली
76. खून की होली: क्रांतिकारियों की रोमांचक गाथाएँ, सुखसागर सिन्हा
77. तीन महान क्रांतिकारी, नरेंद्र कुमार
78. भगत सिंह: व्यक्तित्व और विचार, नरेश सूरीध्रागिनी मिश्रा, मोहिनी गुप्ता, राधा पब्लिकेशस, दिल्ली
79. श्स्वतंत्रता संग्राम और भगत सिंह, डॉ रघुबीर सिंह, राधा पब्लिकेशंस, दिल्ली
80. क्रांतिवीर भगत सिंह, सत्यभक्त, कानपुर, 1932
81. तीन क्रांतिकारी शहीद: शहीद भगत सिंह, आर. एल. बंसल, भारती भवन, आगरा, 1962
82. इन्कलाबी यात्रा, छबीलदास, सीता देवी, एन.बी.टी., दिल्ली, 2006
83. सूरज का सफर (भगत सिंह), दीपचंद निर्मोही, इतिहासबोध, 2007
84. भगत सिंह से दोस्ती, सं. विकास नारायण राय, इतिहासबोध, 2007
85. भगत सिंह पर चुनींदा लेख, सं. एम.एम. जुनेजा, हिसार, 2007
86. स्मारिका: अर्द्ध शताब्दी, सं. बनारसी दास चतुर्वेदी, आगरा, 1981
87. भगत सिंह होने का मतलब, मुद्राराक्षस, इतिहासबोध, 2008
88. क्रांतिवीर भगत सिंह: लालबहादुर सिंह चौहान, आत्माराम एंड संज, दिल्ली, 2006
89. क्रांतिकारी भगत सिंह: सुभाष रस्तोगी, सूर्यभारती, दिल्ली, 2000
90. भगत सिंह और उनका युग, मन्मथ नाथ गुप्त, लिपि प्रकशन, दिल्ली, 1985
91. भगत सिंह एक जीवनी, हंसराज रहबर, वाणी प्रकाशन, दिल्ली, 1988
92. भगत सिंह विचारधारा, हंसराज रहबर, दिल्ली
93. बंदी जीवन, शचिंद्रनाथ सान्याल, आत्माराम एंड संज, दिल्ली
94. संस्मृतियाँ, शिव वर्मा, निधि, दिल्ली, 1983
95. अमर शहीदों के संस्मरण, राजाराम शास्त्री, साधना, कानपुर, 1961
96. यश की धरोहर, शिव वर्मा 'माहौर' मल्कापुरकर, आत्माराम एंड संज, दिल्ली, 1988
97. एक क्रांतिकारी के संस्मरण, राजेंद्रपाल सिंह वारियार शहीद समारक, लखनऊ
98. मेरे भाई शहीद सुखदेव, मथुरादास थापर, प्रवीण प्रकाशन, दिल्ली 1998
99. अमर शहीद भगत सिंह, विष्णु प्रभाकर, किताबघर, दिल्ली
100. शहीद भगत सिंह: क्रांति में एक प्रयोग, कुलदीप नायर, डायमंड, दिल्ली, 2001
101. मैं भगत सिंह बोल रहा हूँ (तीन खंड) राजशेखर व्यास, प्रवीण प्रकाशन, दिल्ली, 2001
102. मृत्युंजय भगत सिंह, राजशेखर व्यास, ग्रंथ आकादमी, नई दिल्ली, 2007

103. भगत सिंह: स्मृति में प्रेरणा, विचारों में दिशा, सं. अजय कुमार, उद्भावना, दिल्ली, 2008
104. सिंहावलोकन, यशपाल, लोकभारती, इलाहाबाद, 1994
105. क्रांतिकारी बैकुंठ शुक्ल का मुकदमा, राजकमल, दिल्ली, 2002
106. अमर शहीद सरदार भगत सिंह, जितेंद्रनाथ सान्याल, नेशनल बुक ट्रस्ट, 2005
107. शहीद-ए-आजम भगत सिंह, सुरेशचंद्र श्रीवास्तव, साधना, दिल्ली, 2005
108. शहीद सम्राट सरदार भगत सिंह, सोहनलाल सिंगारिया, सम्यक्, दिल्ली, 2005
109. शहीद भगत सिंह : इन्कलाब का सफर, सुधीर विद्यार्थी, जनसुलभ बरेली, 2006
110. लेनिन और भारत, लेण्मित्रोखिन, प्रगति, मास्को, 1087
111. फाँसी लाहौर की (काव्य), संण्गुरदेव सिंह सिद्धू, नेशनल बुक ट्रस्ट, दिल्ली, 2006
112. क्रांतिकारी भगत सिंह (काव्य) शाति स्वरूप कुसुम, साहित्य वीथी, दिल्ली, 1997
113. अमर शहीद भगत सिंह (काव्य), शांति स्वरूप कुसुम, साहित्य वीथी, दिल्ली, 1996
114. वीर भगत सिंह (काव्य), हीराप्रसाद ठाकुर, आगरा
115. इन्कलाब (उपन्यास) मृणालिनी जोशी, प्रभात प्रकाशन, दिल्ली, 2005
116. शहीद-ए-आजम (उपन्यास), बच्चन सिंह, आत्माराम एंड संज, दिल्ली, 2006
117. अनित्य (उपन्यास), मृदुला गर्ग, नेशनल दिल्ली, 2004
118. राष्ट्र नायक भगत सिंह, दीपंकर भट्टाचार्य, समकालीन, पटना, 2006
119. भगत सिंह, राजगुरू और सुखदेव, जन नाट्य मंच, दिल्ली, 2006
120. शहीद-ए-आजम भगत सिंह, शहीद यादगार समिति, कोलकाता, 2002
121. शहीदों की वसीयत और विरासत, भूपेंद्र हूजा, जयपुर, 2002
122. शहीदे आजम भगत सिंह, सव्यसाची, मथुरा
123. अमर शहीद सरदार भगत सिंह, रामसिंह बघेले, ग्वालियर 1982
124. शहीदे आजम भगत सिंह: एक गंभीर अध्येता, रघुवीर सिंह, उद्भावना, दिल्ली, 2007
125. हवा में रहेगी मेरे खयाल की बिजली, मनोज शर्मा, उद्भावना, दिल्ली, 2007
126. शहीदे आजम भगत सिंह, सरला माहेशवरी, उद्भावना दिल्ली, 2007
127. नव उपनिवेशवाद के खतरे और भगत सिंह की क्रांतिकारी विरासत, चमन लाल, 2007, उद्भावना, दिल्ली
128. शहीद भगत सिंह की चुनी हुई कृतियाँ, सं. शिव वर्मा, समाजवादी साहित्य सदन, कानपुर, 1987
129. भगत सिंह और उनके साथियों के दस्तावेज, जगमोहन सिंह, चमन लाल, राजकमल प्रकाशन, दिल्ली, 1986

130. भगत सिंह के संपूर्ण दस्तावेज, सं. चमन लाल, आधार, पंचकूला, 2004
131. भगत सिंह के राजनीतिक दस्तावेज, सं. चमन लाल, नेशनल बुक ट्रस्ट, दिल्ली, 2007
132. शहीद भगत सिंहः दस्तावेजों के आईने में, सं. चमन लाल, प्रकाशन विभाग, भारत सरकार, नई दिल्ली, 2007
133. भगत सिंह और उनके साथियों के संपूर्ण उपलब्ध दस्तावेज, संण्सत्यम, राहुल फाउंडेशन, लखनऊ, 2006
134. युगद्रष्टा भगत सिंह, शहीद भगत सिंह सेवा समिति, हैदराबाद, 2007
135. शहीदे आजम भगत सिंहः क्रांतिकारी संघर्ष का वैचारिक उत्कर्ष, रघुवीर सिंह, कन्फ्लुऐंस प्रकाशन, 2008
136. भगत सिंहः व्यक्तित्व और विचारः मोहिनी गुप्ता, राधा पब्लिकेशन्स, नई दिल्ली
137. आयरिश स्वतंत्रता युद्ध डान व्रीन (अनुवाद : भगत सिंह) प्रताप कार्यालय, कानपुर, 1928
138. मेरी कहानी (अनुवाद : भगत सिंह), राजशेखर व्यास निधि, दिल्ली, 1989
139. भगत सिंह का रास्ता, गीतेश शर्मा, मानव प्रकाशन, हावड़ा, 2008
140. खयालात की बिजलियां, डॉ रणजीत-अनूप कपूर लोकभारती, इलाहाबाद 2008
141. शहीदे आज़म भगत सिंह., ए.पी. कमल, राज पाकेट बुक्स दिल्ली, 2002
142. 'मुक्ति' (भगत सिंह : विशेषांक), सं. त्रिनेत्र जोशी, सुरेश सलिल, मंगलेश डबराल, दिल्ली
143. कलम आज उनकी जय बोल, जगदीश जगेश, प्रचारक ग्रंथमाला बनारस
144. लाहौर षडयंत्र अर्थात भगत सिंह, कुंवर सिंह, बनारस सिटी, (जब्त) 1930
145. शेर भगत सिंह, मा. के. एल. गुप्ता, (जब्त) 1931
146. मर्दाना भगत सिंह, प्रभुदयाल डंडेवाला, दिल्ली, 1931
147. शहीद भगत सिंह, चंद्रावती देवी, लाहौर, 1931
148. लाहौर के शहीद, गोकुलदास प्रिंटिग प्रेस, अलीगढ़
149. भगत सिंह की वार्ता, राधेशयाम प्रकाशन, कोलकाता 1931
150. लाहौर की सूली, प्रताप नारायण मिश्र, बनारस, (जब्त) 1931
151. अमर शहीद सरदार भगत सिंह, बद्री प्रसाद, हिंदी साहित्य मंदिर, मथुरा, (जब्त) 1937
152. क्रांतिकारियों के संस्मरण, झारखंडे राय, पी.पी.एच. दिल्ली, 1970
153. भारतीय क्रांतिकारी आंदोलन, झारखंडे राय, पी.पी.एच. दिल्ली, 1970
154. सरदार भगत सिंह (नाटक), भगवान दास माहौर, झांसी, 1980
155. सरदार भगत सिंह (नाटक), देवी प्रसाद विकल, चैतन्य प्रकाशन कानपुर, 1962

156. गगन दमामा बाजयो (नाटक), पीयूष मिश्र, इतिहास बोध प्रकाशन, इलाहाबाद, 2002
157. शहीद भगत सिंह, लालचंद जैन, पुस्तक भंडार, जयपुर, 2000
158. भगत सिंह का आल्हा, सुदर्शन चक्र, कानपुर
159. क्रांति का देवता सरदार भगत सिंह, विष्णु दत्त, 1962
160. भगत सिंह का गुमशुदा पत्र, संपादक डॉ. ब्रह्मेश्वर दयाल, प्रकाशन संस्थान दिल्ली, 2007
161. शहीद भगत सिंह, भवान सिंह राणा, डायमंड दिल्ली, 2006
162. क्रांति के पथ पर, शचिन्द्रनाथ बख्शी, लोकहित, लखनऊ, 2003
162. भारत में सशस्त्र क्रांति की भूमिका, तारिणीशकर चक्रवर्ती, क्रांतिकारी प्रकाशन, मिर्जापुर, 1972
164. क्रांतिकारियों की कहानियां, श्रीकृष्ण सरल, उज्जैन, 1980
165. शहीद भगत सिंह, क्रांति का साक्ष्य, सं. सुधीर विद्यार्थी, राजकमल, 2009
166. क्रांतिकारी महानायक, भगत सिंह, गोदारण (अलीगढ़) सं. भरत सिंह, 2008
167. अमर शहीद भगत सिंह, अखिल भारतीय कांग्रेस कमेटी
168. भगत सिंह, कृष्ण माधव साखवलाकर, पंजाब सरकार, चंडीगढ
169. क्रांतिकारी प्रेरणा के स्रोत, रतनलाल जोशी, 1971
170. मृत्युंजयी, रतनलाल जोशी, 1985
171. भगत सिंह, चमन लाल, मेधा बुक्स दिल्ली, 2009
172. शहीदे आजम भगत सिंह के असली वारिस कौन? एल. आर. ण्बाली, भीम पत्रिका पब्लिकेशज, डॉ. अंबेडकर मार्ग, जालंधर-144 003
173. शहीदे-ए-आजम भगत सिंह—ए. आई. डी. एस. ओ. कार्यालय, कारोल बाग, नई दिल्ली
174. भारतीय क्रांतिकारी आंदोलन, शभूनाथ स्नेहिल ब्रह्मचारी, क्लाईमेक्स, नई दिल्ली, 1991
175. भारतीय स्वतंत्रता आंदोलन में क्रांतिकारियों की भूमिका, मांगेराम आर्य, नई दिल्ली, 1991
176. भगत सिंह इतिहास के कुछ पन्ने, प्रेमचंद सहजवाला, दिल्ली, 2009
177. शहीद भगत सिंह, कृष्ण विकल, हिंद पॉकेट बुक्स, दिल्ली, प्र. सं. 2002, पृष्ठ 128, मूल्य 50
178. सरदार भगत सिंह: स्वतंत्रता संघर्ष में योगदान, डॉण्वर्षा आलोक, जया प्रकाशन, न्यू आगरा, पृष्ठ 240, मूल्य 90
179. भगत सिंह होने का मतलब, डॉ. मृणाल, शिल्पायन, दिल्ली 2011

180. सरदार भगत सिंह : व्यक्ति और विचार, विश्व प्रकाश, मोहिनी गुप्त एनमन प्रकाशन दिल्ली, 2009
181. अमर शहीद भगत सिंह, महेश शर्मा , प्रभात प्रकाशन दिल्ली, 2010
182. मैं भगत सिंह बोल रहा हूँ एस. अनिल कुमार, प्रभात, दिल्ली, 2011
183. आधुनिक भारत के सपूत: भगत सिंह, रमेश एहसास, शिलालेख, दिल्ली
184. भगत सिंह, मीनू सिंहल, प्रभात प्रकाशन, दिल्ली, 2011
185. क्रांति का सूर्यरूभगत सिंह, राजेन्द्र शर्मा, सुबोध पाकेट बुक्स, दिल्ली, 2004
186. चाहि, एक और भगत सिंह, आशा रावत, हिन्दी साहित्य निकेतन
187. शहीदे आजम भगत सिंह, विनोद तिवारी, मनोज पाकेट बुक्स, दिल्ली, 2004
188. शहीद भगत सिंह, सरस्वती ज्ञानमाला
189. सरदार भगत सिंह, जगत राम आर्य, किताबघर, दिल्ली
190. शहीदे आजम भगत सिंह, बड़ा प्रिंट
191. क्रांतिकारी सरदार भगत सिंह, सुरेश चंदर श्रीवास्तव, 1975
192. सरदार भगत सिंह, पथिक, 1956
193. सरदार भगत सिंह, जयप्रकाश भारती, 1965
194. मृत्युंजय सरदार भगत सिंह, रत्न लाल बंसल, आगरा
195. तीन क्रांतिकारी शहीद, वही, 1954
196. शहीद भगत सिंह, मनमोहन सहगल, 1971
197. क्रांतिवीर भगत सिंह, राजासिवी, राजा पाकेट बुक्स
198. भगत सिंह, रेणु सरन, डायमंड, दिल्ली, 2012
199. भगत सिंह, व्यथित हृदय, पेंगुइन, 2002
200. गांधी और भगत सिंह, अवतार सिंह जसवाल, अनामिका, दिल्ली, 2012

Punjabi Readings

1. Likhtan: Shaheed Bhagat Singh Ate Saathi, ed. Amarjit Chandan, Balraj Sahni Yaadgar Pustakmala Amritsar, 1974
2. Shaheed Bhagat Singh Ate Unah de Saathiyan Diyan Likhtan: Edited. Jagmohan Singh, Chetna Prakashan, Ludhiana, 2000 ed.
3. Shaheed Bhagat Singh Dian Kujh Chonvian Likhtan, ed. M. S. Waraich, Tarakbhart, Barnala, 2006
4. Bhagat Singh Shaheed: Chonven Mazmun Ate Kavitavan, Zafar Cheema, Dayal Singh Foundation, Lahore, 2007
5. Shaheed Bhagat Singh: Jeevan Ate Krantikari Marg, by S. S. Azad, Manpreet Prakashan, Delhi, 2007
6. Bhagat Singh Di Soch Walio: by Mohindar Soomal, Chetna, Ludhiana, 2007

7. Chhipan Ton Pehlan (Drama on Bhagat Singh), Devendar Daman, 1982
8. Shaheed Bhagat Singh di Vapsi: (Drama on Bhagat Singh), by Sagar Sarhadi, Deepak Publishers Jalandhar, 1983
9. Bhagat Singh Shaheed (Play), Charan Das Sidhu, Shilalekh Delhi, 1998
10. Dhote Munh Chaped (Play), Jagjit Komal, Literature House Amritsar, 2004
11. Inqualab Zindabad (Drama on Bhagat Singh), Gursharn Singh
12. Shaheed Bhagat Singh (Kav), Prof. Didar Singh, Bhagat Singh Khoj Committee Ludhiana, 1984
13. Kissa Shaheed Bhagat Singh, Prof. Didar Singh, ed. M. S. Waraich, Tarakbharti, Barnala, 2006 (Ist ed. 1968)
14. Singh Garjna (Poetry on Bhagat Singh martyrdom), ed. Gurdev Singh, Publication Bureau, Punjabi University, Patiala, 1982
15. Shaheede-azam-Bhagat Singh (Poetry on Bhagat Singh), N. B. T. Delhi, 2005
16. Sohile Shaheed Bhagat Singh (Poetry), ed. Gurdev Singh Sidhu, NBT, New Delhi, 2008
17. Bandi Bol (Poetry Collection), ed. Gurdev Singh Sidhu, NBT, New Delhi, 2008
18. Virlap – com, Amarnath Ahluwalia, (banned), 1931
19. Ghoriyaan: Shaheed Bhagat Singh, ed. Gurdev Singh Sidhu, Lokgeet Chandigarh, 2006
20. Sutluj di Hawa (Novel), Gyani Ajit Singh, 2007
21. Satluj Vehnda Riha (Novel on Shaheed Bhagat Singh), by Baldev Singh, 2007, Chetna Prakashan, Ludhiana
22. Karachi Congress ate Bhagat Singh di Shahidi, Lokgeet Chandigarh, 2007
23. Inqlab (Biography Bhagat Singh), Tejinder Virli, Kuknoos Jalandhar, 2006
24. Jithe Suraj Ugiya (Biography), Ram Lal Premi, Mukti Prakashan Moga, 2006
25. Shaheed Bhagat Singh Vichardhara, Ed. Balbir Parwana, Chetna Ludhiana, 2006
26. Shaheed Bhagat Singh (Biography), G. S. Deol, Punjabi University, Patiala, 1973
27. Shaheed Bhagat Singh de Inqlabi Tajarbe, Kuldip Nayar, Singh Brothers, Amritsar, 2000

28. Bhagat Singh nal Merian Mulkaatan, Sohan Singh Josh, Aarsee, Delhi,1988
29. Bhagat Singh Te Sathi Jailan Vich, Dr. Pram Singh, People's Forum, 2007
30. Yug Purush Bhagat Singh ate Unnah de Purkhe, Veerendr Sandhu, Language Deptt., Patiala, 1975
31. Taraksheel Bhagat Singh, Taraksheel Society, Ludhiana, 1996
32. Bhagat Singh, Tirlok Singh
33. Sardar Bhagat Singh, Swarn Singh, Wellwish Publishers, Delhi, 1992
34. Shaheed-e-azam Bhagat Singh di Jail Diary, Punjab Govt., Chandigarh, 2007
35. Shaheed Bhagat Singh di Nastikata, Sufi Amrjit, 2001
36. Bhagat Singh, Kartar Singh Duggal, Publication Division, Delhi, 2001
37. Bhagat Singh Di Pahchaan, DBYC, Jalandhar, 1988
38. Bhagat Singh, Savyasachi, Kuknoos, Jalandhar, 2002
39. Bhagat Singh nal Mulaquaat, Randhir Singh, Amritsir, 1963
40. Jo Satluj Kandhae Sarh Gaye, Yuvak Kendar, Jalandhar, March, 1969
41. Quami Lehar (Monthly), Jalandhar, Bhagat Singh issue, March, 1971
42. Sanvad (Toronto), Ed. Sukhindar, Bhagat Singh Issues, 2000-2006
43. Nazria: Bhagat Singh, Special Issue, Malerkotla, Ed. S. Tarsem, 2007, published as book, 'Bhagat Singh:Sangharsh te Shahadat'
44. Jagriti, Punjab Govt., Chandigarh, Bhagat Singh Special Issue, September, 2007
45. Punjab Rang (Quarterly), Ed. Zafar Cheema, Lahore, Bhagat Singh Special Issue, 2007
46. Inqualaabi Itihas De Sunehari Panne, Chaman Lal, Taraksheel Barnala, 2005
47. Bhagat Singh: Jiwan ate Adarsh, Ahmad Salim, Islamabad, 2008
48. Shaheed Bhagat Singh, Mohd. Sadiq, Lokgeet, Chandigarh
49. Shaheed Bhagat Singh di Jai Notebook, Tr. Rajinderpal singh, Lokgeet, Chandigarh, 2005
50. Ek Supna Ek Samvad (Poetry), Lakhwinder Johl, 2007
51. Main Bhagat Singh Han te Main Phir Awanga (Play), Chetna Ludhiana, 2008
52. Kehdi Maan ne Bhagat Singh Jammia (Poetry collection), Eds. Ahmad Salim/Shabnam Ishaque, Sanjh, Lahore, 2008
53. Azadi da Parwana, Mohinder Singh Sethi, 1962
54. Azad Hind da Pehla Quami Shaheed Sardar Bhagat Singh (novel), Mehar Singh and Sons, Amritsar

55. Charhda Suraj Bhagat Singh, Avtar Jawanda, Deepak Publishers Jalandhar, 1983
56. Masiha Suli te Muskraya (Play), Harcharn Singh, Lahore Book Shop Ludhiana, 1980
57. Shaheed Bhagat Singh: Anthak Jiwangatha (Epic), Inderjit Nandan, Chetna Ludhiana, 2008
58. Bhagat Singh Kav Sangrah, (Poetry), Ed. Baldev singh Badhan, Deepak Publishers Jalandhar, 2008
59. Amar Shaheed Bhagat Singh: Kav Shardhanjli, Ed. Baldev Singh Badhan, Gurmat Parkashan, Patiala, 2006
60. Inqlab da Bani: Bhagat Singh, Sohinderbir, Kasturi Lal & Sons, Amritsar, 2008
61. Shaheed Bhagat Singh Chintan, Ed. Kirat Singh Inqlabi, National Book Shop Delhi, 2008
62. Suraj, Suli te Shayar, Ed. S. Tarsem, Nazaria Prakashan, Malerkotla, 2008
63. Quami Shaheed Bhagat Singh (Poetry), Jangir Singh Brar, Udaan, Mansa, 2006
64. Vihvin Sadi da Mahanaik-Shaheed Bhagat Singh, Shyam Sunder Dipti, Prerna, Amritsar, 2008
65. Shaheed Bhagat Singh di Vichardhar, Eds. - Shyam Sunder Dipti/ Anup Singh, Prerna, Amritsar, 2007
66. Shaheed Bhagat Singh da Chintan, Eds. same, 2007

English Readings

1. Jail Notebook & Other Writings of Bhagat Singh: Compiled & Introduction, Chaman Lal, Leftword, Delhi, 2007
2. The Trial of Bhagat Singh, A. G. Noorani, O. U. P. Delhi, 2005
3. The Hanging of Bhagat Singh: Vol. I, (Judgement) M. S. Waraich & G. S. Sidhu, Unistar Chandigarh, 2005
4. — do —— Vol.-II (Proceedings), Chandigarh, 2008
5. — do —— Vol.-III (Confessions, etc.), Chandigarh, 2007
6. — do —— Vol.-IV (Banned Literature), Chandigarh, 2007
7. Revolutionaries in Dialogue, M. S. Waraich, Chandigarh, 2007
8. Selected Writings of Bhagat Singh, Ed. Shiv Verma, N. B. C. Delhi, 1986
9. A Martyr's Notebook, Ed. Bhupendra Hooja, I. B. C., Jaipur, 1994
10. The Eternal Rebel, M. S. Waraich, Publication Divi, G. O. I. Delhi, 2007

11. Shaheed Bhagat Singh, Jatindernath Sanyal, Vishvabharti, Nagpur, 1983 (Banned-1932)
12. Selected Collections on Bhagat Singh, M. M. Juneja, Modern, Hisar, 2007
13. A Revolutionary's Quest for Sacrifice, Srirajayam Sinha, Bhartiya Vidya Bhavan, Mumbai, 1993.
14. Bhagat Singh: Liberation's Blazing Star, PMS Grewal, Leftword, 2007
15. To Make the Deaf Hear, S. Irfan Habib, Three Essay Collections, Delhi, 2007
16. Bhagat Singh, Contemporary portrayals, K. C. Yadav/Babar Singh, Hope India, Gurgaon, 2006
17. Shaheed Bhagat Singh: An Immortal Revolutionary, Ashok Dhawle, 2007
18. Bhagat Singh: Pages from the Life of a Martyr, A. B. Bardhan, PPH, Delhi, 1984
19. Why I am an Atheist, Introduction, Bipin Chandra, PPH, Delhi and NBT, Delhi, 1993, 2007
20. NBS and HSRA, Comrade Ram Chand, G-3, Anand Niketan, Delhi, 1986
21. Road to Freedom: Revealing Sidelights, Com. Ram Chand, Geetanjli Prakashan, Delhi, 1980
22. Ideology and Battle Cries of Indian Revolutionaries, Com. Ram Chand, G-3 Anand Niketan, Delhi, 1989
23. Shaheed Bhagat Singh: Balbhadra Bharti, Jaipur, 1993
24. Bhagat Singh: The Man & His Ideology, Kamlesh Mohan, Jaipur, 1993
25. Under the Shadow of Gallows, Gulab Singh. Rupchand, Delhi, 1963
26. They Lived Dangerously, Manmath Nath Gupta, PPH, Delhi,1968
27. Militant Nationalism in Punjab, Kamlesh Mohan, Manohar, Delhi, 1985
28. In Search of Freedom, Jogesh Chatterji, Firma K. L., Kolkata, 1967
29. Selected Speeches and Writings of Bhagat Singh, D. N. Gupta, NBT, 2007
30. Bhagat Singh Today, Ed. Dr. P. R. Kalia, Canada, 2007
31. They Died so That Country may Live, Brochure Pb. Govt., Chandigarh, 1981
32. Martyrdom of Shaheed Bhagat Singh, Koonar/Sindhra, Unistar, Chandigarh, 2005
33. Without Fear, Kuldip Nayar, Harper & Collins, Delhi, 2007

34. Martyrs as Bridegroom: A Folk Reprsentation of Bhagat Singh, Anthem Press, Delhi, 2008.
35. Inqualaab Zindabad! (Banned), Lahore, 1930.
36. The Man & His Ideas, Gopal Thakur, PPH, Delhi, 1965.
37. In Search of Revolutionary Ideology. S.N. Majumdar, PPH, Delhi, 1965
38. Shaheed Bhagat Singh and His Ideology, S.R. Bakshi, Capital, Delhi, 1981
39. Shaheed Bhagat Singh, K. K. Khullar, Hem, Delhi
40. Shaheed Bhagat Singh, Prince of Martyrs, L. P. Mathur, Avishkar, Jaipur
41. Shaheed Bhagat Singh Legendary Martyr, Omesh Sehgal, Gyan Books, Delhi, 2002
42. Shaheed Bhagat Singh, Unique Martyr, S. Ram
43. Shaheed Bhagat Singh, G. S. Deol, Deep Prakashan, Ludhiana, 1977
44. Bhagat Singh and His Comrades, Ajay Kr. Ghosh, Mumbai, 1945
45. Bhagat Singh, Rana Bhagwan Singh
46. Bhagat Singh (Banned), C. S. Venu, Madras, 1931
47. Bhagat Singh or Roar on Scaffold, T. S. Kanakasabai, Madras (Banned), 1931
48. Life of Sardar Bhagat Singh (Banned), Shrichand Ramhari Palnitkar, Akola (Maharashtra), 1931
49. Celebrating Bhagat Singh, Ed. N. Ram (Frontline Special Issue) November, 2007, Chennai
50. Gandhi and Bhagat Singh, V. N. Datta, Rupa, Delhi, 2008
51. Famous and Historic Trials, Khalid Latif Gauba (K. L. Gauba), Lion Press, Lahore, 1946
52. Bhagat Singh and His Ideology, Foreword, Emily C. Brown, G. S. Deol, Deep. Nabha, 1978
53. Bhagat Singh: Path to Liberation, Bharti Pustakalayan, Chennai, 2007
54. Bhagat Singh and His Legend, Ed. J. S. Grewal, World Punjabi Centre, Patiala, 2008

Urdu Readings

1. Bhagat Singh aur Unki Inqlaabi Jaddojahad, Kuldeep Nayar, translation Fahmida Riyaz, O. U. P., Karachi
2. Bhagat Singh aur Uske Saathi, Ibte Hasan, Karachi
3. Bhagat Singh Zindgii aur Khyalaat, Ahmed Salim, Riktab Karachi, 1986
4. Irtiqa-44 (2007), Bhagat Singh Khasusi, Ed. Wahid Bashir, etc., Karachi
5. Bhagat Singh aur Datt ki Amar Kahaani, Chamanlal Azad, Delhi, 1965

6. Sham-E-Aazadi ke Teen Parvaane, Shambhu Dayal Mishra (Banned), 1931
7. Ghodi Bhagat Singh Shaheed, Jalandhar
8. Shaheedan-i-Vatan urf Kurbanii Azam, Nazar Ahmad Hindi, Amritsar (Banned)
9. Naara –E-Jung, Sayyad Ali Hussain, 1932, Lyalpur (Banned).
10. Lutfe Shahadat ke Teen Shaheed, Bharat Bhushan or Aflatoon, 1932, Lahore
11. Amulle Lal, M. S. Kavi Panchhi, Sailkot, 1931
12. Qatliye-Begunah urf Shahadat e watan, Lahore, (Banned), 1931
13. Drama Bhagat Singh, Datt and Jatindar Das, Mahasha, Ashanand Bhajnik, Rawalpindi, (Banned), 1930
14. Inqlabi lahar urf Toofan e Hind, (Poetry), Bhai Shiv Prasad Seth, (Banned)
15. Sardar Bhagat Singh, Sukhdev Varma, Lahore, Banned, 1931
16. Watan ke Shaheedan ka Bepanah Khoon, Ashanand Bhajnik, Rawalpindi, (Banned), 1931
17. Pyara Bhagat Singh, Meher Ilamuddin Hindi, Lahore, (Banned), 1931
18. Shahid-e-Azam Bhagat Singh (Opera), Avtar Singh Daler, 1962

Marathi Readings

1. Samagra Vangmayaa, Ed. Chaman Lal, translation Dr. Datta Desai, Diamond Books, Pune, 2007
2. Shaheed Bhagat Singh Jeevan va Karya, Ashok Chouslkar, Kolhapur University, 2006
3. Bhagat Singh: Tarun Manacha Krantikaari Hunkaar, By Sachin Mali, Nirmiti Vichaar Manch, Kolhapur, 2006
4. Amar Shahid sa Bhagat Simha, Krishna Madhav Sakhavalkar, 1968
5. Manza Krantii swapan, Ed. Girish Kasid, Kolhapur, 2005
6. Bhagat Singhacha Povada, Sankar Varvarkar, Nashik, 1931
7. Bhagat Singhacha Powada, Narayan Khandekar, Mumbai, 1932 (Banned)
8. Bhagat Singhacha Povada (Ballad) Banned, 1931
9. Bhagat Singh, Rajguru Va Sukhdev (Poetry)
10. Sardar Bhagat Singh, Manmohan, Mumbai, (Banned), 1932
11. Jeevan Marg, Ed. Prabhakar Sanjhgru, Mumbai, 2007
12. Krantivir Chander Shekhar Azad ani Sardar Bhagat Singh, Vishnu Shridhar Joshi, Mumbai, 1978
13. Inqlab (Novel), Mrinalini Joshi, Snehla Prakashan, Pune, 1993

Tamil Readings

1. Bhagat Singh Thuku Alankaram, K. Sundarraju Chettiyar, Tanjore, (Banned), 1931.
2. Bahadur Bhagat Singh Pattu, W. Natraj Pillai, (Banned), 1931
3. Desiya Geetangal, T. K. Durairajan, Madras, (Banned), 1932
4. Sardar Bhagat Singh. Manmargudi, Madras, (Banned), 1932
5. Sutanandir Nadam, R. B. S. Mani, Madras, (Banned), 1931
6. Santamil Mairi, K. Tutralam Pillai, Madras, (Banned), 1931
7. Congress Pattu, V. A. Thiagaraja Chettiyar, Madras, (Banned), 1932
8. Parithapa Geetam, T. M. Thirumalai Swami, Madras, (Banned), 1931
9. Congress klerthanai or Swarajya Path. K.V. Meenakhisundram Chettiyar, Madras, (Banned), 1931
10. Bhagat Singh Kirtanaurtam, V. Natraj Pillai, Madras, (Banned), 1931
11. Na Nattikan En? (Tamil translation of Why I am an Atheist), P. Jeevanadam, 1934, Latest edition, 2005, Madras
12. Tukkile Pakatcin, Ka Vellimalai, 1982

Gujrati Readings

1. Shaheed Bhagat Singh kee Jeevan Katha (Banned), Chamanlal Ishwarlal Mehta, Ahmedabad, 1931.
2. Bhagat Singh Kaun? (Biography), (Banned), by Chamanlal Ishwarlal Mehta, Ahmedabad, 1931

Telugu Readings

1. Naa Nethuru Vrudha Kadu (Selected writings of Bhagat Singh).
2. Shaheed Bhagat Singh Jeevancharittar, C. Krishnaswamy, Madras (Banned), 1935
3. Bhagat Singh Shat Jayanti Ank, Ed. -Nirmlanand "Jan Sahiti", Hyderabad, 2000 and 2007

Bengali Readings

1. Fansi. Mahendra Nath Das, Calcutta (Banned), 1931.
2. Sukhdev, Bhagat Singh aur Rajguru ki Faansi, Pt. Shambhu Prasad Mishra, Calcutta (Banned), 1931
3. Shaheed Bhagat Singh, Pt. Shambhu Prasad Mishra, Calcutta (Banned), 1931
4. Inqlab Zindabad, Lokender Kumar Sengupta, 1970
5. Shaheed Bhagat Singh, Bisva Biswas, 1971

Sindhi Readings

1. Inqlaab Zindabad! (Biography of Bhagat Singh), Dwarkadaas Ruchi Ram, Hyderabad (Sindh), (Banned), 1931
2. Fansi ke Geet, Hoondraj Leelaram, Larkana (Banned), 1931
3. Bhagat Singh khe Phasi (Sangeet Nataku), Sheikh Ayaz, Niyu Fild, Hyderabad (Sindh), 1986

Sanskrit

1. Hutatma Bhkatsingh Charitarm, Krishan Lal Sharma Sudan, Saharnpur
2. Sri Bhakatsimhacharitarm, Svayam Prakash Sharma Shastri, Meerut, 1978
3. Bhagatsinghcharitamartam, Chuni Lal Sudan
4. Bharatrashtarratnam, Yageyeshwar Shastri,
(Updated on 5th November, 2008)

Photo Gallery

BHAGAT SINGH AND HIS FAMILY MEMBERS

Aunt Hukam, Mother Vidyawati, Grandmother Jai Kaur, Aunt Harnam, sister Amar(sitting)

BS grandpa Arjun Singh

Kishan Singh

College group photo of Bhagat Singh

Uncle Ajit Singh

Uncle Swarn Singh

Four original photographs of Bhagat Singh

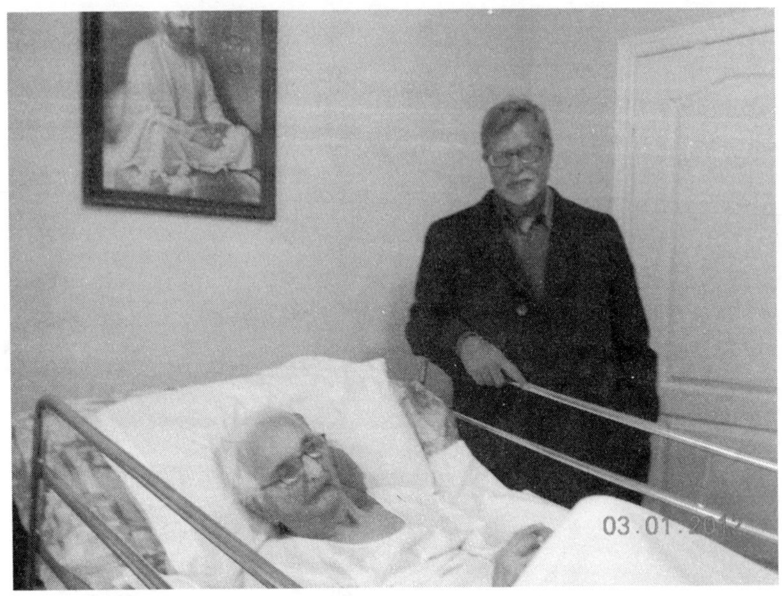

Writer with Bhagat Singh's sister Prakash Kaur in Toronto

COMRADES OF BHAGAT SINGH

Chandershekhar Azad

Bhagwaticharan Vohra-Durga Bhabhi-Shachi

Sukhdev

Rajguru

Jatin Das

Mahavir Singh

Bejoy Sinha

Jaidev Kapoor, Shiv Verma, Surinder Pandey

BS Mahour

Vishawnath Vaishampayan

Com. Ram Chander

Harikishan

Jatinder Sanyal

Pt. Kishori Lal

Kishori Lal, Agya Ram, Shiv Verma and Ajoy Ghosh

Raja Ram Shastri

Ramsaran Dass

Sarabha

MONUMENTS AND LOCATIONS

Arya Sabha HQ Port Louise, Mauritius

Arya Samaj Schools-Institutions, Fiji—Bhagat Singh Photo

Bhagat Singh photo in Vancouver Union office

PROCLAMATION

"SHAHEED BHAGAT SINGH"

"SHAHEED BHAGAT SINGH DAY"

Bernaby-BC-Canada Notification of Bhagat Singh Centenary Day

Berkeley Campus, University of California

BS House-Chak No.105

Bhagat Singh's Primary School-Chak No.105, Lyallpur Bange

Bhagat Singh painting board on highway to Faislabad

Bradlaugh Hall, Lahore

Front of SSP office—Saunders killing location in Lahore

Phansighat Lahore

Gallows Central Jail, Lahore

BS Khatkarkalan Ancestoral House

Cells of Delhi Jail–BS and Dutt kept in 1929

Hussainiwala Memorial

The Daily Bandematram, Lahore.

Live and Constitutional Bombs in Assembly.

Latest Photo of Sardar Bhagat Singh and Bhut Keshwar Datt.

Bhagat Singh.

Bhut Keshwar Dutt.

Hon'ble Mr. PATEL, President Legislative Assembly.

Who threw a Bombshell upon the Government by ruling the Public Safety Bill

Bande Matram 12.4.1929, first publication of BS-Dutt photos

Index